STARRING
FRED ASTAIRE

STARRING
FRED ASTAIRE

STANLEY GREEN/BURT GOLDBLATT

DODD, MEAD & COMPANY, NEW YORK

Acknowledgment is made to the following for permission to reprint copyrighted material:

Irving Berlin Music Corp. for lyrics to "Isn't This a Lovely Day" © copyright 1935 Irving Berlin, © copyright renewed; "Let's Face the Music and Dance" © copyright 1935, 1936 Irving Berlin, © copyright renewed; "A Fella with an Umbrella" © copyright 1947, 1948 Irving Berlin.

Chappell & Co., Inc. for lyrics to "Let's Call the Whole Thing Off" copyright © 1937 Gershwin Publishing Corp., copyright renewed; "They Can't Take That Away From Me" copyright © 1937 Gershwin Publishing Corp., copyright renewed Gershwin Publishing Corp. & New Dawn Music; "They All Laughed" copyright © 1937 Gershwin Publishing Corp., copyright renewed; "That's Entertainment" copyright © 1953 Chappell & Co., Inc.; "Paris Loves Lovers" copyright © 1954 Cole Porter, Chappell & Co., Inc., publisher; "It's a Chemical Reaction, That's All" copyright © 1954 Cole Porter, Chappel & Co., Inc., publisher; "Stereophonic Sound" copyright © 1954 Cole Porter, Chappell & Co., Inc., publisher.

Leo Feist Inc. for lyrics to "Here's to the Girls" copyright © 1944 Loew's Inc., renewed 1971 Metro Goldwyn Mayer Inc., rights controlled by Leo Feist, Inc.; "Too Late Now" copyright © 1950 Loew's Inc., rights controlled by Leo Feist, Inc.; "Oops" copyright © 1945 Loew's Inc., rights controlled by Leo Feist, Inc.

Harry Warren Music Inc. for lyrics to "Shoes with Wings On" © copyright 1948, 1949 Harry Warren Music Inc.; "Manhattan Downbeat" © copyright 1948, 1949 Harry Warren Music Inc.; "I Wanna Be a Dancin' Man" © copyright 1952 Harry Warren Music Inc.

Famous Music Corp. for lyrics to "Can't Stop Talking" copyright © 1950 Paramount Music Corp.; "Jack and the Beanstalk" copyright © 1950 Paramount Music Corp.

Commander Publications for lyrics to "Something's Gotta Give" copyright © 1954 Robbins Music Corp., copyright © 1965 Commander Publications.

ISBN: 0-396-06877-4
Library of Congress Catalog Card Number: 73-13041

Designed by Burt Goldblatt
Text by Stanley Green

For Ann Geilus Astaire
who knew before anyone else

ACKNOWLEDGMENTS

We greatly appreciate the cooperation of many people who have aided in the creation of this book. Foremost—naturally—are Fred and Adele Astaire, who have been generous in making available personal photographs and theatrical memorabilia. Those who have worked with Fred Astaire have also responded helpfully to our inquiries. They include Irving Berlin (whose tribute to Fred was written specially for this volume), Howard Dietz, Dorothy Fields, Ira Gershwin, Burton Lane, George Oppenheimer, and Harry Warren.

To Don Koll go our special thanks for screening films and for checking the manuscript. Other valued sources of information have been DeWitt Bodeen, the late Buddy Bradley, Robert Cushman, Hugh Fordin, Chico Hamilton, Edward Jablonski, Robert Kimball, Chester Kopaz, Miles Kreuger, and Alfred Simon. For the Discography, we are indebted to Howard Levine for his painstaking work. We are also grateful for the assistance of Theodore Jackson, Hilda Schneider, and Helmy Kresa of the Irving Berlin Music Corp.; Vivien Friedman and Philip Wattenberg, Chappell Music, Inc.; Marshall Robbins, Commander Publications; Sidney Herman, Famous Music Corp.; Edward Slattery, Leo Feist, Inc.

The Lincoln Center Theater Collection of the New York Public Library has, as usual, been indispensable. We appreciate the help of curator Paul Myers, and assistants Dorothy Swerdlove, Monte Arnold, Donald Fowle, Maxwell Silverman, and Betty Wharton. Madeline Nichols of the Library's Dance Collection has also been most cooperative.

The following were all helpful in securing films and photographs: Herb Graff; Richard T. Koll; Sid Weiner and Joe Abruscato of Screen Gems; John Greenleaf and Francine Cao of MCA; the late Haven Falconer and Dan Terrell of M-G-M; Warner Bros., Inc.; the American Film Institute; Irving Adler and Fred Berman of Paramount Pictures; Arthur Perles; Fred Lugo; Susan Levenson; Ernie Smith; Maureen Solomon; Chris Steinbrunner; Charles Turner; Robert E. Lee; Eugenia Winter of the Omaha Public Library; for assistance in production, Leslie and Heather Goldblatt.

Brief quotations from Fred Astaire's autobiography, *Steps in Time* (Harper, 1959) appear throughout the book, and there are also excerpts from Mr. Astaire's comments on his working habits which were in Morton Eustis' article, "Fred Astaire—the Actor-Dancer Attacks His Part," *Theatre Arts,* May 1937. Other quotations are from the following: "There's No One Quite Like Astaire" by John O'Hara, *Show,* October 1962; "Ginger: She Wanted to Be a Moooooovie Star" by Garson Kanin, *The New York Times,* January 29, 1967; *The Memoirs of an Amnesiac* by Oscar Levant (Putnam, 1965); "There'll Always Be an Encore" by Judy Garland, *McCall's,* January 1964; *Memo from David O. Selznick* (Viking, 1972).

Our respective families also deserve our deep appreciation for their understanding during a period when it must have seemed that the only actor who ever starred on the silver screen was named Fred Astaire.

Stanley Green/Burt Goldblatt

CONTENTS

STARRING
FRED ASTAIRE

It's nothing new to say that Fred Astaire is a great dancer. We all know that. But what was even more important to those of us who ever wrote songs for him was that he was also a great singer. Remember, I'm talking about writers of the caliber of Jerome Kern, Cole Porter, George and Ira Gershwin, Vincent Youmans, Harold Arlen, Johnny Mercer, Dorothy Fields, Howard Dietz, Arthur Schwartz, Harry Warren, Alan Jay Lerner, Burton Lane, and many others. Fred introduced and was responsible for more hit songs than many of the top singers. He knew the value of a song and his heart was in it before his feet took over.
—Irving Berlin

Fred Astaire makes it look easy only by taking the greatest of pains. He works harder than any newcomer. He never lets up. You'd think his entire life and future depended upon the outcome of each dance. He keeps at the top because he does the impossible—he improves on perfection.
—Rouben Mamoulian

He is endowed with the physical equipment of a decathlon champion, the imagination of an artist, the perserverance of an expert in dressage, the determination of a gyrene drill sergeant, the self-confidence of a lion tamer, the self-criticism of a neophyte in holy orders, the pride of a man who has created his own tradition—and the ability to go home when he has done his job.
—John O'Hara

There never was a greater perfectionist, there never was, or never will be, a better dancer, and I never knew anybody more kind, more considerate, or so completely a gentleman. I love Fred and I admire and respect him. I guess it's because he's so many things I'd like to be, and am not.
—Bing Crosby

With assistant Hermes Pan during a rehearsal (1936). According to
Fred, "Just follow the white lines and anyone can dance it."

In a career that has spanned over sixty-five years, Fred Astaire is, quite simply, the premier dancing actor of our time, both on stage and on screen. Indeed, there has never been a Broadway musical-comedy star who has ever enjoyed anything like Fred's popularity, prestige, and longevity as a motion picture performer.

Although Astaire has occasionally played nondancing and non-singing roles, his image as a dancer is indelible and unalterable. But the image takes in more than his dancing. It's everything about him —his bobbing, jaunty walk, the way he twirls a cane, his light, intimate way of singing, even the cut of his clothes. Watching Astaire on the screen we *knew* he was special. But there was always something about him that was approachable; he had elegance without the frosting. He projected the personality of the shy but talented kid next door, pleased to give pleasure, but a bit surprised at all the fuss. He made every dance step not only seem effortless but as normal and as natural as breathing. He was so very much the embodiment of movement—nimble, lithe, graceful, lambent move-ment—that it was impossible to believe it wasn't all spontaneous.

That, of course, was what we were supposed to believe. That was the public Astaire. The private Astaire, however, was a painstaking artist who devoted long, tedious hours to preparing and perfecting every step he took. He was totally dedicated to making each move not only the right one but the only one. He never faked. To Astaire there was no substitute for hard work to get the results he wanted, and he would spend months creating, rehearsing, and polishing his routines for each picture.

In working out his routines, Astaire needed only a rehearsal room, a pianist (Hal Borne in the early days), and a dance director (usually Hermes Pan), whose job was to remember all the details. At first Fred would stand in the middle of the room listening to a tune from his new movie, letting his feet ramble idly until he hit on something he liked. He might develop it, vary it, or abandon it and go on to something else. Eventually, after many trials and many errors, he would get the routine firmly fixed. With the basic pattern set, he would devote days, even weeks, to refining his movements, gestures, and expressions until he reached a point when he wouldn't even have to think of what came next. If the dance required a partner, Fred would then teach her the steps. It was only after every detail had been thoroughly worked out that the couple would venture the difficult transition from practice clothes to costumes. Once the number was ready for shooting, Astaire and his partner would walk through the dance, step by step, for the benefit of the director, cameramen, and technicians.

In an interview with Morton Eustis published in *Theatre Arts* in 1937, Astaire explained his method of filming a dance: "I always try to run a dance straight through in the movies, keeping in view the full length of the dancer or dancers, and retaining the flow of the movement intact. In every kind of dance, even tap, the movement of the upper part of the body is as important as the legs. By keeping the whole body always in action before the camera, there are certain obvious advantages that the screen has over the stage. You can concentrate your attention directly on the dancer, so that the audience is able to follow intricate steps that would be all but lost behind the footlights. Each person in the audience sees the dance from the same perspective and, I think, gets a bigger reaction. He has a larger, clear, better-focused view, and so derives a greater emotional response."

The same article also pointed out that Astaire always tried to keep the audience from ever being aware of the camera. He had it placed at eye level and let it shoot the dance as straight as possible. Usually, he would have a sequence filmed with three cameras shooting simultaneously. The "A" camera was allotted the position he thought would work best, with the "B" and "C" cameras placed on either side for alternate angles. Each take would then be recorded in its entirety on three rolls of film. After viewing the rushes, Astaire would choose the best sequences to be pieced together. However, as the dancer has explained, "The sequence of the dance is never broken. The audience may be conscious of a change of angle but it will never be conscious that the flow of the dance has been interrupted."

To date, Fred Astaire has appeared in eleven musicals on the New York stage, four in London (actually adaptations of his Broadway hits), thirty-five motion pictures (of which four were nonmusical), and numerous radio and television shows, both musical and dramatic. Of all his screen appearances, however, the ones that most clearly established his worldwide fame and influence were the nine he made with Ginger Rogers during the period from late 1933 through early 1939.

Five of these nine—*The Gay Divorcee, Top Hat, Follow the Fleet, Swing Time,* and *Shall We Dance*—unquestionably represent the flowering of the Astaire-Rogers years. Each had its special appeal yet all had a tone and flavor that created a unique singing and dancing world. Let's call it Astairogersland.

In Astairogersland, no matter the locale, the settings were always elegantly artificial, never intended as literal reproductions of London (*The Gay Divorcee, Top Hat*), or Venice (*Top Hat*), or San Francisco (*Follow the Fleet*), or New York (*Swing Time, Shall We Dance*), or Paris (*Shall We Dance*). All hotels were dazzling white, appointed with quilted, modernistic furnishings. Ocean liners were floating palaces in which staterooms had sliding glass doors opening onto the decks. Nightclubs were huge and amply chandeliered, and usually high in the sky. Private homes were surrounded by grounds so vast they could easily accommodate outdoor dance floors. Even dime-a-dance dance halls were spotless and decorous and had their own lush gardens.

Whenever we visited Astairogersland, we always saw Fred before we saw Ginger. And they always met by accident—whether on a Southampton pier (*The Gay Divorcee*), or in a London hotel suite (*Top Hat*), or in a San Francisco dance hall (*Follow the Fleet*), or on a New York street (*Swing Time*), or in a Paris apartment (*Shall We Dance*). One look was just about all that was needed for Fred to fall completely in love. Ginger, however, was usually annoyed at first at Fred's brashness, but she soon began to melt once Fred sang or twirled her around a dance floor. That still was never quite enough to prevent future misunderstandings, although it was always Ginger, never the constant Fred, who got huffy about something or other. Rifts might occur because of Ginger's mistaking Fred for another man (*The Gay Divorcee, Top Hat*), or Fred's backfiring attempts to help Ginger's career (*Follow the Fleet*), or the appearance of suspected rivals (*Swing Time, Shall We Dance*).

The world of Astairogersland was exceedingly moral. Fred never had anything less than matrimony on his mind right from the start (on one occasion, *Shall We Dance*, he decided to marry Ginger even before he met her). It was also a world in which husbands suspected of philandering had to be taught a lesson (*Top Hat*), promiscuous women always lost out (*Follow the Fleet, Shall We Dance*), an engaged man was honor-bound never to make a play for another girl (*Swing Time*)—and a newspaper photograph of a couple in bed together was accepted as irrefutable evidence that they were husband and wife (*Shall We Dance*). Scandals were to be avoided at all costs since they could not only spell ruin for a show (*Top Hat*), they could also cause the cancellation of an entire ballet company's New York engagement (*Shall We Dance*). On the other hand, it was quite all right for a girl to be found *in flagrante delicto* with a professional corespondent (*The Gay Divorcee*), gambling was encouraged as long as the participant kept winning (*Swing Time*), and it was jolly good sport to prevent a rival—particularly if he was Latin—from being married (*Top Hat, Swing Time*).

Everyone knew the importance of clothes in Astairogersland. The proper attire for gentlemen after six was either tuxedo or full dress, for ladies it was an evening gown. Such dress was suitable for dining, dancing, or—as in *The Gay Divorcee*—keeping a midnight rendezvous. It was also of vital concern whether a gentleman chose a square end or a butterfly-shaped formal bow tie (*Top Hat*), that the striped trousers of his formal cutaway coat be in the latest fashion (*Swing Time*), and that he wear a dinner jacket at a dance audition (*Swing Time*). As for the ladies, parading about in a couturier's elegant clothes was a sure way of winning customers for the designer (*Top Hat*), and changing into an evening gown could instantly transform a dowdy into a dazzler (*Follow the Fleet*).

It was not true, however, that the two leading citizens of Astairogersland were always rich. Fred might be a sailor (*Follow the Fleet*), or temporarily penniless (*Swing Time*); Ginger might be social but impoverished (*Top Hat*), or a dance-hall entertainer (*Follow the Fleet*), or a dance instructor (*Swing Time*). But no matter their station, they always managed to associate with people of means.

Though Ginger was a professional dancer on no more than three out of the five occasions, Fred was always a professional (even, as in *Follow the Fleet*, while temporarily in the Navy). His work habits, however, were rather casual. Rehearsals could be overlooked (*Top Hat*), or kidded (*Follow the Fleet*), or avoided (*Shall We Dance*). As for auditions, they could be ruined by a glass of bicarbonate of soda (*Follow the Fleet*), or even held in the wrong location (*Swing Time*)—which didn't seem to matter at all.

Major conflicts in Astairogersland arose from the most blissfully illogical situations—such as Fred's unaccountable failure to reveal his identity (*The Gay Divorcee, Top Hat*), or his being conned into having cuffs put on his formal striped trousers (*Swing Time*), or his inability to convince anyone that he was not married to Ginger (*Shall We Dance*). As for marriage itself, the laws of Astairogersland were so liberal that it was never any problem to find someone to perform the ceremony at a moment's notice (*The Gay Divorcee, Top Hat, Shall We Dance*).

There were no real villains in Astairogersland. Apart from Fred and Ginger, it was mostly populated by especially appealing comic characters—fluttery Alice Brady (*The Gay Divorcee*), droll Helen Broderick (*Top Hat, Swing Time*), prissy Edward Everett Horton (*The Gay Divorcee, Top Hat, Shall We Dance*), cherubic Victor Moore (*Swing Time*), unctuous Eric Blore (*The Gay Divorcee, Top Hat, Swing Time, Shall We Dance*), and flamboyant Erik Rhodes (*The Gay Divorcee, Top Hat*). Among the more—or less—normal folks were Randolph Scott and Harriet Hilliard (*Follow the Fleet*), Georges Metaxa and Betty Furness (*Swing Time*), and Jerome Cowan and Ketti Gallian (*Shall We Dance*). In addition to other activities, various members of the community were called upon to provide a certain balance to the relationship between Fred and Ginger. Fred always had a close male chum (Horton, Scott, or Moore), and Ginger always had a close female chum (Brady, Broderick, or Hilliard)—except in *Shall We Dance* when her friend turned out to be Jerome Cowan.

In Astairogersland, though they might kiss (*Top Hat, Swing Time*) or embrace (*Follow the Fleet, Shall We Dance*), Fred and Ginger never smooched. Their romances were always developed through the dance. Among the numbers that served this purpose were "Night and Day" in *The Gay Divorcee*; "Isn't This a Lovely Day?" and "Cheek to Cheek" in *Top Hat*; "Let Yourself Go" and "I'm Putting All My Eggs in One Basket" in *Follow the Fleet*; "Pick Yourself Up" and "Never Gonna Dance" in *Swing Time*; and "They All Laughed" and "Shall We Dance" in *Shall We Dance*. (And wasn't it fortunate that such estimable song creators as Cole Porter, Irving Berlin, Dorothy Fields and Jerome Kern, and George and Ira Gershwin were available to call the tunes?)

What was the magic of Astairogersland? As Garson Kanin once wrote, "It cannot be explained; it can only be felt. Astaire and Rogers created a style, a mood, a happening. They flirted, chased, courted, slid, caressed, hopped, skipped, jumped, bent, swayed, clasped, wafted, undulated, nestled, leapt, quivered, glided, spun—in sum, made love before our eyes."

STAGE CAREER

Looking down Douglas Street in Omaha, Nebraska,
at the turn of the century.

Adele at nine, Fred at eight.

Adele at six.

One wintry morning in 1904, in the city of Omaha, Nebraska, Mrs. Frederick Austerlitz finished packing her bags, kissed her husband good-bye, and bundled her two children, four-and-a-half-year-old Fred and six-year-old Adele, onto an eastbound train heading for New York City. Her mission: to enroll her progenies in a dancing school to prepare them for a professional stage career.

Every community has its precocious tots and every community has its mothers who dream of theatrical stardom for their offsprings. Few do anything about it. Particularly if they live far from the hub of the entertainment industry. Particularly if their husbands take home decent salaries. Particularly if their children haven't even started public school. And particularly, as in this case, if the male half of the future dancing team has shown nary a glimmer of talent or interest in either dancing, singing, or acting.

But events were to prove that, through some miraculously accurate divining power, Ann Geilus Austerlitz knew what she was doing. Both of her children did have talent. Extraordinary talent. And while they may never have enjoyed what is generally considered a normal family life, there was no indication that they were unhappy or abused or that they missed the more accustomed pleasures and pains of childhood. Nothing traumatic happened because they were sent out on the stage to earn a living at such tender ages. They danced and they sang and they made people happy and they enjoyed themselves. And they turned out to be the most highly acclaimed Broadway dance team of the twenties.

Fred Astaire, né Austerlitz, was born in Omaha on May 10, 1899. His stagestruck father, an Austrian immigrant who worked for a brewery, and his practical-minded, ambitious mother enrolled sister Adele in a local dancing school by the time she was four. Within two years, she became the featured attraction in the school's dance recitals and was hailed as something of a local prodigy. Fred's only contact with the school took place when he would accompany his parents there either to deposit or pick up his sister.

Once in New York, the Astaire siblings were sent to the Alvienne School of the Dance. While there, Fred played Roxane to Adele's Cyrano de Bergerac. They also performed a bride-and-groom routine on a prop wedding cake, with Fred wearing top hat, white tie, and tails—over a pair of black silk knickers. After about a year at the school, the dancing Astaires made their professional debut in Keyport, New Jersey, earning fifty dollars for a split-week engagement.

Papa Astaire, who had legally changed his name, journeyed East as often as his job would allow. It was he who got his kids their first real break—a twenty-week tour on the Orpheum Circuit that took them all the way to Los Angeles. Following a second tour, Fred and Adele outgrew their material and were unable to get bookings. Forced into temporary retirement, the veteran vaudevillians moved to Highwood Park, New Jersey, where they attended the local grammar school.

After a two-year hiatus from the world of show business, the youngsters were enrolled in the Ned Wayburn Studio of Stage Dancing. (This would be their final formal dance school training, though Adele later took lessons from choreographer Robert "Buddy" Bradley.) Fred and Adele's first appearance in New York was at a benefit at the Broadway Theatre, and their first booking was at Proctor's 5th Avenue Theatre. That was in 1911—and they were such a resounding flop that the manager cancelled their act after the first performance. For about two years the Astaires had to be content with small town bookings in the Midwest. Their luck began to turn when they met Aurelia and Minnie Coccia, a vaudeville dance team, who taught them the tango and the waltz and with whom they toured for about six months. Later they played the Interstate Circuit in Texas at $175 per week, and then returned to the Orpheum Circuit which now paid them $225. (It was during this engagement that Fred first met Rita Hayworth's father, Eduardo Cansino, the star dancing attraction on the bill.)

Fred and Adele made their final vaudeville tour during the season 1915–16. (Some lists have included their names in the cast of a 1915 Mary Pickford film, *Fanchon, the Cricket*. Mr. Astaire, however, recalls only watching the movie being made while he and his

Claude Alvienne.

Fred played Roxane to Adele's Cyrano in
an Alvienne School production (1905).

Adeline Genee, the Danish ballerina, was the
first great dancer Fred and Adele ever saw.
To study her technique, the Astaires went to see her in
The Soul Kiss twenty-eight times.

Fred and Adele launched their vaudeville career
with a bride-and-groom act in 1906.
Note Fred's top hat, white tie and tails.

13

Fred at ten.

On Adele's 12th birthday.

Choreographer Ned Wayburn.

Fred and Adele in Wayburn's act, "A Rainy Saturday."

The Fifth Avenue Theatre, where the Astaires had their
first New York booking—and their first flop.

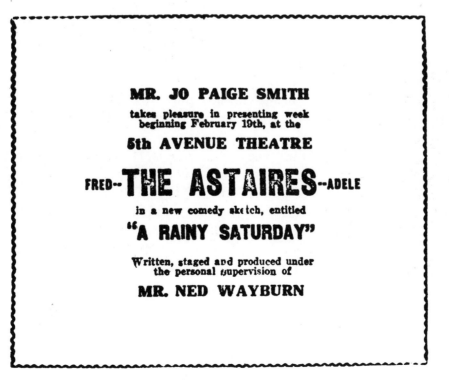

MR. JO PAIGE SMITH

takes pleasure in presenting week
beginning February 19th, at the

5th AVENUE THEATRE

FRED--**THE ASTAIRES**--ADELE

in a new comedy sketch, entitled

"A RAINY SATURDAY"

Written, staged and produced under
the personal supervision of

MR. NED WAYBURN

15

sister were spending the summer at Delaware Water Gap, Pa. The possibility that Fred and Adele might have been in some of the footage cannot be ascertained since all prints of the film have, apparently, been lost.)

The Astaires were now such a success—even though they never did get to play the Palace—that they were signed for their first appearance in a Broadway musical. It was the Shubert revue, *Over the Top*, a wartime show with a score by Sigmund Romberg that played at—according to the program— the Forty-fourth Street Theatre Roof Theatre. Justine Johnstone was the featured attraction, and Ed Wynn joined the cast during the run. The debut of the seventeen-year-old Fred Astaire and his sister did not go unnoticed. "One of the prettiest features of the show," wrote Lewis Sherwin in the *Globe*, "is the dancing of the two Astaires. The girl, a light, sprite-like little creature, has really an exquisite floating style in her capering, while the young man combines eccentric agility with humor."

The program for the revue contained this illuminating heading: "To Make the Lucidity of the Libretto 'Conspicuous' the Following Musical Interruptions Take Place"—and it then listed, among other such interruptions, three dances performed by Fred (in one place referred to as "Ted") and Adele Astaire. *Over the Top* did not go over too well, remaining on Broadway for less than three months before embarking on a brief tour.

The Astaires were not idle for long. Their next Broadway appearance, a July entry, was *The Passing Show of 1918*, again produced by the Shubert brothers and again featuring a score by Sigmund Romberg. This was a more successful and elaborate revue than *Over the Top*, with one scene depicting a London air raid that included the destruction of two German planes. It also entertained audiences with the comic gifts of Frank Fay, Charles Ruggles, and Willie and Eugene Howard, plus the fetching sight of what a handbill termed a "Wiggling Wave of Winsome Witches."

Reviewing the revue in the *Tribune*, Heywood Broun wrote: "In an evening in which there was an abundance of good dancing, Fred Astaire stood out. He and his partner, Adele Astaire, made the show pause early in the evening with a beautiful, careless, loose-limbed dance, in which the right foot never seemed to know just

The Astaires on the Orpheum Circuit, 1914.

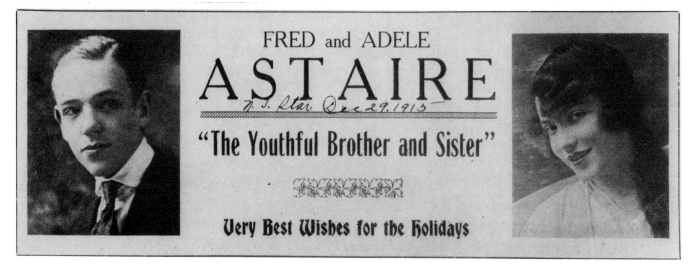

An ad in the *New Jersey Star*, December 29, 1915.

what the left foot was going to do, or cared, either. It almost seemed as if the two young people had been poured into the dance." Similar appreciation was voiced by Alan Dale in the *American*: "Fred Astaire, with Adele of the same name, danced all evening in knots, and it made one swelter to look at them. Fred is an agile youth, and apparently boneless, like that nice brand of sardines." And in the words of Charles Darnton in the *Evening World*: "The eye followed with delight Fred and Estelle [*sic*] Astaire, who danced so cleverly and put so much originality into their steps that they scored the hit of the show."

After five months in New York, *The Passing Show of 1918* went on the road. When Frank Fay left the cast, Fred took over his assignments in the sketches, thus marking his first appearances in speaking roles.

Producer Charles Dillingham, who had admired the Astaires during their tour of *Over the Top*, signed them to appear in *Apple Blossoms,* with a book by William LeBaron and a score created in almost equal parts by Fritz Kreisler and Victor Jacobi. The operetta was based on a story by Alexandre Dumas, but updated to chronicle the escapades of a young married couple in Greenwich Village. John Charles Thomas and Wilda Bennett played the couple, with the Astaires on view in only two dance routines: "On the Banks of the Bronx" (by Jacobi) and "A Girl, a Man, a Night, a Dance" (adapted from Kreisler's *Tambourin Chinois*). The musical opened on October 7, 1919, to favorable notices, particularly for the Astaires. "Fred Astaire and his pretty sister, Adele," wrote Charles Darnton in the *Evening World*, "danced as though they were twins, and scored the biggest hit they've ever made." "In all frankness," confessed Heywood Broun in the *Tribune*, "we must admit that to us quite the most stirring event of the evening was the remarkable dancing of the Astaires." *The Times'* Alexander Woollcott was equally impressed: "There should be a half-dozen special words for the vastly entertaining dances by the two Adaires [*sic*], in particular for those by the incredibly nimble and lackadaisical Adaire named Fred. He is one of those extraordinary persons whose senses of rhythm and humor have been all mixed up, whose very muscles, of which he seems to have an extra supply, are downright facetious." Mr. Woollcott, however, was far less taken with the show's leading lady, Wilda Bennett, who apparently had an attack of first-night jitters. "Doubtless she will do much better,"

Aurelia and Minnie Coccia. Fred credits Coccia with having the greatest influence on him of any dancer.

The New York Press unanimously declare

FRED AND ADELE ASTAIRE

(The Brother and Sister)

A HIT

with

"Over The Top"

The Latest Shubert Production

Over the Top was the Astaires' first Broadway show.

The "Twit, Twit, Twit" song in the "Birdland" scene from *The Passing Show*.

Producer Charles B. Dillingham.

. . . and in *The Love Letter*.

Fred and Adele in *Apple Blossoms* . . .

20

he wrote, "when she is not saying to herself: 'I am singing songs by the great Fritz Kreisler and there he is in the seventh row on the aisle. I think I'm going to faint.'"

Dillingham tried to repeat his *Apple Blossoms* success two years later with *The Love Letter*. Again John Charles Thomas was the star, again the Astaires were the featured dancers, again William LeBaron was the librettist, and again Victor Jacobi was the composer. But Fritz Kreisler was missing, and apparently a number of other things. As Fred Astaire wrote in his autobiography: "It was one of those cumbersome vehicles, very well meant and planned, but it had a concept that couldn't be conquered for musical purposes."

The Astaires, however, won their customary high praise. In the *World*, Louis DeFore wrote: "When the pace became slow, the dancing Astaires came gracefully to the rescue. Their own little triumph was won with the grotesque number, 'Upside Down,' one of the most captivating bits in the musical." The uncredited *Herald* appraiser referred to the Astaires "getting four encores for their entertaining singing and nutty dancing to 'Upside Down,' and revealing in this and in other whirlwind numbers that they have developed a penetrating comedy touch with their lips as well as their always ambitious feet." And from the equally anonymous *Sun* critic: "One of the best bits was a clever and amusing 'nut' dance by Fred and Adele Astair [*sic*]."

What in the world is a "nut" dance? Actually, it was the team's first attempt at what would become their familiar "runaround" trademark. The whole thing was director Edward Royce's idea. He had Adele put her arms in front of her as if she were on a bicycle holding the handlebars, and run around in a large circle looking as if she were grimly intent on getting somewhere. Fred was then instructed to join her, shoulder to shoulder, and they simply trotted around three or four times, their faces expressionless, to the accompaniment of a series of oompahs-oompahs from the pit orchestra. The Astaires used this runaround exit from then on in every show they appeared except for *The Band Wagon*, and it never failed to bring down the house. Years later, Fred even had Gracie Allen revive it in the movie *A Damsel in Distress*.

During the run of *The Love Letter*, Fred Astaire met Alex Aarons, a young producer who wanted to cast the brother and sister act in his next show, *For Goodness Sake*. Though the score was originally to have been the work of George and Ira Gershwin, a previous commitment limited their contributions to three songs. The story was all about a husband who suspects his wife of flirting and feigns suicide to win her back. Fred and Adele played friends of the married couple, and while they received no better than sixth billing, they were, unquestionably, the hit of the show. In the words of Alan Dale of the *American*: "The two Astaires are the principal assets of *For Goodness Sake*. They can speak a little, act a little, and dance quarts. . . . Miss Astaire is a pleasant little body, with a sense of humor, and Mr. Astaire has the lank lissomeness necessary for his 'line of work.'" Robert Benchley, the *Life* magazine critic, was similarly taken by the team: "There isn't much to say about *For Goodness Sake* that you couldn't say about most musicals except that the Astaires (perhaps late of 'Astaire and Down') are in it. When they dance everything seems brighter and their comedy alone would be good enough to carry them through even if they were to stop dancing (which God forbid!)."

The unidentified *Herald* man reported that "Fred and Adele Astaire received the ovation of the evening. This refreshing pair won encore after encore until it seemed they'd get the ague. Brother and sister stamped themselves as the best dancing pair for eccentric comedy by their agility as well as their modest and unsophisticated air of having just escaped from high school." The team's unsophisticated air was also noted by Charles Darnton of the *Evening World*, who wrote: "Here are those young favorites, the gangling Fred and the pert Adele. As they amble into view and mix with the youngsters they don't look as though they were anything more than somebody's children. But when they dance—oh, boy, and likewise girl! With ease, grace, rhythm, charm and humor, youth becomes a wonderful thing, and you realize all this in watching the Astaires. They happen to be the best of their kind."

Fred was not yet twenty-three and Adele no more than twenty-four when *For Goodness Sake* opened early in 1922. They were obviously the ones who had turned an average little musical into a fair success. They scored heaviest with two of their three numbers: "Oh Gee, Oh Gosh" ("Oh golly, I love you"), and "The Whichness of the Whatness" ("And the whereness of the who"), the latter being the "nut" number for their runaround hop. The show closed after 103 performances, caused primarily by the severe summer heat that season.

Broadway's *For Goodness Sake* became an even bigger hit in London as *Stop Flirting*.

QUEEN'S · THEATRE
SHAFTESBURY AVENUE. W.

Licensed by the Lord Chamberlain to
General Manager

ALFRED BUTT
OSCAR BARRETT

EVERY EVENING at 8.30
MATINEES : WED. & SAT. at 2.30

ALFRED BUTT
WITH
ALEX A. AARONS
PRESENTS

STOP FLIRTING

A MUSICAL FARCE
By FRED JACKSON

Music by WILLIAM DALY and PAUL LANNIN.   Additional Numbers by GEORGE GERSHWIN.
Play Produced by FELIX EDWARDES

| FRED AND ADELE ASTAIRE |
| JACK MELFORD |
| HENRY KENDALL |
| H. R. HIGNETT |
| GEORGE de WARFAZ |
| MIMI CRAWFORD |
| MARJORIE GORDON |

With Noël Coward in London, 1923. Fred staged two numbers in Coward's revue, *London Calling!*

Fred hated both the song and the wig in the "Pale Venetian Moon" number in *The Bunch and Judy*.

A flyer heralding the first stop for the touring *Lady, Be Good!* in 1925.

Adele and Fred in *Lady, Be Good!*

Fred and the girls in *Funny Face*.

Fred's first appearance with a top-hatted male chorus
was the "High Hat" number in *Funny Face*.

Though they had appeared in *For Goodness Sake* under the aegis of Alex Aarons, Fred and Adele were still under contract to Dillingham. Now that the team had become well established, Dillingham decided to build an entire show around them. But even with a Jerome Kern score, *The Bunch and Judy* quickly became known as *The Bust and Judy*. And while the musical gave the Astaires their biggest roles to date, another brother and sister team, comedians Johnny and Ray Dooley, scored equally as well.

Among the critics, there were some doubts expressed that Fred and Adele could carry an entire show. But they still had their champions, including Heywood Broun, who offered this opinion in the *World*: "Fred and Adele are the most graceful and charming young dancers available in the world of musical comedy. Indeed, the Astaires are distinctly attractive even when they are not in motion, and once they begin to dance they are among the immortals." Helping them maintain this exalted position was the usual nut number with the runaround trot, this time known as "How Do You Do, Katinka?"

While they were staggering through the two-month run of *The Bunch and Judy*, the Astaires got an offer from Alex Aarons to repeat their roles in the London version of *For Goodness Sake*, renamed *Stop Flirting*. The team sailed on the *Aquitania* in March 1923, rehearsed for five weeks, toured Liverpool, Glasgow, and Edinburgh, and opened in the West End on May 30. Principally because of Fred and Adele, the entertainment became a resounding hit and made the two dancers the most popular American attraction London had seen since Edna May appeared in *The Belle of New York* twenty-five years before. In *The Nation and Athenaeum*, Francis Birrell observed: "In their tireless high spirits, their unfailing delight in their own concerns, their litheness and unceasing activities, Fred and Adele Astaire ceased to be human beings to become, as it were, translated into denizens of an Elizabethan forest." Of remarkably similar mind was Sydney Carroll, who wrote in the *London Times*: "They typify the primal spirit of animal delight that could not restrain itself—the vitality that burst its bonds in the Garden of Eden. . . . They are as lithe as blades of grass, as light as gossamer, and as odd as golliwogs."

Stop Flirting opened at the Shaftesbury Theatre, was transferred to to the Queen's, and eventually ended up at the Strand. During the

"We play hoops!" in *The Band Wagon*.

Fred, Adele and Tilly Losch.

The Band Wagon's first-act finale, "I Love Louisa," with Tilly Losch, the Astaires, Frank Morgan, and Helen Broderick.

The Astaires and chorus in the "White Heat" number in *The Band Wagon*.

Adele and Fred in the
Chinese party scene in *Smiles*.

pantomime season at Christmas, the show played Birmingham and then returned to the Strand in March 1924. The total run of all London engagements was 418 performances, which could easily have been extended had not the Astaires decided that a year and a half was long enough time to be away from Broadway.

Upon their return the team discovered that Alex Aarons had secured the services of George and Ira Gershwin to write the entire score for the next Fred and Adele show. The new production also marked the beginning of Aaron's production association with Vinton Freedley, a former actor who had played the romantic lead in *For Goodness Sake*. Everything augured well for this maiden effort which began life as *Black Eyed Susan* but which was known as *Lady, Be Good!* by the time it reached Broadway.

The tale dreamed up by co-librettists Guy Bolton and P. G. Wodehouse was a frothy bit about a brother and sister—Dick and Susie Trevor, played by the Astaires—who, after being dispossessed in the opening scene, are forced to do their singing and dancing in the homes of well-heeled friends. They finally come into the money when Susie masquerades as a Spanish heiress to collect four million dollars.

The Gershwin score was crowded with hits. In addition to the near-title song, "Oh, Lady Be Good," which was sung by Walter Catlett, there were duets for Fred and Adele that included "Hang on to Me" (a chins-up piece the couple perform in the street following their eviction), "Fascinating Rhythm" (with Cliff Edwards), and "Swiss Miss" (the old runaround bit again). Fred also had his first solo number: "The Half of It, Dearie, Blues." One casualty, however, was "The Man I Love" which, though written for *Lady, Be Good!*, was dropped during the tryout.

The Times' critic lavished most of his praise on Adele ("as charming and entertaining a musical comedy actress as the town has seen on display in many a moon"), while curiously almost ignoring brother Fred ("Fred too gives a good account of himself"). But the other appraisers were careful to divide the honors. In the *American*, Alan Dale wrote: "They dance, they sing and they have been jellied into some sort of plot which eludes me, as such plots invariably do, and I never worry." "The insouciant Astaires recaptured the hearts of New York," welcomed Arthur Hornblow in *Theatre Magazine*. "Adele is, if anything, more piquant and impish and her brother Fred more blithe and joyous. Their nimble feet twinkle faster than ever, and they came near carrying off all the honors of the sprightly new show."

After appearing in *Lady, Be Good!* on Broadway until September 1925, the Astaires toured in it in ten cities, and took it to London, where it opened the following April, and became another triumph. Wrote Hubert Griffith in the *Evening Standard*: "Adele Astaire is, I think, the most attractive thing on any stage." And according to the *Daily Sketch*: "Fred and Adele have only to appear and everyone is blissfully happy. . . . Their dancing was uproarious." Nine months later the show was forced to close because the Empire Theatre, in which it was playing, was to be torn down to make way for a cinema.

Upon completion of their tour through England, Wales and Scotland, Fred and Adele Astaire returned to New York in June 1927, to start preparing for their next opus: *Smarty*, with a book co-authored by Robert Benchley and a score by George and Ira Gershwin. Only before the show reached Broadway, the title had been changed to *Funny Face*, Victor Moore had joined the cast as a timorous jewel thief, Allen Kearns had succeeded Stanley Ridges in the romantic lead, seven numbers had been dropped, five were added, and Benchley no longer had anything to do with it. Among the musical replacements that helped turn a shaky venture into a solid hit were two show-stoppers for Fred and Adele, "Funny Face" and "The Babbitt and the Bromide" (this year's runaround), plus a duet for lovers Adele Astaire and Allen Kearns, "He Loves and She Loves" (which took the place of "How Long Has This Been Going On?", Adele's duet with Ridges.) Other musical pleasures: the sibilant duet, " 'S Wonderful," and Fred's specialty, "High Hat," in which, for the first time, the dancer led a contingent of tapping, top-hatted chorus boys. (The title and lyric, however, dealt less with apparel than with the proper method of treating girls to make them "come around.")

Funny Face, which opened on Broadway November 22, 1927, was the first attraction to be housed in the newly built Alvin Theatre (the name combined the first syllables of Aarons' and Freedley's first names). It was a particularly auspicious occasion for almost all concerned. Writing in the *World*, Alexander Woollcott mused: "I do not know whether George Gershwin was born into this world to write rhythms for Fred Astaire's feet or whether Fred

Astaire was born into this world to show how the Gershwin music should really be danced. But surely they were written in the same key, those two." *Judge*'s judge, George Jean Nathan, handed down this verdict: "The Astaire team lifts the evening as they have lifted equally dubious vehicles in the past and sends the show gaily over. If there are better dancers anywhere I must have been laid up with my old war wounds when they were displaying themselves."

In the *Sun*, Gilbert Gabriel was positively ecstatic: "It's a light-hearted and light-toed musical comedy, charged with winsome Gershwin tunes, droll as droll could reasonably or seasonbly be, and a rhapsody of the magical and flying motions of Brother and Sister Astaire. When Harlequin puts on a grey derby hat and Columbine delights in a particularly impudent snub nose, you have the two Astaires. . . . They are a sort of champagne cup of motion, those Astaires. They live, laugh and leap in a world that is all bubbles. They are sleek, long-shanked, blissfully graceful, both of them. Their dance steps flash and quiver with an intricacy which declines to be taken seriously but which is none the less a maker of marvels."

The book of *Funny Face* was generally dismissed as "dull," "scrambled," "tedious," "perishable," and "flat." But no matter. The musical chalked up a successful 250-performance engagement, and even won a Paramount screen test for Fred and Adele, though nothing came of it. What did come of it was the, by now, inevitable London production. And the inevitable London success. In the *Sketch*, the reviewer greeted the event by predicting: "There is no mistaking the fact that London is about to enjoy another out-break of 'Astairia' this winter. Adele's personality has still the same naive and easy-going grace, humour and simplicity. Fred Astaire—that mild and intellectual looking young man—is still the mind of the dance." The West End run bested the Broadway run by thirteen performances.

An offer by Florenz Ziegfeld to co-star with Marilyn Miller in *Tom, Dick and Harry*—later called *Smiles*—brought the brother-and-sister team back to New York. The show, however, turned out to be a disaster, despite the producer's celebrated touch, the appeal of the three stars, and a Vincent Youmans score that included "Time on My Hands" (even that song had to overcome the handicap of Miss Miller warbling a special refrain that began, "What can I say?/ Is there a way/ I can get gay with you? . . . ") *Smile*'s story,

The "Night and Day" dance with Claire Luce in *Gay Divorce.*

Fred, Claire and Erik Rhodes are surprised by Luella Gear.

about a Salvation Army lass involved in high society, struck many as a throwback to a turn-of-the-century musical, *The Belle of New York* (itself eventually transformed into a movie for Fred Astaire), and the show remained for barely two months. Trying to be kind, *The New Yorker*'s Robert Benchley wrote: "Considered as the Golden Calf brought in on the Ark of the Covenant, it was a complete bust. Of course, no show with Fred and Adele Astaire in it could be really considered a *complete* bust. There are moments, such as when Fred is shooting down chorus boys with his stick, or, with Adele, is executing the beloved 'runaround' to the accompaniment of an uncoordinated French band, when the back of your neck begins to tingle and you realize that you are in the presence of something Pretty Darned Swell. Adele is a fine little comedian, and I don't think that I will plunge the nation into war by stating that Fred is the greatest dancer in the world."

That "shooting-down-chorus-boys-with-his-stick" business was, of course, later used for *Top Hat*'s memorable "Top Hat, White Tie and Tails" number. But nothing could help *Smiles*. Fred Astaire once described it as "the kind of flop that even made the audience look bad."

The Astaires snapped back the following year. Ever since *Three's a Crowd*, producer Max Gordon, lyricist Howard Dietz, and composer Arthur Schwartz had clearly established themselves as the foremost creators of smart, sophisticated revues. For their smart, sophisticated follow-up, Gordon signed Fred and Adele Astaire, Helen Broderick, Frank Morgan, and Tilly Losch to star in *The Band Wagon*, a production many still regard as the supreme revue of all times. Following its June 3, 1931, Broadway opening, Brooks Atkinson wrote in *The Times*: "Mr. Schwartz's lively melodies, the gay dancing of the Astaires, and the colorful merriment of the background and staging begin a new era in the artistry of the American revue. When revue writers discover light humors of that sort in the phantasmagoria of American life, the stock market will start to rise spontaneously, the racketeers will all be retired or dead, and the perfect state will be here." As for the particular contributions of Fred and Adele, the *Sun*'s critic, Richard Lockridge, offered this estimate: "There is something utterly audacious about the two of them; there is a lightness and flexibility and dash in whatever they do, whether it is to chase a plump and bearded Frenchman around the revolving stage or to dance in black and white before an immense encircled drum. They may be chatty and intimate, teasing themselves and the audience. They may be bizarre, tantilizing figures from a modernistic nightmare. They are in any case incomparable."

Fred's solo in *The Band Wagon* was "New Sun in the Sky," which he performed while putting on his top hat, white tail, and tails. With sister Adele, he did "Sweet Music" (offered as an antidote to the wolf at the door), "Hoops" (the kids chased the Frenchman in that one), "I Love Louisa," and "White Heat" (in front of the drum). With Tilly Losch, Fred danced the "Beggar Waltz" in a balletic routine that later was to provide partial inspiration for Astaire's "Limehouse Blues" number in the film *Ziegfeld Follies*. For the first time, the Astaires did away with their runaround trademark—though the oompahs were kept in for "I Love Louisa."

It was during the post-New York tour that Adele Astaire permanently retired from the stage to marry Lord Charles Cavendish, the second son of the Duke of Devonshire. This, of course, meant that for the first time Fred Astaire would be on his own without the sibling partner with whom he had danced all of his professional life. As his premier solo starring effort, Fred chose to appear in *Gay Divorce*, with Claire Luce as his new partner and a score by Cole Porter. Though the musical garnered few posies, Fred's dancing and the song "Night and Day" managed to attract sufficient patronage to turn it into a success. Newspaper reviewers, however, could hardly resist comparing Miss Luce to her predecessor. "In the refulgent Claire Luce," commented Brooks Atkinson in *The Times,* "Fred Astaire has found a partner who can match his step for step, and who flies over the furniture in his company without missing a beat. As a solo dancer Mr. Astaire stamps out his accents with that lean, nervous agility that distinguishes his craftsmanship, and he has invented turns that abound in graphic portraiture. But some of us cannot help feeling that the joyousness of the Astaire team is missing now that the team has parted."

By helping transform a weak vehicle into a hit, Fred Astaire proved that he could carry a show all by himself. But he was losing his taste for the Broadway theatre. In an interview at the time with Lucius Beebe in the *Herald Tribune*, Astaire was quoted as saying: "The stage is beginning to worry me a bit. Just why I

The wedding group at Adele's marriage to Lord Charles Cavendish
at Chatsworth, England. Ann Astaire is standing at the left,
and the Duke of Devonshire is at the far right.

Phyllis and Fred Astaire a few months
after their arrival in Hollywood.

Fred and his mother on the set of *Easter Parade.*

cannot say, only perhaps it's getting on my nerves. I don't know what I'm going to do about it either. I feel that I ought to dance just as long as I'm able to do it and get away with it. Lots of people seem to like it and would be disappointed if I should turn to anything else."

The obvious next step was Hollywood. In Hollywood, he could continue as a dancing actor without an eight-performances-a-week schedule that had become both a bore and a chore. As he wrote in his autobiography: "Having had so many years on the stage, I was looking for a change and a chance to prove something brand-new for myself professionally." With agent Leland Hayward handling the contractural details, Astaire was signed by David O. Selznick, then the head of RKO-Radio Pictures, to appear in *Flying Down to Rio* just as soon as he had completed his Broadway engagement.

But first there was time for a more personal event. On July 12, 1933, Astaire married the former Phyllis Baker Potter, with Justice Selah B. Strong performing the ceremony in his Brooklyn chambers. Following a one-day honeymoon aboard Mrs. Payne Whitney's yacht, Mr. and Mrs. Fred Astaire took a Ford tri-motor plane that landed them in Hollywood twenty-six hours later.

When the Astaires arrived, however, Selznick had already left RKO at the urging of M-G-M boss Louis B. Mayer—who was also Selznick's father-in-law at the time—to join his studio as producer. One of his very first productions was *Dancing Lady*, starring Joan Crawford and Clark Gable. Needing a dancer, Selznick simply borrowed Astaire from his old studio which, fortunately, was not yet ready to begin shooting *Flying Down to Rio*.

Selznick, himself, had to overcome some initial doubts about Astaire. After viewing Fred's screentest, the producer, while he was still at RKO, had sent the following memo: "I am still a little uncertain about the man, but I feel, in spite of his enormous ears and bad chin line, that his charm is so tremendous that it comes through even in this wretched test."

BROADWAY MUSICALS

1917 • OVER THE TOP

Producers: Messrs. Shubert. Lyrics: Charles J. Manning, Matthew Woodward. Music: Sigmund Romberg, Herman Timberg. Sketches: Philip Bartholomae, Harold Atteridge. Director: Joseph Herbert. Dance director: Allan K. Foster. Settings: P. Dodd Ackerman. Music director: Frank Tours.

Cast: Justine Johnstone, Mary Eaton, T. Roy Barnes (succeeded by Ed Wynn), Craig Campbell, Ted Lorraine, Joe Laurie, Fred & Adele Astaire, Vivian & Dagmar Oakland, Betty Pierce.

MUSICAL NUMBERS: "Frocks and Frills"—V. Oakland; dance by Astaires/ "My Rainbow Girl"—Johnstone, Campbell/ "The Girl for Me"—Oakland Sisters, Lorraine/ "Posterland"—Johnstone/ "Oh, Galatea" (lyric, Bartholomae)—Campbell; dance by Johnstone & Lorraine/ "That Airship of Mine"—Lorraine/ "Greenwich Village Belle"—Oakland Sisters, Lorraine/ "Over the Top"—Lorraine/ "Golden Pheasant" (lyric, Woodward)—Campbell/ "Algerian Girl"—V. Oakland/ "Where Is the Language to Tell?"—Astaires/ "Justine Johnstone Rag" (music with Frank Carter; lyric, Manning)—Astaires, Oakland Sisters, Pierce, Lorraine/ "A Bit of Airy Camouflage"—Barnes.

Opened November 28, 1917 at the 44th Street Theatre; 78 performances.

1918 • THE PASSING SHOW OF 1918

Producers: Messrs. Shubert. Lyrics & sketches: Harold Atteridge. Music: Sigmund Romberg, Jean Schwartz. Director: J. C. Huffman. Dance director: Jack Mason. Settings: Watson Barratt. Costumes: Cora MacGeachy. Music director: Charles Previn.

Cast: Frank Fay, Willie & Eugene Howard, Charles Ruggles, George Hassell, Sam White, Lou Clayton, Nita Naldi, Fred & Adele Astaire, Dave Dreyer, Jessie Reed, Nell Carrington, Isabel Lowe, Virginia Fox Brooks, Arthur Albro, Dorsha, Edith Pierce, Aileen Rooney, Emily Miles, Olga Roller.

MUSICAL NUMBERS: "I Can't Make My Feet Behave"—A. Astaire/ "Won't You Buy a War Stamp?" (music, Ray Perkins)—Lowe, Ruggles/ "My Baby-Talk Lady"—Fay, Ruggles, Lowe/ "Go West Young Girl" (music, Russell Tarbox)—Brooks/ "Trombone Jazz"—White, Clayton/ "Oh, Those Vampire Girls"—Albro/ "Squab Farm"—F. Astaire/ "The Shimmy Sisters"—Pierce, Rooney, Fay/ "I'll Make an Angel Out of You"—Fay, Lowe/ "Serenade"—Howard Brothers/ "Bring On the Girls"—Miles, Carrington, Astaires, Clayton, White/ "Twit, Twit, Twit"—Astaires/ "My Holiday Girl"—Ruggles/ "Quick Service"—Astaires/ "Galli Curci Rag"—Howard Brothers/ "Smiles" (J. Will Callahan-Max Kortlander)—Carrington/ "The Duchess of Devonshire"—Roller/ "Dress, Dress, Dress"—Roller.

Opened July 25, 1918 at the Winter Garden; 125 performances.

Fred in *Apple Blossoms* .

38

1919 • APPLE BLOSSOMS

Producer: Charles Dillingham. Book & lyrics: William LeBaron. Music: Fritz Kreisler, Victor Jacobi. Director Fred C. Latham. Dance director: Edward Royce. Settings: Joseph Urban. Music director: William Daly.

Cast: John Charles Thomas, Wilda Bennett, Roy Atwell, Fred & Adele Astaire, Rena Parker, Percival Knight, Juanita Fletcher, Alan Fagan, Harrison Brockbank, Florence Shirley.

MUSICAL NUMBERS: "Brothers" (Jacobi)—Fletcher/ "Who Can Tell?" (Kreisler; same melody as later song, "Stars in My Eyes")—Bennett/ "On the Banks of the Bronx" (Jacobi)—Parker, Knight; dance by Astaires/ "I'll Be True to You (Jacobi)— Bennett/ "Nancy's Farewell" (Kreisler)—Bennett/ "Marriage Knot" (Kreisler)—Parker, Atwell/ "When the Wedding Bells Are Ringing" (Jacobi)— Bennett, Fagan/ "Little Girls, Goodbye" (Jacobi) —Thomas/ "You Are Free" (Jacobi)—Bennett, Thomas/ "Phillip's Story" (Kreisler)—Thomas/ "Star of Love" (Kreisler)—Bennett/ "A Girl, a Man, a Night, a Dance" (Kreisler)—Shirley; dance by Astaires/ "I'm in Love" (Kreisler)—Thomas/ "The Second Violin" (Kreisler)—Shirley, Knight, Fletcher, Parker, Brockbank.

Opened October 7, 1919 at the Globe Theatre; 256 performances.

1921 • THE LOVE LETTER

Producer: Charles Dillingham. Book & lyrics: William LeBaron. Music: Victor Jacobi. Director & dance director: Edward Royce. Settings: Joseph Urban. Music director: William Daly.

Cast: John Charles Thomas, Carolyn Thomson, Alice Brady, Marjorie Gateson, Fred & Adele Astaire, Will West, Bessie Franklin, Jane Carroll.

MUSICAL NUMBERS: "To the Girl You Dance With" —chorus/ "Any Girl"—Gateson/ "I'll Say I Love You"—Astaires/ "I'll Return for You"—Thomas, Thomson/ "First Love"—Thomson/ "The Only Girl"—Thomas/ "Scandal Town"—Gateson, West/ "We Were in Love"—Thomas, Thomson/ "Upside Down"—Astaires/ "Canzonetta"— Thomson/ "Rainbow"—Carroll/ "You're Mine"— Carroll/ "Man, Man, Man"—Gateson/ "Dreaming" —Astaires/ "My Heart Beats for You"—Thomas/ "Twiddle Your Thumbs" (Will West)—West.

Opened October 4, 1921 at the Globe Theatre; 31 performances.

1922 • FOR GOODNESS SAKE

Producer: Alex A. Aarons. Lyrics: Arthur Jackson. Music: William Daly, Paul Lannin. Book: Fred Jackson. Director Priestley Morrison. Dance director: Allan K. Foster. Settings: P. Dodd Ackerman. Music director: William Daly.

Cast: John E. Hazzard, Marjorie Gateson, Charles Judels, Vinton Freedley, Helen Ford, Fred & Adele Astaire.

MUSICAL NUMBERS: "All to Myself" (Ira Gershwin-George Gershwin)—Astaires/ "Someone" (Gershwin-Gershwin)—Ford, Freedley/ "Tra-La-La" (Gershwin-Gershwin)—Gateson, Hazzard/ "When You're in Rome"—F. Astaire, Gateson, Judels/ "Every Day" (music, Daly alone)—Ford, Freedley/ "Twilight" (music, Daly alone)—chorus/ "The Greatest Team of All"—Ford, Freedley, Judels/ "Oh Gee, Oh Gosh"—(music, Daly alone)— Astaires/ "In the Days of Wild Romance"— Hazzard/ "When Somebody Cares"—Ford, Freedley/ "French Pastry Walk" (lyric, Jackson, Ira Gershwin)—Judels, F. Astaire, Freedley/ "The Whichness of the Whatness"—Astaires.

Opened February 20, 1922 at the Lyric Theatre; 103 performances.

1922 • THE BUNCH AND JUDY

Producer: Charles Dillingham. Lyrics: Anne Caldwell. Music: Jerome Kern. Book: Anne Caldwell & Hugh Ford. Director Fred G. Latham. Dance director: uncredited. Settings: Gates & Morange. Music director: Victor Baravalle.

Cast: Fred & Adele Astaire, Johnny Dooley, Ray Dooley, Grace Hayes, Roberta Beatty, Philip Tonge, 6 Brown Brothers, Carl McBride, Augustus Minton, Patricia Clark.

MUSICAL NUMBERS: "Silenzio"—McBride, Beatty/ "The Naughty Nobleman"—Minton/ "Pale Venetian Moon"—Astaires/ "Peach Girl"—Astaires/ "Morning Glory"—A. Astaire/ "Lovely Lassie"— Beatty/ "Every Day in Every Way"—Astaires/ "Times Square"—A. Astaire, R. Dooley, Clark, J. Dooley, F. Astaire/ "How Do You Do, Katinka?"— Astaires/ "Have-You-Forgotten-Me-Blues"— Hayes.

Opened November 28, 1922 at the Globe Theatre; 65 performances.

1924 • LADY, BE GOOD!

Producers: Alex A. Aarons & Vinton Freedley. Lyrics: Ira Gershwin. Music: George Gershwin. Book: Guy Bolton & Fred Thompson. Director: Felix Edwardes. Settings: Norman Bel Geddes. Music director: Paul Lannin. Orchestrations: Stephen Jones.

Cast: Fred & Adele Astaire, Walter Catlett, Alan Edwards, Cliff Edwards, Gerald Oliver Smith, Kathlene Martin, Patricia Clark, Phil Ohman & Vic Arden (duo-pianists).

MUSICAL NUMBERS: "Hang on to Me"—Astaires/ "A Wonderful Party"—chorus/ "The End of a String"—chorus/ "We're Here Because"—Clark, Smith/ "So Am I"—A. Astaire, A. Edwards/ "Fascinating Rhythm"—Astaires, C. Edwards/ "Oh, Lady Be Good!"—Catlett/ "Weather Man"—chorus/ "Rainy Afternoon Girls"—chorus/ "The Half of It, Dearie, Blues"—Martin, F. Astaire/ "Juanita"—A. Astaire/ "Little Jazz Bird"—C. Edwards/ "Carnival Time"—chorus/ "Swiss Miss"—Astaires.

Opened December 1, 1924 at the Liberty Theatre; 330 performances.

1927 • FUNNY FACE

Producers: Alex A. Aarons & Vinton Freedley. Lyrics: Ira Gershwin. Music: George Gershwin. Book: Fred Thompson & Paul Gerard Smith. Director: Edgar MacGregor. Dance director: Bobby Connolly. Settings: John Wenger. Costumes: Kiviette. Music director: Alfred Newman. Choral director: Frank Black.

Cast: Fred & Adele Astaire, William Kent, Victor Moore, Allen Kearns, Betty Compton, Ritz Quartette, Gertrude McDonald, Dorothy Jordan, Phil Ohman & Vic Arden (duo-pianists).

MUSICAL NUMBERS: "Birthday Party"—Compton, McDonald/ "Once"—Kent, Compton/ "Funny Face"—Astaires/ "High Hat"—F. Astaire, boys/ "He Loves and She Loves"—A. Astaire, Kearns/ "Let's Kiss and Make Up"—Astaires/ "In the Swim"—girls/ " 'S Wonderful"—A. Astaire, Kearns/ "Tell the Doc"—Kent/ "My One and Only"—F. Astaire, McDonald, Compton/ "Sing a Little Song"—Ohman & Arden, Ritz Quartette/ "Blue Hullabaloo"—Compton, McDonald/ "The Babbitt and the Bromide"—Astaires.

Opened November 22, 1927 at the Alvin Theatre; 250 performances.

1930 • SMILES

Producers Florenz Ziegfeld. Lyrics: Clifford Grey, Harold Adamson, Ring Lardner. Music: Vincent Youmans. Book: William Anthony McGuire. Director: William Anthony McGuire. Dance director: Ned Wayburn. Settings: Joseph Urban. Costumes: John Harkrider. Music director: Frank Tours.

Cast: Marilyn Miller, Fred & Adele Astaire, Tom Howard, Eddie Foy, Jr., Paul Gregory, Larry Adler, Claire Dodd, Georgia Caine, Edward Raquello, Kathryn Hereford, Adrian Rosley, Aber Twins, Bob Hope, Virginia Bruce.

MUSICAL NUMBERS: "Blue Bowery" (Adamson)—Aber Twins/ "Say, Young Man of Manhattan" (Adamson, Grey)—F. Astaire, boys/ "Rally 'Round Me" (Lardner)—Miller/ "Hotcha Ma Chotch" (Adamson, Grey)—A. Astaire, Foy/ "Time on My Hands" (Adamson, Mack Gordon)—Gregory/ "What Can I Say?" (Lardner; same melody as "Time on My Hands")—Miller/ "Be Good to Me" (Lardner)—Astaires/ "Chinese Party" (Lardner)—chorus/ "Clever These Chinese" (Adamson, Grey)—Hereford, Foy/ "Anyway, We Had Fun" (Lardner)—Miller, Astaires/ "Something to Sing About" (Lardner)—chorus/ "Here's a Day to Be Happy" (Lardner)—Gregory/ "If I Were You, Love" (Lardner)—Astaires/ "I'm Glad I Waited" (Adamson, Grey)—Miller, F. Astaire/ "La Marseilles" (Adamson, Grey)—Miller/ "Why Ain't I Home?" (Lardner)—Foy/ "Dancing Wedding" (Lardner)—chorus.

Opened November 18, 1930 at the Ziegfeld Theatre; 63 performances.

The Astaires and William Kent (left) in *Funny Face.*

1931 • THE BAND WAGON

Producer: Max Gordon. Lyrics: Howard Dietz.
Music: Arthur Schwartz. Sketches: George S.
Kaufman, Howard Dietz. Director: Hassard Short.
Dance director: Albertina Rasch. Settings: Albert
Johnston. Costumes: Kiviette, Constance Ripley.
Music director: Al Goodman. Orchestrations:
Robert Russell Bennett.

Cast: Fred & Adele Astaire, Frank Morgan, Helen
Broderick, Tilly Losch, Philip Loeb, John Barker,
Roberta Robinson, Francis Pierlot, Jay Wilson,
Peter Chambers.

MUSICAL NUMBERS: "Sweet Music"—Astaires/
"High and Low"—Robinson, Barker/ "When the
Rain Goes Pitter-Patter"—Morgan, Broderick/
"The Flag"—Losch/ "For Dear Old Nectar"—
cast/ "A Nice Place to Visit"—Broderick/ "Hoops"
—Astaires/ "Confession"—chorus/ "New Sun in
the Sky"—F. Astaire/ "Miserable with You"—A.
Astaire, Morgan/ "I Love Louisa"—Astaires, cast/
"Again"—Loeb, Wilson, Chambers/ "Dancing in
the Dark"—Barker; dance by Losch/ "Nanette"—
Morgan, Loeb, Pierlot, Chambers/ "Where Can
He Be?"—Broderick/ "The Beggar Waltz"—
dance by F. Astaire, Losch/ "White Heat"—
Astaires.

Opened June 3, 1931 at the New Amsterdam
Theatre; 260 performances.

1932 • GAY DIVORCE

Producer: Dwight Deere Wiman & Tom Weatherly.
Lyrics & Music: Cole Porter. Book: Dwight Taylor.
Director: Howard Lindsay. Dance directors:
Carl Randall, Barbara Newberry. Settings: Jo
Mielziner. Costumes: Raymond Sovey. Music
director: Gene Salzer. Orchestrations: Hans
Spialek, Robert Russell Bennett.

Cast: Fred Astaire, Claire Luce, Luella Gear,
G. P. Huntley, Jr., Betty Starbuck, Erik Rhodes,
Eric Blore, Roland Bottomley.

MUSICAL NUMBERS: "After You, Who?"—Astaire/
"Why Marry Them?"—Starbuck/ "Salt Air"—
Huntley, Starbuck/ "I Still Love the Red, White
and Blue"—Gear/ "Night and Day"—Astaire,
Luce/ "How's Your Romance?"—Rhodes/ "What
Will Become of Our England?"—Blore/ "I've Got
You on My Mind"—Astaire, Luce/ "Mister and
Missus Fitch"—Gear/ "You're in Love"—Astaire,
Luce, Rhodes.

Opened November 29, 1932 at the Ethel Barry-
more Theatre; 248 performances.

Fred and Adele in *The Bandwagon.*

LONDON MUSICALS

1923 • STOP FLIRTING (FOR GOODNESS SAKE)

Producer: Alfred Butt. Director: Felix Edwardes. Dance director: Gus Sohlke. Settings: Phil Harker. Music director: Jacques Heuvel.

Cast: Fred & Adele Astaire, Jack Melford, Mimi Crawford, Marjorie Gordon, Henry Kendall, George de Warfaz.

MUSICAL NUMBERS: "All to Myself"—Astaires/ "Someone"—Crawford, Kendall/ "I'll Build a Stairway to Paradise" (B. G. DeSylva, Ira Gershwin-George Gershwin)—Gordon, Melford, Crawford, Kendall, Astaires/ "Every Day"—Melford, Gordon/ "The Best of Everything" (DeSylva, Arthur Jackson-Gershwin)—Kendall, Crawford/ "Oh Gee, Oh Gosh"—Astaires/ "It's Great to Be in Love" (DeSylva, Jackson-Gershwin)—A. Astaire, Crawford, Gordon/ "The Whichness of the Whatness"—Astaires.

Opened May 30, 1923 at the Shaftesbury Theatre; 418 performances.

1926 • LADY, BE GOOD!

Producer: Alfred Butt, with Alex A. Aarons & Vinton Freedley. Director: Felix Edwardes. Dance director: Max Scheck. Settings: Joseph & Phil Harker. Music director: Jacques Heuvel.

Cast: Fred & Adele Astaire, William Kent, Buddy Lee, George Vollaire, Ewart Scott, Sylvia Leslie, Glori Beaumont, Irene Russell.

MUSICAL NUMBERS: "Buy a Little Button"—chorus/ "We're Here Because"—Beaumont, Scott/ "Hang on to Me"—Astaires/ "A Wonderful Party"— chorus/ "The End of a String"—chorus/ "Fascinating Rhythm"—Astaires, Lee/ "So Am I"—A. Astaire, Vollaire/ "Oh, Lady Be Good!"—Kent/ "Linger in the Lobby"—chorus/ "I'd Rather Charleston" (lyric, Desmond Carter)—Astaires/ "The Half of It, Dearie, Blues"—Russell, F. Astaire/ "Juanita"—A. Astaire/ "Carnival Time"— chorus/ "Swiss Miss"—Astaires.

Opened April 14, 1926 at the Empire Theatre; 326 performances.

1928 • FUNNY FACE

Producers: Alfred Butt & Lee Ephraim, with Alex A. Aarons & Vinton Freedley. Director: Felix Edwardes. Dance director: Bobby Connolly. Settings: Joseph & Phil Harker. Music director: Julian Jones.

Cast: Fred & Adele Astaire, Leslie Henson, Bernard Clifton, Rita Page, Sydney Howard, Eileen Hatton, Jacques Frey & Mario Braggiotti (duo-pianists).

MUSICAL NUMBERS: "Birthday Party"—Page, Hatton/ "Look at the Damn Thing Now"—Henson, Page/ "Funny Face"—Astaires/ "High Hat"— F. Astaire, boys/ " 'S Wonderful"—A. Astaire, Clifton/ "Let's Kiss and Make Up"—Astaires/ "In the Swim"—girls/ "Imagination"—A. Astaire, Clifton/ "Tell the Doc"—Henson/ "My One and Only"—F. Astaire, Hatton/ "The Babbitt and the Bromide"—Astaires.

Opened November 8, 1928 at the Prince's Theatre; 263 performances.

1933 • GAY DIVORCE

Producer: Lee Ephraim. Director: Felix Edwardes. Dance directors: Carl Randall, Barbara Newberry. Settings: Joseph & Phil Harker. Music director: Percival Mackey.

Cast: Fred Astaire, Claire Luce, Olive Blakeney, Claud Allister, Eric Blore, Joan Gardner, Erik Rhodes, Fred Hearne.

MUSICAL NUMBERS: "After You, Who?"—Astaire/ "Salt Air"—chorus/ "Never Say No"—Joan Gardner/ "Where Would You Get Your Coat?"— Blakeney/ "Night and Day"—Astaire, Luce/ "How's Your Romance?"—Rhodes/ "Waiters Versus Waitresses"—Blore/ "I've Got You on My Mind"—Astaire, Luce/ "I Love Only You"— Rhodes/ "Mister and Missus Fitch"—Blakeney/ "You're in Love"—Astaire, Luce, Rhodes.

Opened November 2, 1933 at the Palace Theatre; 108 performances.

MUSICAL NUMBERS
STAGED BY FRED ASTAIRE

Noël Coward and Gertrude Lawrence in "You Were Meant for Me" and Noël Coward in "Sentiment," both performed in *London Calling!*, Duke of York Theatre, London, 1923.

Marilyn Miller and Boys in "The Wedding Knell," performed in *Sunny*, New Amsterdam Theatre, New York, 1925.

Ginger Rogers and Allen Kearns in "Embraceable You," performed in *Girl Crazy*, Alvin Theatre, New York, 1930.

Fred and Adele on the roof of the Savoy Hotel just prior to the London opening of *Stop Flirting*.

FILM CAREER

DANCING LADY

CAST

Janie Barlow	Joan Crawford
Patch Gallagher	Clark Gable
Todd Newton	Franchot Tone
Grandma Newton	May Robson
Rosette LaRue	Winnie Lightner
Fred Astaire	Fred Astaire
Ward King	Robert Benchley
Steve	Ted Healy
Stooges	Moe Howard, Jerry Howard, Larry Fine
Singer	Art Jarrett
Vivian Warner	Gloria Foy
Jasper Bradley	Grant Mitchell
Junior Bradley	Maynard Holmes
Singer	Nelson Eddy
Pinky (librettist)	Sterling Holloway
Another Librettist	Harry Hayden
Judge	Francis Pierlot
Actress with Southern Accent	Eunice Quedens (Eve Arden)
Her Agent	Matt McHugh
Miss Allen (secretary)	Cecil Cunningham
Chorus Girl	Lynn Bari

Producer: David O. Selznick for Metro-Goldwyn-Mayer. Director: Robert Z. Leonard. Lyrics: Harold Adamson, Dorothy Fields, Lorenz Hart, Arthur Freed. Music: Burton Lane, Jimmy McHugh, Richard Rodgers, Nacio Herb Brown. Screenplay: Allen Rivkin, P. J. Wolfson, from novel by James Warner Bellah. Dance directors: Sammy Lee, Eddie Prinz. Art Director: Merrill Pye. Costumes: Adrian. Music director: Louis Silvers. Orchestrations: Maurice DePackh. Cameraman: Oliver T. Marsh. Editor: Margaret Booth. Release date: December 2, 1933. Running time: 90 minutes.

MUSICAL NUMBERS: "Hey, Young Fella" (Fields-McHugh)—burlesque chorus/ "Hold Your Man" (Freed-Brown)—Lightner/ "Everything I Have Is Yours" (Adamson-Lane)—Jarrett/ "My Dancing Lady" (Fields-McHugh)—Jarrett; dance by Crawford, chorus/ "Heigh-Ho, the Gang's All Here" (Adamson-Lane)—chorus, Astaire & Crawford; dance by Astaire & Crawford/ "Let's Go Bavarian" (Adamson-Lane)—chorus, Astaire & Crawford/ "That's the Rhythm of the Day" (Hart-Rodgers)—Eddy; dance by Crawford, chorus.

A new Broadway musical, *Dancing Lady*, is in rehearsal. Janie Barlow, fresh from the chorus line, has been tapped to replace the star of the show and director Patch Gallagher wants her to run through a number with her leading man:

PATCH: Freddy.

FRED: Yes, Patch.

PATCH: Show Miss Barlow the routine for the opening number, will you?

FRED: I'd love to.

JANIE: Good evening, Mr. Astaire.

FRED: Miss Barlow. Do you know the routine?

JANIE: I've seen it often enough. I'll try.

FRED: That's fine. Oh, Harry, give us the pickup on the "Gang" number, will you please? Thanks.

And so, following his first words on the screen, Fred Astaire dances for the first time on the screen. But not for long. After less than forty seconds, the "Gang" number is abruptly halted when Janie collapses because of a severe pain in her ankle (fortunately, it turns out to be only a sprain).

Fred Astaire's introduction to movie audiences in *Dancing Lady* (a previously scheduled appearance in a short sponsored by the Lambs Club was never made) was both casual and brief. He was simply brought on as himself, Fred Astaire, Broadway song-and-dance man. With Clark Gable playing Patch Gallagher and Joan Crawford as Janie Barlow he even had the added prestige of being welcomed to screenland by two authentic members of Hollywood royalty. But best of all, he was being seen in a major motion picture without the responsibility of carrying any part of the story. All that was required of him was to ease into the scene (Astaire later described his impression of himself as "knife-like"), and give a sample demonstration of the kind of work he had been doing almost all of his life.

But that wasn't all there was of Fred Astaire in *Dancing Lady*. For the climax of the film—the Broadway open-

Joan Crawford resists a demonstrative patron at the International Burlesque Theatre.

A note and a fifty dollar bill from socialite Franchot Tone impress Joan and her roommate Winnie Lightner.

Ted Healy and the Three Stooges
all set to give Joan the brushoff.

"Now listen, the show as it stands
is Spanish-American-War stuff." Director Clark Gable
tells off librettist Sterling Holloway.

ing of the stage musical—he danced in two numbers that were joined together as only Hollywood could join two disparate routines (their sole link was that both songs referred to beer-drinking, a timely topic following Prohibition's repeal). In the first, "Heigh-Ho, the Gang's All Here" (originally sung in the Broadway revue, *Earl Carroll Vanities* of 1931), the formally clad boys and girls of the chorus sing the words as they prance about a circular bar. Presently, Fred Astaire—in top hat, white tie, and tails—and Joan Crawford come bounding in, arm-in-arm, to reprise the number and perform a rhythmic, strutting dance. Then —miracle of miracles—Fred and Joan are raised on a platform above the heads of the partygoers, fly up through the roof and sail merrily across a starry sky to land—where else?—in Bavaria. (Of course, they are still in the same theatre before the same audience.) Here, in a setting reminiscent of the "I Love Louisa" number in Astaire's stage success, *The Band Wagon,* the frolicking dirndl-and-lederhosen crew joyously propose "Let's Go Bavarian," with the similarly attired Astaire and Crawford joining in for a rousing oompah ending. ("How'm I doing?" asks Crawford of Gable after the number. "So far so good" is the raspy reply.)

Fred Astaire's guest appearance paid off. Not only did he gain experience in dancing in front of a camera, he also received encouraging notices in the country's press. *Motion Picture Daily* even made a prediction: "Fred Astaire links an attractive screen personality to ace dancing and should go somewhere in celluloid."

The story depicted in *Dancing Lady* was, by then, familiar Hollywood fare —ever since, earlier the same year, Warner Brothers had struck gold with its classic backstage saga, *42nd Street* (and had quickly followed it up with *Gold Diggers of 1933* and *Footlight Parade*). There were, in fact, certain

49

Astaire, Crawford and Gable run through Fred's introductory
scene for director Robert C. Leonard . . .

. . . which leads into Fred's
first on-camera dance routine,
performed with Joan.

startling similarities between *Dancing Lady* and *42nd Street*—which, to begin with, was all about a musical called *Pretty Lady*. Both movies told the story of a Broadway-bound musical from its inception to opening night. Both showed stage directors as hard-driving, totally dedicated men, ruthless in their demands for perfection, and anxious to weed out anything that smacked of being old-fashioned. In both films, chorus girls took over the leading roles from the supposedly aging stars (in *Dancing Lady* not once but twice). Both had their productions financed by wealthy angels attracted to the leading ladies, and both shows had to be temporarily cancelled when the backing was withdrawn (the angel flew back in *42nd Street,* but plucky Patch had to raise the money himself in *Dancing Lady*). And both films ended with scenes focusing on the pell-mell pace of modern city life (*42nd Street* had its "42nd Street," *Dancing Lady* its "Rhythm of the Day"). There was also another link, though not apparent at the time. Ginger Rogers was in *42nd Street* and Fred Astaire was in *Dancing Lady*.

But in spite of its unblushing closeness in theme to its trailblazing predecessor, *Dancing Lady* did have the star appeal of Crawford and Gable, M-G-M's lavish hand, and a well-varied assortment of talented players. In addition to Astaire, there were humorist Robert Benchley as a diffident Broadway columnist forever losing his pencil and feigning disinterest in gossip items; sour-faced Ted Healy as Gable's loyal sidekick (you know he's loyal because he always calls Gable "boss"); Crawford's good-time chum Winnie Lightner (in her final screen appearance); and tony Franchot Tone as Gable's romantic rival. In minor roles were Nelson Eddy who sang the finale, and Eve Arden (then Eunice Quedens) in an unbilled appearance as a southern-accented actress. The studio even threw in The Three Stooges for little reason other than their long-time association with Healy.

Franchot Tone takes a well-chaperoned Joan Crawford to Havana.

Newspaper columnist Robert Benchley confides to Gable that it was Tone who got the producer to close the show.

52

Heigh-Ho, the Gang's All He[re.]

[Jo]an and Fred soaring through the clouds above the theatre.

What viewers today, however, will doubtlessly find even more incongruous is that Miss Crawford's all-knees-and-elbows audition could have landed her the dancing lead in such a major Broadway extravaganza. (Commenting on the lady's performance, Philip Scheuer wrote in the *Los Angeles Times:* "She frowns, cajoles, swallows hard, tap dances, sings a bit, and makes stars come out of her eyes at the least provocation.")

The genesis of *Dancing Lady* was a novel by James Warner Bellah which Claire Luce, Astaire's dancing partner in *Gay Divorce,* claimed to have been based on her early experiences breaking into the theatre. In chronicling the quick rise of Janie Barlow from striptease dancer in a burlesque house to the star of a glittering Broadway musical, the film indulged in some of the choicest bits of what the screen was then offering as authentic backstage jargon. In one scene, Patch summons a slightly nervous Janie into his office following a rehearsal:

PATCH: I've been thinking things over.

JANIE: Yes, sir.

PATCH: You're through with the unit.

JANIE: Sorry I didn't make the grade, Mr. Gallagher. I worked awfully hard.

PATCH: That's right. That's why I'm taking you out of the unit.

JANIE: Because I worked hard?

PATCH: No, because I want to put you in the top spot.

JANIE: The . . . what?

PATCH: The top spot.

JANIE (*in a world of her own*): Top spot . . .

PATCH: Yes, yes, yes. The top spot. Where if you drop you got twice as far to fall. Aw, maybe I'm a sap for tryin'. But maybe I can make something of you if you can stand up when I'm through with you.

JANIE: I've got good legs, Mr. Gallagher.

PATCH: Yeah, so I've noticed. But don't let 'em run away with you.

JANIE: I won't. I'm stickin' right here.

Janie does stick, of course, and everything looks just dandy—until smooth-talking socialite Todd Newton (Franchot Tone), who is secretly backing the show because he loves Janie, figures that the only way she'll marry him is to get the nominal producer, Jasper Bradley (Grant Mitchell), to call off the production. But that doesn't stop Patch. Although Janie takes off with Todd on a well-chaperoned trip to Cuba, Patch decides to produce the show himself and even rehires the actress whom Janie had replaced. On Janie's return to New York, however, she discovers what a low-down trick Todd has pulled. Just one night before the scheduled opening, she rushes to Patch's apartment to discover the director so disheartened about the show's prospects that he is in the process of getting himself smashed:

JANIE: Oh, Patch, if it's gonna be a bust let me be there when it happens.
PATCH: Aw, it's too late. We open tomorrow night.
JANIE: But I know the routines. Please let me go back in.
PATCH: Aw, forget about it, duchess. It can't be done. Life's too short.
. JANIE: So the great Patch Gallagher's layin' down, huh? So life's too short. So the first opus he's got his own dough in is a flop.
PATCH: Awww . . .
JANIE: All the wisies on Broadway'll say it wasn't Gallagher, it was Bradley . . .
PATCH: What?
JANIE: Without Bradley, Gallagher's a washout.
PATCH: What was that Bradley crack?
JANIE: Yeah, that's what they'll say. They'll put you on the pan and keep you there until Bradley takes you off.
PATCH (threateningly): Why, I've got a notion to . . .
JANIE: If that's what it takes to get you on your feet, GO AHEAD!

The "Let's Go Bavarian" number.

The show finale, with Nelson Eddy singing "That's the Rhythm of the Day" . . .

... and a kaleidoscopic merry-go-round.

That does it. He'll do it. With Janie again in the top spot, the show goes on and, of course, scores a triumph. For the musical's—and the movie's—finale, "That's the Rhythm of the Day" (by Rodgers and Hart), the dance director seems to have been strongly influenced by Busby Berkeley. After beginning with a stately minuet performed in an eighteenth-century garden, Nelson Eddy—clad in top hat, white tie, and tails—bursts in ha-ha-ha-ing at their elegant ways. "You're old-fashioned, You're passé/ Rhythm's in the air today," he sings. Then, like the "Heigh-Ho-Bavaria" mismatch, only with a bit more logic, the scene changes: the minuet dancers doff their silks and satins and don modern apparel as a noisy, frenetic city street is rolled into view. The crowds rush on foot or speed along in cars and buses, the policemen dance, and old women enter a beauty salon where—in silhouette—they are hammered, drilled, and scissored into young and beautiful shapes. The scene is capped by a psychedelic effect that has a kaleidoscopic carousel whirling the girls round and round.

The curtain falls. Thunderous applause. And Janie and Patch end in a clinch.

Fred Astaire wasn't the only one to benefit from an appearance in *Dancing Lady*. In an indirect way, it also proved a boon to Clark Gable's career. Upset that his role was secondary to Joan Crawford's, Gable complained constantly to the front office. To teach him a lesson, Louis B. Mayer agreed to loan the actor to Columbia—Hollywood's Siberia—for an insignificant comedy that was sure to send the insubordinate Gable back to Metro a much chastened and humbled man. But it didn't work out that way, and Gable returned with even more demands than before. The Columbia picture? *It Happened One Night*.

FLYING DOWN TO RIO

CAST

Belinha de Rezende	Dolores Del Rio
Roger Bond	Gene Raymond
Julio Rubeiro	Raul Roulien
Honey Hale	Ginger Rogers
Fred Ayres	Fred Astaire
Dona Elena	Blanche Friderici
Mr. Hammerstein	Franklin Pangborn
Assistant Hotel Manager	Eric Blore
Sr. de Rezende	Walter Walker
Singer at Casino	Etta Moten
Greeks	Roy D'Arcy, Maurice Black, Armand Kaliz
Mayor of Rio de Janeiro	Paul Porcasi
Casino Manager	Luis Alberni
Haitian Caddy	Clarence Muse
Hotel Guests	Betty Furness, Movita Casteneda
Belinha's Friend	Mary Kornman
Alfredo	Reginald Barlow
Musicians	Eddie Borden, Jack Rice, Ray Cooke
Casino Orchestra	The Brazilian Turunas

Producer: Louis Brock for RKO Radio Pictures. Director: Thornton Freeland. Lyrics: Edward Eliscu & Gus Kahn. Music: Vincent Youmans. Screenplay: Cyril Hume, H. W. Hanemann, Erwin Gelsey, from play by Anne Caldwell, based on story by Louis Brock. Dance director: Dave Gould. Assistant: Hermes Pan. Art directors: Van Nest Polglase, Carroll Clark. Costumes: Walter Plunkett. Music director: Max Steiner. Cameraman: J. Roy Hunt. Editor: Jack Kitchin. Release date: December 20, 1933. Running time: 89 minutes.

MUSICAL NUMBERS: "Music Makes Me"—Rogers/ "The Carioca"—Moten, two uncredited singers; dance by Astaire & Rogers, Brazilians, with Turunas/ "Orchids in the Moonlight"—Roulien; dance by Astaire & Del Rio/ "Flying Down to Rio"— Astaire; dance by flying chorus.

On June 25, 1933—even before Fred Astaire had completed his Broadway engagement in *Gay Divorce*—newspapers carried a brief item revealing that RKO Radio was sending a camera unit to Brazil to film background and aerial scenes for its new movie, *Flying Down to Rio*. Prominent in the cast would be Fred Astaire, Helen Broderick, Raul Roulien, Chick Chandler, and Arline Judge. One month later, another item announced the acquisition of Ginger Rogers and Joel McCrea. By the time actual shooting began, however, the story had been so drastically altered that Broderick, Judge, Chandler, and McCrea were out, and Dolores Del Rio and Gene Raymond (presumably inheriting McCrea's part) were in.

Obviously, the plot of *Flying Down to Rio* was going to count far less than the exotic locale and the musical spectacles. Also obviously, this was going to be a major effort. RKO, which had come into existence only five years earlier when Joseph P. Kennedy persuaded RCA's David Sarnoff to go into the motion-picture business, had been having little success until David O. Selznick was put in charge of the studio. One of Selznick's pet projects was a musical film that would utilize a South American background in combining songs and dances with aviation. Shortly before production began, however, Selznick left RKO to join M-G-M. Merian C. Cooper succeeded him as studio boss, and Louis Brock, who had supplied the original story idea for the movie, was named producer, with Thornton Freeland chosen to direct.

Eric Blore and Franklin Pangborn of Miami's Hotel Hibiscus warn band vocalist Ginger Rogers not to become familiar with the guests.

In the hotel's Date Room, Ginger sings "Music Makes Me." Fred's on the accordian and Gene Raymond is leading the band.

Dolores Del Rio says goodbye to aunt, Blanche Friderici,
before flying off with Gene Raymond.

In Rio de Janeiro, Fred comes to pick up Gene to hear the
"Turuna Turuna Band." Gene's friend, Raul Roulien, is at the right.

Nothwithstanding its songs, spectacles and locale, *Flying Down to Rio* became a major film for one reason only: it provided the first occasion for Fred Astaire and Ginger Rogers to get together on a dance floor. Like Astaire, Miss Rogers had been in show business almost all of her life. Born Virginia Katherine McMath in Independence, Missouri, she adopted her stepfather's name when, in her 'teens, she won a Charleston contest and launched a vaudeville act—"Ginger Rogers and the Redheads"—that toured the Interstate Circuit in Texas. After reaching New York as a vocalist with Paul Ash's Orchestra, Ginger, then eighteen, won a leading role in a Broadway musical called *Top Speed*. (In the chorus was Hermes Pan who would be associated with Fred Astaire in most of his best-known films.) Miss Rogers' performance as Babs Green led to her first movie, *Young Man of Manhattan*, made at Paramount's Astoria, Long Island, studio. The part gave nonsmoker Ginger a briefly quoted catch-phrase—"Cigarette me, big boy. Well liiight it"—and a song—"I've Got IT but IT Don't Do Me No Good." The picture title even inspired a song title, "Say, Young Man of Manhattan." This was the Vincent Youmans number that Fred Astaire sang and danced to—and shot down chorus boys to—in *Smiles*.

But there was even closer contact between Ginger Rogers and Fred Astaire during 1930. After her initial screen appearance, Ginger was cast in the Gershwin musical, *Girl Crazy*, which also gave Ethel Merman her first chance to shake the rafters in a Broadway theatre. The show was produced by Alex A. Aarons and Vinton Freedley, the sponsors of two of Astaire's biggest hits, *Lady, Be Good!* and *Funny Face*. Because they were dissatisfied with the way Ginger's song-and-dance duet, "Embraceable You," was being directed, the producers called in old buddy Fred to restage it.

Shooting "The Carioca" number, with Ginger and Fred atop seven pianos.
Below, "The Carioca," Ginger and Fred's first screen dance together.

Ginger and Fred play it cool after he's been thrown
out of a restaurant for talking to Dolores Del Rio.

For a while Fred and Ginger dated,
but once *Girl Crazy* closed in June
1931, Ginger was off to Hollywood.
Before making *Flying Down to Rio,*
she had appeared in a total of nineteen
films, the best known being *42nd
Street* (in which she played Anytime
Annie) and *Gold Diggers of 1933* (in
which she sang "We're in the Money"
in Pig Latin).

Early in 1933, Merian Cooper
placed Ginger under contract at RKO.
In his autobiography, Fred Astaire
wrote: "The cast for *Flying Down to
Rio* had not been entirely decided upon
when I arrived at RKO. . . . I had no
idea for two days with whom I would
be dancing, if anybody. The third day
I was told that Ginger Rogers might
be in the cast. This was great news, of
course, although I wondered whether

or not she really wanted to work with
me." Ginger's recollection of how the
Astaire-Rogers team was launched is
equally vague. "I was suddenly called
and asked if I would like to take the
role," she once said. "I was under contract to RKO then so I had to more or
less do what they asked me anyway.
The next thing I knew I was facing an
old friend from the New York stage
and I was delighted to see Fred again.
But I don't know whose idea it was
that Fred and I should dance together."

In fashioning a screenplay to fit the
titular specifications of combining a
Brazilian setting with air travel, the
writers (no less than five were involved) came up with a slim tale concerning a Brazilian beauty (played by
Mexican Dolores Del Rio) who is torn
between her love for a North American

At the Aviation Club, the chorus dances to "Orchids in the Moonlight."

band leader-songwriter-aviator with blond wavy hair (Gene Raymond) and the local lad (Raul Roulien, a real Brazilian) to whom she has been affianced. Fred Astaire played Gene's best friend, Fred Ayres (an obvious attempt to establish Astaire's name with movie audiences), and Ginger Rogers was Honey Hale, the band's vocalist. The best-remembered line in the film, however, was delivered by bit player Mary Kornman in an early scene in the Date Room of Miami's Hotel Hibiscus. Jealous of the way her friend Dolores has successfully flirted with band leader Raymond, Mary innocently asks another friend, "What have these South Americans got below the equator that we haven't?"

Happily, all the melodies supposedly created by Gene Raymond in the movie were actually melodies created by Vincent Youmans. They included the infectious "Music Makes Me" (when introduced from the bandstand, Raymond announced that it would have "a complete vocalization by the charming, bubbling, effervescent little lady, Miss Honey Hale"); the languid tango, "Orchids in the Moonlight," sung by Sr. Roulien to Srta. Del Rio as a variety of orchids and tropical beach scenes were flashed in the background; and the buoyant title song. (Gene's inspiration came when, after hatching a scheme to fly Dolores from Miami to Rio, he exclaimed: "Flying down to Rio! Boy, what a name for a new song!")

The last-named piece served an important development in the movie's plot. Raymond's band is in Rio de

Janeiro to furnish the music for the opening of the new Hotel Atlantico, owned by Dolores Del Rio's father. But because of the machinations of three unscrupulous Greeks (who are always seen as shadows), the hotel is denied an entertainment permit for the opening day. This means that Dolores's father will be ruined! Gene, however, looks to the sky and gets a bright idea: if they can't have the entertainment *in* the hotel they'll have it *above* the hotel. With the help of Ginger and Fred, he persuades all the girls hired for the opening day's floor show to join him in a daring and dangerous plan. After Fred and the band musicians enter the hotel with their instruments carefully concealed, the featured acts and chorus girls take off on a fleet of airplanes. But instead of being inside the planes, they are on top of them, strapped to the wings. At a signal, Fred leads the band in playing "Flying Down to Rio," and the planes fly the performers high above the hotel for a series of leggy if somewhat constricted maneuvers. Trapeze artists fly through the air. Apache dancers dance. One aerialist falls from one plane and is caught on the wings of another that swoops right under it. The show is a high-flying success and so, of course, is the hotel.

But moviegoers found even that spectacular finale less exciting than the sight of Fred Astaire and Ginger Rogers dancing to "The Carioca," the only number they did together in the picture. Actually, neither the scene nor the song had much to do with what was going on in the story and its inclusion seems to have been motivated simply by the desire to put Mr. Astaire on the same dance floor with Miss Rogers. Reason enough. They worked it into the action on the pretext of Fred wanting buddy Gene to hear the music of a native band, the Turunas, who perform at an outdoor spot called the Carioca Casino. Building up the anticipation for Fred's and Ginger's forthcoming ballroom display, the musicians in Gene's orchestra first express amazement at the gyrations of the dancers and the compelling beat of the music. Fred and

Fred, Dolores and "Orchids in the Moonlight."

Getting ready for the aerial floorshow.

Ginger are particularly intrigued at the sight of all the foreheads being pressed together:

GINGER: What's this about the forehead?

FRED: Mental telepathy.

GINGER: I can tell what they're thinking about from here. *(She continues to study the movements.)* The trick is to keep your mind a blank.

FRED: With that music?

GINGER: Oh, Freddy, is my mind red!

And so, with Ginger's "We'll show 'em a thing or three," Astaire takes Rogers by the hand and they sprint onto the dance floor to join the dancers who deferentially back away to give them room. After the team's solo, twenty-five couples in native dress take to the floor accompanied by the successive singing of three girls, one of whom was Etta Moten. These dancers are replaced by sixteen North Brazilian Negro couples, who execute more animated variations on the theme. Then Fred and Ginger come dashing back again for a finale that finds them dancing on the tops of seven grand pianos arranged to form a circular dance floor.

Although Astaire and Rogers had roles subordinate to the main triangular romance, it was clear after the film's release that they were the ones who sent people flying down to *Flying Down to Rio*. Still, of the two, it was Fred Astaire who garnered most of the critical favor. Philip Scheuer of the *Los Angeles Times* wrote: "Astaire, being hailed as a 'find,' electrifies in a tap specialty and in the rhumba-like 'Carioca' (with Miss Rogers)." "The chief point of interest," claimed Thornton Delehanty in the *New York Post,* "is that it has Fred Astaire in the cast. Thanks to that, and to that alone, the picture is worth seeing." This view was similarly stated by Sid Silverman in *Variety*: "The main point of *Flying Down to Rio* is the screen promise of Fred Astaire.... Not that Astaire threatens to become an ocean-to-ocean rage, but here he shows enough to indicate what he could do with good material. He's assuredly a

"My Rio, Rio by the sea-o . . ."

"Flying Down to Rio"

Ride 'em Ginger.

bet after this one, for he's distinctly likable on the screen, the mike is kind to his voice, and as a dancer he remains in a class by himself."

Astaire, however, was not completely satisfied with his work. He was, in fact, delighted to bid farewell to Hollywood after the shooting was completed, and head for London where he successfully repeated his role in the musical *Gay Divorce*. Certain that he would never again be offered another chance on the screen, Astaire was amazed to receive a cablegram from RKO executive Pandro S. Berman which read: "YOU WERE A SWELL SUCCESS IN PREVIEWING FLYING DOWN TO RIO LAST NIGHT." Other encouraging cables followed. *Flying Down to Rio* was turning into one of the top-grossing pictures of the year.

It went against all the rules. The shy, lanky fellow with the prominent forehead and the pointed chin was hardly the type from which movie stars were being made. But in this one appearance he proved conclusively that the screen was his perfect medium, and that his easygoing charm and unsurpassed footwork would score even more impressively on film than they could in the theatre. *Flying Down to Rio* even gave him an added bonus: a partner to rival sister Adele. Though they appeared together in only one number, by the time the former Frederick Austerlitz and the former Virginia Katherine McMath walked off the dance floor they had become America's dancing sweethearts.

THE GAY DIVORCEE

CAST

Guy Holden	Fred Astaire
Mimi Glossop	Ginger Rogers
Hortense Ditherwell	Alice Brady
Egbert Fitzgerald	Edward Everett Horton
Rodolfo Tonetti	Erik Rhodes
Waiter	Eric Blore
Cyril Glossop	William Austin
Hotel Guest	Betty Grable
Guy's Valet	Charles Coleman
Singer	Lillian Miles
French Headwaiter	Paul Porcasi
Chief Customs Inspector	E. E. Clive

Producer: Pandro S. Berman for RKO Radio Pictures. Director: Mark Sandrich. Lyrics: Cole Porter, Herb Magidson, Mack Gordon. Music: Cole Porter, Con Conrad, Harry Revel. Screenplay: George Marion, Jr., Dorothy Yost, Edward Kaufman, from stage musical, *Gay Divorce,* by Dwight Taylor. Dance director: Dave Gould. Assistant: Hermes Pan. Art directors: Van Nest Polglase, Carroll Clark. Costumes: Walter Plunkett. Music director: Max Steiner. Cameraman: David Abel. Editor: William Hamilton. Release date: October 3, 1934. Running time: 107 minutes.

MUSICAL NUMBERS: "Don't Let It Bother You" (Gordon-Revel)—French chorus; dance by Astaire/ "A Needle in a Haystack" (Magidson-Conrad)—Astaire; dance by Astaire/ "Let's K-nock K-nees" (Gordon-Revel)—Grable & Horton; dance by Grable & Horton, hotel guests/ "Night and Day" (Porter)—Astaire; dance by Astaire & Rogers/ "The Continental" (Magidson-Conrad)—Rogers, Rhodes, Miles; dance by Astaire & Rogers, chorus.

Now that RKO had so potentially valuable a team the question was what to do with it. Of all the major film studios this would seem to be the one least likely to come up with the right answer. Never an innovative outfit, except during David Selznick's brief tenure as production boss, the company had built its small cadre of stars by signing up veteran performers at the termination of their contracts with other studios. With Fred Astaire and Ginger Rogers, however, it was faced with the responsibility of nurturing and promoting the freshest, most exciting musical-comedy team in movies. And it succeeded beyond anyone's expectation.

RKO would have liked nothing better than to capitalize on the *Flying Down to Rio* triumph by quickly following it up with another Astaire-Rogers musical. But since early November 1933, Astaire was appearing in London in the stage musical, *Gay Divorce,* and the studio would simply have to bide its time until the engagement was over (which wouldn't be until the following April). Wait a minute! That's it! How about putting Fred and Ginger in a movie version of *Gay Divorce?* The story was no great shakes, but the musical *had* been a hit on Broadway and it *was* doing great business in London. Almost everyone was familiar with the show's title, and its chief song, "Night and Day," was well on its way to becoming a standard. How could it miss? Producer Pandro S. Berman, then only twenty-nine, was put in charge of the film (he would also produce seven of the eight subsequent movies Astaire made at RKO), and Mark Sandrich, who had won praise for two innovative musicals, *So This Is Harris* and *Melody Cruise,* was assigned to direct (in all, Sandrich directed six Astaire films, five at RKO and one at Paramount).

Playing with finger dolls in a Paris Night club.

On the Southampton pier, Fred comes to the aid of Ginger, whose skirt has been caught in her aunt's steamer trunk.

70

At the seaside resort, Betty Grable coaxes Horton
to join her in the number, "Let's K-nock K-nees."

First, however, there had to be a few changes. When the studio submitted the title for approval to the Hays Office, the industry's self-regulating arbiter of cinematic morals, the verdict was handed down that a divorce could never be gay. However a compromise was reached: although a gay divorce was impossible, a gay divorcee was perfectly acceptable. So, thanks to this rather hazy logic, the title was altered to *The Gay Divorcee*, which actually turned out to be more euphonious and even more appropriate. One minor and equally fitting alteration was the profession of the character played by Fred Astaire: on stage he had been a novelist, on screen he was a dancer. The studio also decided that since "Night and Day" was the only song people knew from the original Cole Porter score, it would be the only song people would hear from the original score. So two local songwriting teams were called in to provide four new numbers.

For the most part the picture stuck closely to the original story as it told of the complications that arise when Ginger (as Mimi Glossop) mistakes Fred (as Guy Holden) for the professional corespondent hired by an English lawyer to help provide grounds for her divorce. Adding to the faithfulness of the screen adaptation were two actors repeating their original stage roles: Erik Rhodes as the real professional corespondent and Eric Blore (he'd already been seen briefly in *Flying Down to Rio*) as a Wodehouse-type waiter at the British resort where most of the action takes place. (The hotel, which is unaccountably given the Italianate name of Bella Vista, is situated in "Brightbourne," a mythical locale created by combining the Channel resort cities of Brighton and Bournemouth.) Edward Everett Horton played the bumbling lawyer (he was never referred to as a solicitor), and Alice Brady was Ginger's feather-brained aunt ("I adore Paris. It's so much like Chicago that I enjoyed every minute of it"). Also on hand, wearing white satin beach pajamas was singing-and-dancing Betty Grable. ("Blonde kid number leader in 'Let's K-nock K-nees' shows lots of prom-

72

Eric Blore as the waiter.

"Like the beat beat beat of the tom-tom. . ."

ise," reported *Variety*'s Abel Green, who somehow neglected to mention the blonde kid's name.)

Although RKO had chosen a pre-tested property for Fred's and Ginger's first co-starring vehicle, the studio was still taking a chance in offering the moviegoing public a story that must have raised many eyebrows. For whether it was about a gay divorce or a gay divorcee, the picture *was* dealing with the rather sordid and dishonest theme of a girl being caught *in flagrante delicto* with a paid corespondent. That the movie never seemed tasteless was a tribute to its players and its general air of innocence and unreality. When Rodolfo Tonetti, the corespondent, shows up at the resort for his assignment, he is revealed as an opera-spouting dandified Italian who quickly reassures lawyer Egbert Fitzgerald that his work is completely professional: "My slogan—'Your wife ees safe weeth Tonetti. He prefers spaghetti.'" Mimi, who doesn't know what Tonetti looks like, has been told that he will identify himself by the password, "Chance is the fool's name

73

Dancing to "Night and Day."

Professional corespondent Erik Rhodes arrives to ruin the evening for Fred and Ginger.

Fred's brilliant scheme to deceive Rhodes by cutting out the silhouette of a dancing couple from a magazine.

for fate." That night, after dancing with Guy, she hears him use the line —which happens to have been from his last show. Having no idea what Guy's profession is, Mimi is shocked:

MIMI: You? You??
GUY: Me? Why, yes, of course it is.
MIMI: So you're the man I've been waiting for.
GUY: None other.
MIMI: I'll be waiting for you in my room. 216. At midnight.

Taken aback by Mimi's seemingly brazen invitation, Guy shows up—in top hat, white tie, and tails—at the appointed hour. But then Mimi makes the thoroughly confused chap sit on the far side of the room:

MIMI: Some people will do anything for money.
GUY: Oh, it's not as bad as all that. After all, I do bring pleasure to thousands of people.
MIMI: Thousands?
GUY: Yes, tens of thousands. I bring romance to tens of thousands of shop girls, servant girls, stenographers . . .
MIMI: You might spare me, Mr. Bluebeard.

Guy soon reveals his true identity, but Mimi must still cope with Tonetti, who arrives on the job and insists on remaining. The corespondent, however, is a good family man and promptly telephones his wife. Hearing a strange voice in the background he is at first suspicious but is quickly reassured. "What do you theenk?" he asks Mimi and Guy. "My leetle son, Rodolfo, only nine years old and already hees voice is changing."

Everything is straightened out the following morning when Mimi's husband barges in—and is revealed by the waiter to be leading a double life with another spouse. Once everyone has gone, Mimi and Guy dance merrily over the furniture and trip gaily out of the room with Guy sporting a bellboy's top hat at a rakish angle.

Two views of "The Continental" chorus.

Unlike most musicals of the time, *The Gay Divorcee* did make a conscientious effort to have at least two of the five songs flow naturally from the dialogue and the situation. Early in the film, after he has met, fallen for, and lost the lovely Mimi, Guy confides to Egbert, "I'll find that girl if it takes me from now on." To which his friend replies: "Well, it shouldn't be difficult. After all, there are only three million women in London." And that's all the setup Guy needs to reveal his dilemma in song and dance: "It's just like looking for a needle in a haystack. . . ."

When Guy finally does discover Mimi at the resort, she is embarrassed to be seen there and runs away to a deserted area overlooking the water. Guy dashes after her, determined that she won't get away from him this time. He pleads with her: "Don't go. I have so many things to say to you." But instead of saying them he sings, "Like the beat beat beat of the tom-tom . . ." —thus launching into the throbbing confession, "Night and Day." The singing concluded, Mimi tries to leave but Guy blocks her path. Again she heads for another exit but again he steps in front of her. He takes her hand and begins to sway to the music. Reluctantly at first, then almost in a trance, Mimi sways with him. In her desperation to break free she even slaps Guy's face and sets him reeling. But she is powerless to resist; the music and Guy's dancing weave their spell and Mimi becomes a willing and active partner, matching Guy step for step. Once the dance is concluded, she sinks into a chair and Guy nonchalantly wipes his hands together and offers her a cigarette.

Here, for the first time on the screen, we have the classic Fred Astaire wooing-and-winning dance ritual. No need for dialogue or self-conscious clinching. Through the words of the song and, most especially, through the movements of the dance Astaire is able to reverse the girl's feelings from reluctance or even antagonism to compliant love. It is a routine that would be included, though always with variations appropriate to each situation, in

78

Ginger and Fred dancing to "The Continental."

almost every Astaire-Rogers film, and would still be used in *Silk Stockings,* the last musical in which Astaire played the romantic lead.

The more or less unmotivated "set" pieces included "Don't Let It Bother You," sung by a bevy of chorus girls performing a finger-doll dance in a Parisian nightclub, and "Let's K-nock K-nees" (originally intended for the 1931 *Ziegfeld Follies* but cut during its tryout), which offered the unlikely sight of cuddly Betty Grable making a play for prissy Edward Everett Horton with such sentiments as "My heart's so tick-tock-tickable,/ Your lips are so lipstickable." For the film's final number, those in charge deliberately set out to surpass "The Carioca" with another dance-celebrating chorus-crowding, senses-staggering spectacle. The occasion inspired songwriters Herb Magidson and Con Conrad to come up with a seventy-two-bar marathon called "The Continental," which, as performed in the picture, contained some fifteen variations of assorted lengths, went on for a full seventeen minutes, and won the first Academy Award ever bestowed on a movie song (runner up: "The Carioca").

The main theme of the song is first heard in the background as Guy complains to Mimi in her hotel suite that Tonetti, who insists they remain in the suite, makes him feel like a prisoner. The two saunter over to the balcony to watch the dancers on the patio below:

GUY: Hel-lo, hel-lo. This doesn't sound like "The Prisoner's Song" to me. Not a bad tune. What is it?

MIMI: It's the newest thing over here. It's called "The Continental."

GUY: "The Continental"?

MIMI: Mm-hmm.

GUY: Oh, I like it. It's the second thing I've found I'd like to take home with me. Know the words?

MIMI: Mm-hmm. *(And she sings them.)* "Beautiful music . . . Dangerous rhythm . . ."

Accompanied by a few whistling interpolations by Guy, Mimi finishes the song, and the two try out a few dance steps. Then Guy gets the kind of inspiration that could exist only in musical comedy. Since Tonetti is discreetly sitting in the adjoining room, Guy cuts out two dancing figures from a magazine cover and affixes them to a phonograph turntable. Once he adjusts the angle of a floor lamp shade the cutout figures appear to be dancing shadows, which Tonetti, poor boob, accepts as that of Guy and Mimi dancing 'round and 'round.

With Tonetti thus craftily deceived, Mimi quickly changes into a feathery gown and makes her escape with Guy. Once on the patio, they join the dancing throng, which deferentially backs off to give them enough room for their opening routine. Presently the chorus descends to the dance floor from three revolving doors, the boys in black dancing with the girls in white and the boys in white dancing with the girls in black. Even Tonetti ardently warbles the refrain accompanying himself on a concertina, and singer Lillian Miles follows with a patter itemizing all the spots in Europe where "The Continental" has become the rage. Now the chorus girls have returned in black-and-white bathing suits to dance with the boys in black-and-white blazers and flannels. Guy and Mimi lead them through a tango and a Russian dance, and end up gaily sprinting through the center revolving door.

The Gay Divorcee was a box-office sensation and was greeted by universal critical encomia. In the *New York American,* Regina Crewe gushed: "It is difficult to recall any dancing on the screen compared to that of Mr. Astaire who, in addition to his inexpressible terpsichorean talents, endows the picture with a charm and personality, a gay subtlety, a very definite class which the screen must never allow to escape. He is a brilliant star, more than welcome to the film firmament." Abel Green also used the celestial theme in his *Variety* notice, referring to Astaire as "a new marquee satellite. The picture unquestionably will set the musical comedy star for the celluloid firmament. . . . All through the picture there is charm, romance, gayety and eclat."

André Sennwald, *The New York Times* man, called it "an entirely agreeable photoplay which sings, dances and quips with agility and skill. Both as a romantic comedian and as a lyric dancer, Fred Astaire is an urbane delight and Miss Rogers keeps pace with him even in his rhythmic flights over the furniture." The *Post*'s Thornton Delehanty and the *Herald Tribune*'s Richard Watts, Jr., put *The Gay Divorcee* in the company of the all-time greats of the cinema musical. "For a Grade A blend of music, dancing and comedy," wrote Mr. Delehanty, "you need look no further than the Radio City Music Hall, where the incomparable Fred Astaire and his almost incomparable partner, Ginger Rogers, head the cast of a brisk and opulent picture. . . . In *The Gay Divorcee,* you will have, unless you were never meant for this world, the almost perfect screen musical." And from Mr. Watts: "In addition to being a magnificent dancer, Mr. Astaire is an excellent comedian and an engaging leading man. For a second virtue, the photoplay gives the freshly charming Miss Ginger Rogers an opportunity to prove that she is almost as perfect an example of feminine desirability in musical comedy as Miss Myrna Loy is in straight dramatic works. . . . The film has a dash, a polished humor, an air of fresh tunefulness, and a genial charm of playing that makes it one of the most delightful examples of its type of cinema that has ever been devised."

RKO had gambled and had won. *The Gay Divorcee* not only affirmed the star qualities of Fred Astaire and Ginger Rogers, it established them as the studio's number one box-office attraction. But the film achieved even more. Without deliberately trying to pioneer, the film company had set the pattern for a new, imaginative form of intimate musical comedy on the screen.

At breakfast, lawyer Horton is surprised to find both Fred and Erik Rhodes with Ginger. Alice Brady is at the left.

81

Lucille Ball surrounded by some
of the other mannequins.

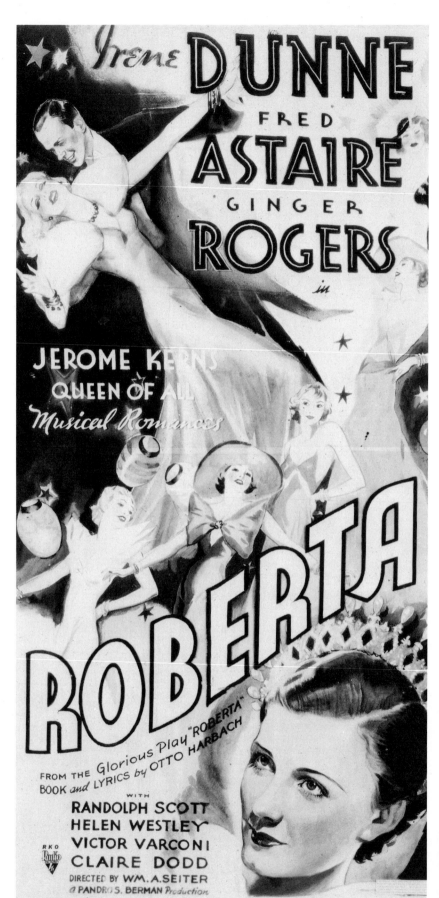

82

ROBERTA

CAST

Stephanie	Irene Dunne
Huckleberry "Huck" Haines	Fred Astaire
Countess Tanka Scharwenka (née Lizzie Gatz)	Ginger Rogers
John Kent	Randolph Scott
Roberta (Aunt Minnie)	Helen Westley
Ladislaw	Victor Varconi
Sophie Teale	Claire Dodd
Alexander Petrovich Moscovich Voyda	Luis Alberni
Lord Henry Delves	Ferdinand Munier
Albert	Torben Meyer
Girl in Salon	Lucille Ball
Restaurant Cossacks	Mike Telegen, Sam Savitsky
Wabash Indianians	Candy Candido, Muzzy Marcellino, Gene Sheldon, Howard Lally, Hal Borne, Charles Sharpe, Ivan Dow, William Dunn, Phil Cuthbert, Delmon Davis

Producer: Pandro S. Berman for RKO Radio Pictures. Director: William A. Seiter. Lyrics: Otto Harbach, Dorothy Fields. Music: Jerome Kern. Screenplay: Jane Murfin, Sam Mintz, Glenn Tryon, Allan Scott, from the stage musical, *Roberta*, by Otto Harbach, adapted from the novel, *Gowns by Roberta*, by Alice Duer Miller. Dance director: Hermes Pan. Art directors: Van Nest Polglase, Carroll Clark. Costumes: Bernard Newman. Music director: Max Steiner. Cameraman: Edward Cronjager. Editor: William Hamilton. Release date: February 12, 1935. Running time: 105 minutes.

MUSICAL NUMBERS: "Indiana" (Ballard Macdonald-James F. Hanley)—Indianians/ "Let's Begin" (Harbach-Kern)—Astaire, Candido; dance by Astaire, Candido, Sheldon/ "Russian Song" (traditional)—Dunne/ "I'll Be Hard to Handle" (Bernard Dougall-Kern)—Rogers; dance by Astaire & Rogers/ "Yesterdays" (Harbach-Kern)—Dunne/ "I Won't Dance" (Fields, Oscar Hammerstein, 2nd-Kern)—Astaire & Rogers; piano playing by Astaire; dance by Astaire/ "Smoke Gets in Your Eyes" (Harbach-Kern)—Dunne; reprised as dance by Astaire & Rogers/ "Fashion Show" (background, "Don't Ask Me Not to Sing")—Astaire, with models/ "Lovely to Look At" (Fields-Kern)—Dunne, male chorus; reprised by Astaire & Rogers; dance by Astaire & Rogers. Background: "The Touch of Your Hand," "You're Devastating."

Since RKO had chosen wisely in adapting the Broadway musical, *Gay Divorce*, as the first Fred Astaire–Ginger Rogers vehicle, it was almost mandatory that the company executives again look to Broadway for the next item on the dancing team's agenda. They found it in *Roberta*, one of the major theatre successes of 1933. Like *Gay Divorce*, this was a modern, "sophisticated," attractively mounted production with a score by another acknowledged musical giant (Jerome Kern), including another acknowledged musical classic ("Smoke Gets in Your Eyes"), and which, by common consent, had an equally dismal libretto.

The studio planned *Roberta* as an even more opulent and star-studded musical than *The Gay Divorcee* (it was budgeted at $750,000), with the main locale, a couturière's salon in Paris, lending itself to the introduction of the latest in feminine finery. As for the story, all it needed was some fresh dialogue and some tinkering with the script to make it fit not only Fred Astaire and Ginger Rogers but also the patrician Irene Dunne, one of RKO's few genuine star attractions.

The studio's approach to filming *Roberta* differed from its approach to filming *Gay Divorce* on two main counts. Unlike its predecessor, the new picture did not utilize the services of any of the actors who had appeared in the stage production. Astaire's role had originally been played by Bob Hope, Ginger Rogers' by Lyda Roberti, Irene Dunne's by Tamara, Randolph Scott's by Ray (then Raymond) Middleton, Helen Westley's by Fay Templeton, and Ferdinand Munier's by Sydney Greenstreet. George Murphy had also been in the show on Broadway but his role was eliminated.

On the other hand, RKO was far more considerate of *Roberta*'s composer, Jerome Kern, than it had been of *Gay Divorce*'s composer, Cole Porter. Only "Night and Day" had been retained for *The Gay Divorcee*, whereas the movie version of *Roberta* not only kept "Smoke Gets in Your Eyes" (no question about that one) but also "Let's Begin," "Yesterdays," and "I'll

84

At the French pier, Fred and Randolph Scott cannot persuade Luis Alberni to hire Fred's Wabash Indianians instead of the authentic Indians he had cabled to play in his café.

Even their "Organ Number" fails to impress him. (That's Candy Candido at Fred's left.)

Be Hard to Handle," with "You're Devastating," "The Touch of Your Hand," and "Don't Ask Me Not to Sing" used as background music. And when two additional songs were needed, producer Pandro Berman took the unusual step of going directly to Kern himself to supply them. The assignment also marked the composer's first association with lyricist Dorothy Fields, who up to then had been writing songs almost exclusively with Jimmy McHugh. Then two new pieces: a staccato declaration of contrariness, "I Won't Dance" (which, with a different lyric by Oscar Hammerstein, 2nd, had been introduced in a 1934 London musical, *Three Sisters*), and a lilting, cascading ballad called "Lovely to Look At." The brevity of the second melody—a mere sixteen bars, not counting the verse—rather disturbed producer Berman, who asked the composer if it were at all possible to make the song just a wee bit longer. "That's all I had to say," Kern shrugged—and he wouldn't add another note.

The fact that the movie used four of the original *Roberta* songs did not mean that it was also required to use all of the original Otto Harbach lyrics. The Hays Office was ever on guard to make sure that nothing even slightly off-color would be allowed to sully a Hollywood soundtrack. For example, as sung on stage, "Let's Begin" contained an observation about a young lady having necked till she was wrecked. For the movie, those shocking lines were altered to an innocuous reference to a simple meeting for which there'd be "no reason for vain regret."

For "I'll Be Hard to Handle," a free-spirited young lady had to change her desire from raising hell to raising cain. In the same song, Broadway audiences heard a passage in which "threw a gander" rhymed with "willing to philander," and led up to the girl's confession that she never thought she'd have to be a bride. Wow! How racy can you get? So, for the more innocent ears of filmgoers, the lady admitted, among other faults, to having a terrific temper and being an expert marksman at throwing chairs and tables.

Irene Dunne comes to Randolph Scott's rescue in a stuck elevator.

86

Ginger, posing as a Polish countess, gets Fred
to agree to keep her secret.

Helen Westley, Irene Dunne and Ferdinand Munier.

Not all of the lyric changes resulted from Hays Office pressure. Originally, in "Yesterdays," the aging Roberta recalled the days when youth was hers, truth was hers, and joyous, free, and flaming life forsooth was hers. Forsooth, indeed! For the movie—and only for the movie—these lines were dropped in favor of an almost identically worded sentiment which found the singer pining for the days when "free and gaily flaming life was mine to live."

As for the plot, the main departure was to provide a secondary, rather casual romance involving Fred and Ginger (her role in the original had been that of an energetic vamp who briefly distracted the play's hero), and also give them room enough and reason enough to dance. Actually, their relationship—Fred played Huck Haines, a band leader, and Ginger was Lizzie Gatz, alias Countess Tanka Scharwenka, a nightclub singer—was totally without conflict or even emotion. The only romance audiences were expected to take seriously was that between Irene Dunne as the exiled Russian Princess Stephanie and Randolph Scott as John Kent, a former All-American halfback who inherits his Aunt Minnie's dress salon.

Because M-G-M controls the rights to the musical (they remade it in 1952 as *Lovely to Look At*), RKO's *Roberta* has never been shown on television. Apart from the buoyant Astaire-Rogers routines, however, it is not really a serious loss. Yet in its day *Roberta* was deemed just about the ultimate in screen musicals, with most reviewers venturing the opinion that it was superior to the original (a verdict that had also greeted *The Gay Divorcee*). "With the excellent help of Professor Astaire," André Sennwald wrote in *The New York Times*, "the Kublai Khans at RKO have erected a bright and shimmering pleasure dome. The work is a model of urbanity in the musical films and Mr. Astaire, the debonair master of light comedy and the dance, is its chief ornament. To watch him skipping on effortless cat's feet across a dance floor is to experience one of the major delights of the contemporary cinema. . . . If there is a flaw in the photoplay it is the unfortunate circumstance that Mr. Astaire and his excellent partner, Miss Rogers, cannot be dancing during every minute of it." Mr. Sennwald's praise of Astaire was echoed in the verdict turned in by Richard Watts, Jr., of the *New York Herald Tribune*: "What Cole Porter lyrically called the nimble tread of the feet of Fred Astaire is gorgeously present, and the superb dancing of the First Dancer, at the top of his form, is enough to make the new photoplay worthy of applause and obeisances."

Most of the other critics also turned encomiasts for the occasion. Joe Bigelow in *Variety* called it "musical picture-making at its best"; *Liberty* magazine maintained that it "stands in a good way of being the best musical comedy to come out of Hollywood"; William Boehnel in the *New York World-Telegram* held it to be "the last word in screen musical comedy entertainment. . . . As usual, it is Fred Astaire, more than ably assisted by Ginger Rogers, who provides most of the joy. If there has ever been more thrilling prancing than the two offer in this 'wow' attraction then I haven't seen it or even heard of it."

The script was studded with what was apparently then accepted as sparkling repartee. When the cloddish John Kent—whose sole expression of approval is the word "swell"—first meets his Aunt Minnie (Helen Westley) in Paris, he tells her that he has broken his engagement to his fiancée: "She's given me the air. We had a row." Minnie chuckles: "Oh, I thought you said she'd given you an heir." Upon being introduced to his childhood sweetheart, now masquerading as the Countess Scharwenka, Huck Haines asks what he should call her.

"You may call me Tanka."

"Tanka?"

"You're welcome."

After his aunt dies and John inherits her business, he gets into an argument with the doorman (Victor Varconi),

As Prince Victor Varconi strums,
Irene Dunne sings a tender Russian lullaby.

Fred recalls their carefree days as children in Indiana.

The "I'll Be Hard to Handle" dance routine.

who happens to be a Russian nobleman. "Why, *youuu* Russian prince!" John storms. "I'm still boss of this outfit and you're fired!" To which the prince replies with the princely line: "No, no. I am not fired. I am perfectly cool."

Then there was this sally following some unflattering remarks Huck makes about John's old flame, Sophie Teale (Claire Dodd), who has just turned up in Paris:

JOHN: What do you know about anything anyway?

HUCK: I know about everything everyway.

JOHN: Then you must know Sophie's swell.

HUCK: John, every day you act worse. But today you're acting like tomorrow.

(This seems like an appropriate spot to quote again from Mr. Sennwald of the *Times*: "The libretto, which proved a definite handicap to *Roberta* on the stage, has been visibly brightened by the dialogue polishers in the studio.")

Fortunately, they couldn't keep Fred and Ginger—or Huck and Tanka—off the dance floor for long. The phony countess ("You've got to have a title to croon over here"), complete with phony accent, sings at the Café Russe and even manages to wangle a job there for Huck and his Wabash Indianians. During a rehearsal, she does "I'll Be Hard to Handle" (the "h's" pronounced with a gutteral "ch") and, as an inside joke, interpolates the line "If you vant to be sveet and chot"—purposely recalling the Polish-accented Lyda Roberti, Ginger's predecessor in the part, who had first won fame singing a song called "Sweet and Hot." Then in a joyous, seemingly spontaneous tap routine, Huck and Tanka reminisce about their days as kids together in Indiana, peppering their dance with much giggling and clowning.

Later, during an actual performance at the club, the two join in singing "I Won't Dance." Here too there is an

Fred and Randolph Scott submit to an interview following Randy's inheritance of his aunt's dress business.

Claire Dodd, Scott's old flame, shares a drink with Fred at the Café Russe bar.

Fred leads, Ginger sings "I Won't Dance."

"So I chaffed them and I gaily laughed . . ."
Irene Dunne singing "Smoke Gets In Your Eyes."

"We endorse this polo rig, of course/ And for an added thousand francs, we furnish horse." Fred introduces the mannequins at the fashion show.

"in" reference, with two of the lines inspired by a previous Astaire-Rogers number: "When you dance you're charming and you're gentle/ Specially when you do 'The Continental,' " as a trumpet solo echoes the song's "Beautiful music" theme. Despite his verbal protestations, Huck is firmly escorted onto the dance floor by two burly restaurant Cossacks and performs a lively tap solo.

Because of a spat during Stephanie's singing of "Smoke Gets in Your Eyes," John and Stephanie, now partners in the dress firm, disappear leaving Huck in charge ("Somebody's got to take this ridiculous business off my shoulders. In the four days I've been here my voice is beginning to change"). Stephanie, of course, returns to save the business by planning a mammoth fashion show—complete with song and dance. Decked out in billowy white, she sings the collection's theme, "Lovely to Look At," which, along with "Smoke Gets in Your Eyes," is danced by Huck and Tanka. John also comes back, the fashions are a success, and Tanka even backs Huck into proposing:

TANKA: I guess I'll have to give in to you.
HUCK: To me? I didn't say anything.
TANKA: But I thought you were about to want to marry me.
HUCK: Well, I was.
TANKA: Well, I accept.
HUCK: Well, thanks very much.
TANKA: Well, you're quite welcome, my fine-feathered friend.

Of the six consecutive films Astaire and Rogers starred in together, *Roberta* was the least representative of the kind of movie world the couple inhabited and made their own. Primarily, of course, this was the result of having been given roles that were incidental to the film's main plot, and also the fact that their numbers were no more than specialties without any relevance to characters or situations. Still, they alone make *Roberta* worth seeing again today. If you can find it.

93

Dancing to "Smoke Gets In Your Eyes."

Irving Berlin plays "The Piccolino" for Fred and Ginger

TOP HAT

CAST

Jerry Travers	Fred Astaire
Dale Tremont	Ginger Rogers
Horace Hardwick	Edward Everett Horton
Madge Hardwick	Helen Broderick
Alberto Beddini	Erik Rhodes
Bates	Eric Blore
Flower Shop Manager	Leonard Mudie
Flower Shop Clerk	Lucille Ball
London Hotel Manager	Edgar Norton
Venice Hotel Manager	Gino Corrado
Call Boy	Peter Hobbes

Producer: Pandro S. Berman for RKO Radio Pictures. Director: Mark Sandrich. Lyrics & Music: Irving Berlin. Screenplay: Dwight Taylor & Allan Scott, adapted by Karl Noti from play, *The Girl Who Dared,* by Alexander Farago & Aladar Laszlo. Dance director: Hermes Pan. Art director: Van Nest Polglase. Costumes: Bernard Newman. Music director: Max Steiner. Cameraman: David Abel. Editor: William Hamilton. Release date: August 16, 1935. Running time: 101 minutes.

MUSICAL NUMBERS: "No Strings"—Astaire; dance by Astaire/ "Isn't This a Lovely Day?"—Astaire; dance by Astaire & Rogers/ "Top Hat, White Tie and Tails"—Astaire; dance by Astaire, male chorus/ "Cheek to Cheek"—Astaire; dance by Astaire & Rogers/ "The Piccolino"—Rogers; dance by Astaire & Rogers, chorus. Unused: "Get Thee Behind Me, Satan," Wild About You."

Edward Everett Horton lends a helping hand for Fred's sand dance to "No Strings"...

Top Hat was the quintessential Fred Astaire–Ginger Rogers movie. It has remained a classic of the genre, certainly the first film that comes to mind whenever we think of the team. Everything seemed to fall perfectly into place: the complementing personalities of the two stars; the buoyant, expertly integrated score by Irving Berlin; the glitteringly modern, never-never land settings; the gossamer story with its naively illogical plot devices; the deft playing of the supporting comics; the beautifully staged and perfectly performed dance sequences. It so blithely represented the tone, the style of the entire Astaire and Rogers series that most people accept it as establishing the pattern for all their pictures.

Yet Top Hat, while it may have improved upon the form, did not establish it. The form had already been established by The Gay Divorcee. And it is reasonable to wonder if Top Hat could ever have been created had there been no previous model. Consider:

The Gay Divorcee

The locales are Paris, London, and an English seaside resort.

Fred plays a well-known American dancer.

Edward Everett Horton plays Fred's English friend.

Alice Brady plays Horton's old flame, then his wife.

Ginger plays Brady's niece.

Eric Blore plays a Wodehouse-type waiter.

Erik Rhodes plays a florid Italian co-respondent.

Fred falls for Ginger at first sight.

After falling, Fred reveals his feeling about Ginger by singing and tapping "Looking for a Needle in a Haystack" in a London hotel room.

Fred and Horton go to the resort hotel because of Ginger.

Film's major complication is Ginger's mistaking Fred for Rhodes.

Fred and Ginger, formally attired, perform the romantic "Night and Day" in a deserted part of the resort.

"The Continental," a song about a new dance, is an outdoor production number at the resort.

At film's end, Fred and Ginger gaily scamper out of resort together.

Top Hat

The locales are London and an Italian seaside resort.

Fred plays a well-known American dancer.

Edward Everett Horton plays Fred's English friend.

Helen Broderick plays Horton's wife.

Ginger plays Broderick's friend.

Eric Blore plays a Wodehouse-type valet.

Erik Rhodes plays a florid Italian dress designer.

Fred falls for Ginger at first sight.

Before falling, Fred reveals his feeling about matrimony by singing and tapping "No Strings" in a London hotel room.

Fred and Horton go to the resort hotel because of Ginger.

Film's major complication is Ginger's mistaking Fred for Horton.

Fred and Ginger, formally attired, perform the romantic "Cheek to Cheek" in a deserted part of the resort.

"The Piccolino," a song about a new melody, is an outdoor production number at the resort.

At film's end, Fred and Ginger gaily scamper out of resort together.

. . . which Fred hopes will lull Ginger back to sleep.

And *Top Hat* was supposed to have been based on a play written by two Hungarians! (Actually, though RKO had paid $10,000 for the rights to the play, *The Girl Who Dared,* only one scene, dealing with a girl mistaking one man for another, was used.) Of far more significance was the fact that *Top Hat*'s author, Dwight Taylor, also happened to have been the original librettist of the stage musical from which *The Gay Divorcee* had been adapted. Furthermore, the two films shared the same producer (Pandro S. Berman), director (Mark Sandrich), dance director (Hermes Pan), art director (Van Nest Polglase), music director (Max Steiner), cameraman (David Abel), and editor (William Hamilton). Once again, as so often happens, Hollywood heeded the aphorism: "If at first you do succeed—do it again."

When they did it again this time, however, it was apparent that under director Sandrich's increasingly assured hand, the results turned out to be a gayer, brighter, more dazzling product. It was almost as if those responsible for a Broadway-bound musical, even after a well-received Philadelphia tryout, kept most of the principals and the basic situations but altered the dialogue, rearranged the story line, brought in an entirely new score, and then, under another title, opened the show in New York. And it ran for years.

Among the ingredients that lifted *Top Hat* to its unique place in the pantheon of screen musicals was unquestionably the music and lyrics by Irving Berlin, which the composer still regards as the best score he has ever written. For *Top Hat,* there were no throwaway numbers like "Don't Let It Bother You" or unmotivated routines like "Let's K-nock K-nees" in *The Gay Divorcee.* Each song was created to fit the talents of Fred and/or Ginger and to serve a specific function within the context of the story. "Irving Berlin sat in on all conferences," director Sandrich once told an interviewer,

On the way to the bridle path.

"with the result that all the songs grew out of the scene structure itself. If any of them had to be eliminated—with the possible exception of 'The Piccolino'—dialogue would have had to be substituted." Note that this even applies to "Top Hat, White Tie and Tails" which, though it was a specialty number performed as part of a stage show, actually evolved out of—and capped—the previous scene. The song is equally renowned, of course, both as a tribute to Fred's sartorial trademark and as his own personal musical signature. (There is a touch of irony here, since Astaire wrote in his autobiography: "At the risk of disillusionment, I must admit that I don't like to wear top hats, white ties and tails.")

As for "The Piccolino," it was written to specification: the producer wanted a new dance finale as a successor to "The Carioca" and "The Continental." For his melody, Berlin went back to a bouncy Italian-flavored instrumental he had composed for the first *Music Box Revue* in 1921, and for his lyric he spun the tongue-in-cheek tale of a Brooklyn gondolier who fashions a song that becomes the rage of Italy. The number was not only a properly festive way to end the picture, it was also perfectly suited to the make-believe Venetian locale of the story.

Mark Sandrich began working on *Top Hat* in December 1934, some four months before actual shooting, and Astaire devoted at least five weeks to blocking out and rehearsing the dance routines (this was one of his few movies in which he danced to every song). Of the six principals in the cast, only Helen Broderick (in her second screen role) had not appeared in *The Gay Divorcee*. It turned out to be an inspired bit of casting, since her dry, deadpan personality was in perfect

"Isn't this a lovely day to be caught in the rain? . . ."

comic contrast to Edward Everett Horton's fluttery fussbudget. Briefly seen in the movie (she had been even more briefly seen in *Roberta*) was Lucille Ball, who in 1958 would take control of the RKO-Radio studio for her own television company, Desilu Productions. The chief mishap that occurred during filming involved the gown Ginger Rogers wore in the "Cheek to Cheek" number. The dress was covered with thousands of feathers and as Ginger began to dance the feathers began to molt. Hundreds of them. The scene took on the appearance of a downy snowstorm. Dozens of takes had to be made before the dance was finally shot without any of the flying feathers visible to the camera.

Top Hat begins, not surprisingly, with the credits superimposed over a top hat, which, once our story begins, turns out to be perched on the head of a gentleman entering the exclusive Thackeray Club in London. Inside the hushed, hallowed walls, Jerry Travers (Fred Astaire), an American dancer, is met by his friend Horace Hardwick (Edward Everett Horton), who is producing a new musical in which Jerry is starred. Although the London opening is set for the following night, Horace's sole concern is that Jerry accompany him, not to the theatre for a final rehearsal, but back to his hotel suite. Before leaving the club, however, the dancer performs a brief, explosive tap step that wakes up and shakes up all the old gaffers.

In his suite, Horace pleads with Jerry to remain with him overnight because he has had a tiff with his man-servant, Bates (Eric Blore), over the issue of the proper shape—square end or butterfly—of his formal bow tie (though how Jerry's presence can help resolve the rift is never quite made clear). Horace also tells Jerry that his wife, Madge (Helen Broderick), who is vacationing in Italy, is expecting them to fly down to the Lido to spend the weekend with her. (One must assume that Jerry's show plans no Saturday performances or that by "weekend" Horace really means just Sunday.)

"Top Hat, White Tie and Tails."

Horace further reveals that the main reason for Madge's invitation is that she is anxious to have Jerry meet a young friend who is visiting her. When Jerry airily dismisses the idea of going, Horace tells him he has to because Madge is counting on it. Besides, it's about time he settled down and got married. "No thanks, Horace," says Jerry. "In me you see a youth who is completely on the loose. No yens. No yearnings. No strings. No connections. No ties to my affections..." And before you know it, he's sailing right into the song, "No Strings." Indeed, so happy is he in his stringless, tieless state that Jerry breaks into an exuberant tap dance.

This private performance is a treat for Horace, but Jerry's taps make such a racket they disturb the sleep of a young lady, Dale Tremont (Ginger Rogers), who is occupying the room directly below. She telephones the hotel manager who telephones Horace. Jerry's dancing, however, makes it impossible to hear the message and Horace mistakenly thinks a young lady is awaiting him in the lobby. Smirking with self-satisfaction, he leaves but Jerry keeps right on going. When a piece of plaster falls on Dale, she has had enough; up she marches to the room above to tell off the offending tapper.

Jerry takes one look at Dale and—POW! He's smitten. After she leaves, he tries to make amends by sprinkling sand on the floor and doing an ever so soothing sand dance to help return the lovely lady to her slumber.

So enamored is Jerry that the next morning he orders every flower in the hotel flower shop delivered to Dale with a card reading, "From your Silent Admirer." Jerry also thinks it would be jolly good sport to have the entire purchase put on Horace's hotel bill.

"Cheek to Cheek"

"Heaven, I'm in Heaven . . ."

In the hotel lobby, Jerry approaches Dale, dressed in a riding outfit, and offers to drive her to the stables. No thanks, a hansom cab is there to pick her up, and off she goes in the rather antiquated conveyance. Disturbed by the slowness of the ride, Dale raps open the trapdoor on the roof to signal the unseen driver above—who, of course, is madcap Jerry Travers:

DALE: Driver, can't you go any faster than this?

JERRY: Lord love a duck, miss, oy can. But oy'm not allowed to leave the 'awss.

DALE: I mean the horse, of course.

JERRY: Well, it's like this, miss. Y'see, the 'awss is kinda tired today on account of 'avin' won the Grand National Friday.

DALE: Are you telling me that this is a race horse?

JERRY: Yes, miss. And oy've got 'is pedigree, too. As a matter o' fact, 'is sire was Man o' War.

DALE: Well, who was his dam?

JERRY: Oy beg your pardon, miss.

DALE: I said, who was his dam?

JERRY: Oh, oy don't know, miss. 'E didn't give a . . .

Slam! Dale shuts the trapdoor and the horse, frightened by the noise, gallops off. To let the confused girl in on his little deception, Jerry does a bit of tap dancing on the roof and, when Dale opens the trapdoor again, greets her with a friendly "Peek-a-boo."

Somehow they do manage to reach the stables (Dale: "What is this power you have over horse?" Jerry: "Horse power"), and Dale goes off on her morning ride. A thundershower, however, sends her scurrying for shelter to a nearby bandstand, where Jerry joins her. After being frightened by a sudden thunderclap, she rushes into Jerry's arms:

JERRY: Afraid of thunder?

DALE: Oh, no. Just the noise.

JERRY: You know what thunder is, don't you?

DALE: Of course. It's something about the . . . air. . . .

JERRY: No-no. No. When a clumsy cloud from here meets a fluffy little cloud from there, he billows toward

her. She scurries away and he scuds right up to her. She cries a little. And there you have your shower. He comforts her. They spark. That's the lightning. They kiss. Thunder!

Right on cue, it does thunder again, and Jerry sings: "The weather is fright'ning;/ The thunder and lightning/ Seem to be having their way./ But as far as I'm concerned, it's a lovely day. . . ." Following the song, Jerry struts about, hands in pockets, whistling. Dale copies his movements. He taps. She follows. It's a challenge, with Jerry setting the pace and Dale matching him step for step. And even adding some variations of her own. With another thunderclap, the tempo accelerates and, by the time the number ends, it is clear that the dance has

An enraged Erik Rhodes threatens
to "keell" Edward Everett Horton.

brought the two very close together.

Later in the day, Dale confides to
Alberto Beddini (Erik Rhodes) that
she has danced with and fallen in love
with . . . But she doesn't even know his
name. Beddini is a dress designer, and
Dale, an idle daughter of society down
on her financial luck, has promised to
wear his creations at the Lido so that
her wealthy friends will admire them
and commission Beddini to design
their wardrobes. (Here the scenarists
seem to have availed themselves of a
similar situation in *Irene,* the hit
Broadway musical of the early twenties, which RKO later planned as a
starring vehicle for Ginger Rogers. In
that story, an effeminate French dress
designer hires poor shopgirl Irene to
wear his gowns while posing as a
member of Long Island's social set.)

Now that she is in love, however,
Dale refuses to leave London. A tele-
gram arrives from the Lido: "COME
AHEAD STOP STOP BEING A SAP STOP
YOU CAN EVEN BRING ALBERTO STOP
MY HUSBAND IS STOPPING AT YOUR
HOTEL STOP WHEN DO YOU START
STOP." No, it isn't from Gertrude
Stein, it's from Madge Hardwick, who
just happens to be Dale's best friend.
(Despite this close friendship, how-
ever, Dale has apparently never met
Madge's husband, Horace.) But still
the girl refuses to budge, and Beddini
strides out of the room hurling his
final threat: "Never again weell I al-
low weemen to wear my dresses!"

In the hotel lobby that night, Dale
asks the desk clerk if a Mr. Horace
Hardwick is a guest at the hotel. Oh
yes, she is told, he's in room 404, right

above her's. Hmmm. Spotting Horace alone on the mezzanine at the far side of the lobby, the clerk obligingly points him out. Dale heads toward him but before she crosses the lobby, Jerry has walked up to Horace and sends him back to his room for a telephone call. Not noticing the replacement because a chandelier blocks her view, Dale mistakes Jerry for Horace. Furious at Jerry's apparent deception, she storms up to him and slaps his face.

Back in her room, Dale rages at Beddini. "I hate men!" she screams. "I hate you! I hate all men!" Beddini tries to calm her: "Oh, Cara Mia, you have made beeg mistake. I am no man. I am Beddini!"

The volatile couturier further vows to kill Horace for trifling with Dale's affection. He also convinces Dale that she must go to the Lido to confront Madge with the facts about her philandering mate.

Meanwhile, back in Horace's room, Horace and Jerry are totally bewildered by the slapping incident. (Horace is doubly upset because he is convinced that "one breath of scandal at this time will ruin our show."):

HORACE: You mean to say that that girl slapped your face in front of all those people for nothing?

JERRY: What would you have done, sold tickets?

HORACE: Are you sure you didn't forget yourself in the park?

JERRY: Positive. If I ever forget myself with that girl I'd remember it.

Though almost overlooked, the big event of the evening is still the opening night performance of Jerry's new show. Just before the second act, Jerry is in his dressing room getting ready for his "Top Hat, White Tie and Tails" number. Horace bursts in with the news, "Everybody is crazy about the show. The critics are raving!" He also reads Jerry a telegram he's just received from Madge expressing regret that the two won't be able to fly down to Italy after the performance to meet her friend, Dale Tremont. Dale Tremont??!! Jerry is so excited that he wants to take the first plane in the morning. But Horace—completely and inexplicably reversing his position of

Everything gets straightened out in a gondola ride.

"Gondolier" Eric Blore warns Rhodes, Horton and Helen Broderick that Fred and Ginger are drifting out to sea.

the night before—is now dead set against leaving London:

HORACE: You can't do that. The seats are selling out for four months in advance.

JERRY (*limbering up*): How long does it take to fly there?

HORACE: It takes seven hours. We've got to get back here Monday night for a performance.

JERRY: Listen . . . charter a plane for the weekend. We'll be back in time.

HORACE: I will not jeopardize my position!

JERRY (*dashing out of room*): If you want this show to run two nights, get busy now!

HORACE: What kind of a plane?

JERRY (*sprinting back and kicking one leg high in the air*): One with wings!!

Clutching Madge's telegram, Jerry bounds onstage to make his exultant musical announcement—"I just got an invitation through the mails"—punctuating his staccato words by jabbing at the telegram with the head of his cane. After singing of his anticipated fun-filled formal bash, he begins his dance with a rhythm step (right heel in place with toes tapping right and left), as a top-hatted male chorus struts behind him. Once the boys have left, Jerry does an angular solo with his cane as prop, which, as the stage is darkened, turns snakily slinky. After the boys have marched back again

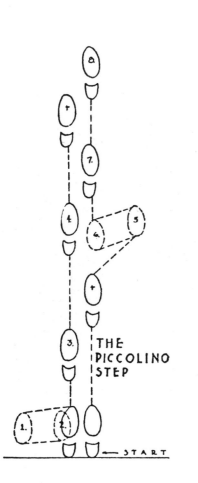

Diagram of "The Piccolino Step."

Dancing to the strains of the catchy "Piccolino."

from the rear, he uses his cane to shoot them down, one by one, with his tapping toes simulating rifle and machine-gun fire. Soon there is only one dancer still standing, but Jerry manages to bring him down by pantomiming a shot with a bow and arrow. (The routine actually dated back to Astaire's 1930 stage flop, *Smiles*, though it was then performed to a Vincent Youmans song called "Say, Young Man of Manhattan." Even earlier, in *Funny Face*, Fred Astaire had led a chorus line of top-hatted male dancers in a number called "High Hat.")

As the theatre's pit orchestra reprises the melody, the scene dissolves and we are at a gleamingly white Lido resort where a mandolin-flavored band is also playing "Top Hat, White Tie and Tails." There Madge Hardwick welcomes her friend Dale and immediately wants to know if her husband had looked her up in London. Dale gulps. When she learns that Horace will be joining them (conveniently for the plot, Madge omits any mention of Jerry coming too), Dale tells her friend that he had sent her a roomful of flowers and chased her in the park. But Madge assures her that Horace flirts with every pretty girl and it doesn't mean a thing.

When Jerry and Horace arrive via seaplane, Dale avoids meeting them (thereby prolonging the misunderstanding). Beddini, however, accosts Horace in the lobby:

BEDDINI (*aggressively*): You are Horace Hardweeck?

HORACE (*flattered to be recognized*): Oh, thank you. I am. How do you do?

BEDDINI: I am very displeased to meet you.

HORACE (*still flattered*): Really? Well . . . (*sudden realization*) What do you mean "displeased"?

BEDDINI: Signor, I warn you. For men of your kind, thees ees not a healthy place.

113

HORACE (*trying to be friendly*): My dear fellow, this is one of the healthiest spots in Europe. The air . . . the breeze . . . the flowers . . .

BEDDINI: Ah so, it ees funny treecks you are being. I warn you, never let your path criss-cross mine again!

At the hotel's outdoor dining room that night, Jerry finds Dale sitting with Madge. Since Horace is obligingly absent and Madge does not refer to Jerry by name, Dale still thinks he is Madge's husband. She is totally confused when Madge suggests they run along and dance and forget all about her. On the dance floor, Dale tries to be philosophical: "Well, if Madge doesn't care I certainly don't." And Jerry responds: "Neither do I. All I know is that it's [and he sings] 'Heaven, I'm in heaven. . . .'" Once having described the thrill that comes only when dancing "Cheek to Cheek," Jerry leads Dale off the dance floor, across a bridge, and onto a deserted part of the hotel. There they perform a romantic *pas de deux,* full of long, lovingly graceful steps and effortless lifts.

At the conclusion of the dance, Jerry asks Dale to marry him. This is just too much—and she again slaps his face, saying, "How could I have fallen in love with anyone as low as you?" Though dazed, Jerry is now *really* in heaven. She loves him!

On a balcony overlooking the canal, Beddini takes the opportunity to propose to Dale: "Why don't you marry Beddini? He'll make you happy. I'm reech. And I'm preetty." In desperation the confused girl says yes—but only on the condition that they get married right away. Not only are they able to have the ceremony performed immediately, they even unwittingly force Jerry and Horace, who had been sharing the bridal suite, to be moved to the room directly above.

Determined to get to the bottom of the mystery, the boys try to explain the situation to Madge. They are interrupted by a telephone call: it's Dale advising Madge that she has just married Beddini. When Madge blames Horace for Dale's rash behavior, it finally dawns upon Jerry that Dale has been mistaking him for Horace

"By the Adriatic waters . . ."

all along. Now he plans direct action. Vowing, "All is fair in love and war and this is revolyooshun!", Jerry dashes over to the bridal suite. Nonchalantly lying on the circular bed, he shows Beddini his room key, but Horace bustles in and gets him to leave. Beddini, furious at the intrusion, warns the hotel manager: "If he returns I weell keell heem! The Beddinis have the motto—'For the woman the keess. For the man the sword!' "

As Dale enters the bridal suite, she hears the familiar sound of Jerry tap dancing in the room above and pleads with Beddini to make him stop. With sword unsheathed, Alberto rushes upstairs—exactly as Jerry had hoped he would. To stall off the enraged husband, Jerry instructs the befuddled Horace to play decoy by taking over the tapping while he climbs over the balcony to the room below. At first Horace is unsure what to do, but quickly gains confidence and, as he continues his club-footed hopping, his expression changes from perplexity to smug satisfaction. Horace's bliss is ended with the appearance of the wild-eyed Beddini threatening to kill him. Madge also enters the room and calmly enjoys the scene ("Go right ahead, Alberto"), but the gallant Latin cannot kill a man in the presence of a lady.

Jerry finally gets the chance to explain the whole mixup to Dale as they glide along in a gondola. Suddenly, however, the gondolier—none other than Bates—falls into the water and the boat drifts out to sea.

The couple somehow manage to get back to the hotel safe and dry—and just in time for the Carnival (remember, this is all happening in one night). First the Venetian revelers sing and dance to the strains of the catchy "Piccolino," with the camera photo-

115

graphing them from above in a variety of geometric patterns, and also catching their reflection in the water. Once Dale has sung a solo to Jerry seated at a table, the two rise to join the dancers, with the camera at first showing only their tapping feet. In their joyous display, the team highlights a circular step featuring backward kicking and heel slapping, and a peasant-type variation performed with hands on hips. As the dance ends, Dale and Jerry are back at their table with their glasses raised in a toast.

But still the movie must tidy up that messy business of Dale's marriage to Beddini. No problem at all. Seems that the faithful Bates merely turned his collar around and passed himself off as a clergyman to perform the ceremony. Now Jerry and Dale can gaily bound out of the hotel together—and also out of the picture.

Top Hat opened at the Radio City Music Hall on August 16, 1935. The film broke all existing records at the showplace, taking in $134,800 the first week, $24,000 more than any other movie in the same period of time. It also established a new three-week record with receipts of $350,000.

The reviewers may have carped a bit at the transparent device of the plot's excessively prolonged misunderstanding, but there was general rejoicing at everything else. In *The New York Times,* André Sennwald greeted the film with: "Irving Berlin has written some charming melodies for the photoplay and the best of the current cinema teams does them agile justice on the dance floor. When *Top Hat* is letting Mr. Astaire perform his incomparable magic or teaming him with the increasingly dexterous Miss Rogers, it is providing the most urbane fun that you will find anywhere on the screen." The *New York Post* man,

116

Thornton Delehanty, claimed the picture to be "the best of the Fred Astaire-Ginger Rogers vehicles, which is to say the tops in screen entertainment. . . . The new attraction has the silken quality of the Fred Astaire personality; it ripples and flows from scene to scene." The *New York Daily News* even saw fit to praise *Top Hat* in its editorial column: "The best thing yet done in movie musical comedy. The music is Berlin at his best; the settings are gorgeous; the lines are among the funniest we've heard; and the dancing and comedy of Fred Astaire and Ginger Rogers are something to go back and see again. Especially the dancing."

Overseas, the reception was equally enthusiastic. In the *Illustrated London News,* Michael Orme penned this tribute: "There is no weak spot to be found in the company's armour, but Mr. Astaire, with no effort, no trace of self-assertion, wears his with a gay and careless *panache* that gives

his work its individuality and its distinction. He embodies the very essence of lighthearted entertainment. He brings something of the rhythm of the dance into the traffic of the comedy passages and translates the emotions of life into terpsichorean terms."

Time magazine, however, was the most observant of all in detecting the minor revolution that the Fred and Ginger pictures had wrought: "When Hollywood revived musical films three years ago, dancing was monopolized by Director Busby Berkeley and his imitators. . . . Thanks more to Fred Astaire than to any other single influence, the character of musicomedy in the cinema has completely changed." Not completely, perhaps, but the Astaire influence did prove that the sight of one expert dancer and his partner was at least as thrilling as the sight of massed formations and geometric designs. And nobody has ever called Fred Astaire camp.

Blore's explanation makes everyone happy—except Erik Rhodes.

FOLLOW THE FLEET

CAST

Bake Baker	Fred Astaire
Sherry Martin	Ginger Rogers
Bilge Smith	Randolph Scott
Connie Martin	Harriet Hilliard
Iris Manning	Astrid Allwyn
Dopey Williams	Ray Mayer
Capt. Hickey	Harry Beresford
Lt. Williams	Addison Randall
Jim Nolan	Russell Hicks
Sullivan (Nolan's assistant)	Brooks Benedict
Kitty Collins	Lucille Ball
Singing Trio	Betty Grable, Joy Hodges, Jennie Gray
Waitress	Jane Hamilton
Hostess	Maxine Jennings
Sailors	Tony Martin, Frank Jenks, Frank Moran, Edward Burns
Weber (dance hall manager)	Herbert Rawlinson
Contest Dancers	Dorothy Fleisman, Bob Cromer

Producer: Pandro S. Berman for RKO Radio Pictures. Director: Mark Sandrich. Lyrics and Music: Irving Berlin. Screenplay: Dwight Taylor & Allan Scott, from play, *Shore Leave,* by Hubert Osborne. Dance director: Hermes Pan. Art director: Van Nest Polglase. Costumes: Bernard Newman. Music director: Max Steiner. Cameraman: David Abel. Editor: Henry Berman. Release date: February 19, 1936. Running time: 110 minutes.

MUSICAL NUMBERS: "We Saw the Sea"—Astaire, sailors/ "Let Yourself Go"—Rogers, with Grable, Hodges, Gray; dance by Astaire & Rogers, Fleisman & Cromer, others; reprised as dance by Rogers/ "Get Thee Behind Me, Satan"—Hilliard/ "I'd Rather Lead a Band"—Astaire; dance by Astaire, sailors/ "But Where Are You?"—Hilliard/ "I'm Putting All My Eggs in One Basket"—piano playing by Astaire; sung by Astaire & Rogers; dance by Astaire & Rogers/ "Let's Face the Music and Dance"—Astaire; dance by Astaire & Rogers. Unused: "Moonlight Maneuvers," "With a Smile on My Face."

119

Viewers of Fred Astaire's first three starring films could hardly be blamed if they went away convinced that Fred Astaire spent almost all of his waking hours in formal attire (in *The Gay Divorcee* he even showed up sporting tile and tails for a midnight rendezvous in Ginger Rogers' hotel suite). Fearful that so glossy an image could not endure indefinitely, the powers at RKO ruled that the time had come to lower his station and limit his wardrobe. Their edict: for his next picture Fred Astaire would be seen as a gum-chewing gob.

But first they had to find a story in which this social and sartorial change could take place. After many conferences, the front office decided to reuse a twice-twice told tale that had already been a play and its movie version, plus a musical adaptation and *its* movie version. The genesis began in 1922 with David Belasco's production of Hubert Osborne's play *Shore Leave*. It starred Frances Starr as Connie Martin, a spinster dressmaker living in a New England seaport, who meets and falls in love with sailor Bilge Smith, played by James Rennie. Though Bilge goes away to sea the very next day, Connie is so smitten that she has a ship salvaged just for him. When Bilge returns two years later, he's too proud to accept her present and takes off for another two years. Eventually, matters are straightened out and Connie gets her man. A silent-screen version was made three years later with Richard Barthelmess as Bilge and Dorothy Mackaill as Connie.

In 1927, librettist Herbert Fields, lyricists Clifford Grey and Leo Robin, and composer Vincent Youmans turned the story into a musical hit, *Hit the Deck*, which included such perennials as "Sometimes I'm Happy" and "Hallelujah." This time the heroine's name was changed to Loulou (possibly because the part was played by Louise Groody) and the action was expanded so that she might travel to China to be near her Bilge (played by Charles King). In 1930, RKO filmed the musical with Polly Walker as Loulou and

Fred sings "We Saw the Sea" on ship (above), and in a landing craft (below). Among the singing gobs: Randolph Scott, Frank Jenks, Ray Mayer, and Tony Martin.

120

Lucille Ball and Betty Grable help transform drab schoolmarm Harriet Hilliard into a sexy dazzler.

Seamen Mayer, Jenks and Martin encourage Ginger and Fred to enter the dance contest.

Jack Oakie as Bilge. (The 1955 M-G-M remake kept the title and most of the songs. However, the story was new, and the theme—three sailors on shore leave—seemed to owe more to *On the Town* for general inspiration than it did to *Hit the Deck*.)

In 1936, when RKO planned its second movie version of *Hit the Deck*, it renamed it *Follow the Fleet*, called in Irving Berlin to create a brand-new score, and cast Fred Astaire and Ginger Rogers in the leads. But not as Bilge and Loulou—or even Connie. Fred and Ginger played two newly dreamed-up characters, Bake Baker, an ex-hoofer turned sailor, and Sherry Martin, his former partner now singing in a San Francisco dime-a-dance ballroom. It was Randolph Scott, Fred's buddy in *Roberta*, who appeared as Bake's buddy, Bilge Smith, and Harriet Hilliard who was cast as Sherry's sister, Connie. In this version, Connie still falls for her Bilge and still salvages a ship for him. But it's Bake and Sherry who really save the old schooner by putting on a show that raises the money needed for its restoration.

Irving Berlin's memorably bright and varied songs for *Follow the Fleet* skillfully fitted in with the surroundings and the characters who introduced them. Since it was Harriet Hilliard who had the more "serious" romance, it was she who got the more "serious" ballads, "Get Thee Behind Me, Satan" and "But Where Are You?", both perfectly mirroring the girl's lovesick emotions. The more ebullient expressions —plus "Let's Face the Music and Dance"—were all first sung by Fred and Ginger, either as solos or as duets.

"We Joined the Navy," which opens the movie, gets things off to a properly nautical, lightly satirical start as Fred

Letting go to "Let Yourself Go."

catalogues his irritations at seeing the world from the deck of a battleship. At the Paradise Ballroom, where Ginger works, she offers an irresistibly rhythmic invitation to the dance, "Let Yourself Go," accompanied by a vocal trio consisting of Betty Grable (something of a comedown after her k-nees k-nocking number in *The Gay Divorcee*), Joy Hodges (she later played ingenues in Broadway musicals and, in 1972, took over the Ruby Keeler role in *No, No, Nanette*), and Jennie Gray (whose career apparently ended at the Paradise Ballroom). Following the vocal rendition, there is an elimination dance contest for the ballroom patrons, all of whom had been recruited by RKO through a series of actual contests held in dancehalls throughout Los Angeles. (The intrepid twosome that made it to the finals with Fred and Ginger were an eighteen-year-old dishwasher and a twenty-year-old stenographer.) The song also served later in the film as the accompaniment to the only solo tap dance Ginger Rogers ever performed in all her ten movies with Astaire.

"I'd Rather Lead a Band," another specialty, is offered by Fred in dress whites aboard ship after he has been called upon to entertain a visiting British admiral and his gushy wife ("I do *so* adore Ameddican music"). Once Fred has expressed his preference for bandleading over anything else in the world, he emphasizes that conviction with a spirited tap solo. Presently, a veritable ship's complement of tapping sailors comes to join him, and Fred puts them through a series of close-order drills, using nothing but his feet to convey his commands. (Apparently this was intended as a follow-up to the all-male tap routine, "Top Hat, White Tie and Tails," in *Top Hat*.)

Harriet and Randy get acquainted.

During his shipboard dancing class,
Fred gives personal attention to Frank Moran.

124

"I'd Rather Lead a Band."

Once Fred gets the idea of putting on a benefit show aboard the S.S. *Connie Martin*, he recruits his cast from his fellow sailors and Ginger's dance-hall friends. During a rehearsal—in a scene frequently cut when the movie is shown on television—Fred ambles over to the piano and starts pecking out the tune of "I'm Putting All My Eggs in One Basket." Ginger, wearing floppy slacks, joins him and the two break into a slap-happy, seemingly spontaneous dance reminiscent of their lighthearted "I'll Be Hard to Handle" routine in *Roberta*. As a running gag, Fred leads Ginger into a step, she follows but then gets so wrapped up in it that, with brows furrowed and shoulders hunched, she continues the step even though Fred has already gone on to another. At the end they spoof the mugging, broad-armed finales favored by applause-milking dance acts.

The team's last number in the film, the exquisite "Let's Face the Music and Dance," is performed as part of the gala entertainment aboard the ship. In it, Fred gets his only opportunity in the picture to don top hat, white tie, and tails, and though the song has nothing to do with the plot, it leads to another variation on Fred's wooing-and-winning dance technique. Fred is first seen at a gambling table at the Monte Carlo Casino, surrounded by lovelies (including Lucille Ball), who desert him once he loses all his money. The curtains close and immediately reopen on the casino terrace. Passers-by all snub the penniless, dejected gambler. He takes a small pistol out of his pocket and is ready to end it all when he sees the elegantly gowned Ginger about to leap off the ledge. He pulls her down, shows her his gun, and throws it away. Then he shows her his empty wallet and throws *that* away.

The inevitable misunderstanding.

At a rehearsal for the big show.

Then he sings, "There may be troubles ahead/ But while there's moonlight and music and love and romance/ Let's face the music and dance. . . ." And so the gambler must dance to give heart to the despondent girl. At first she stiffly tries to ignore the spell of the music and Fred's mesmeric hand-passes. As the gambler keeps dancing around her, the girl slowly begins to succumb. Caught up in the sweep and passion of the compelling melody, the two dance defiantly, even ecstatically, in the face of the troubles they know await them. At the end, bravely kicking their legs and throwing back their heads, they stride gallantly off. Curtain.

Apart from casting Fred as a sailor and Ginger as a dime-a-dance entertainer (they wouldn't dare cast her as a dime-a-dance dancer), *Follow the Fleet* also altered course by reverting to the *Roberta* formula of doing away with the services of any character comedians. But there was plenty of the expected Fred and Ginger banter. In their reunion scene early in the film—and after greeting each other with a series of "Gosh, I'm glad to see you's" and "Same here's"—Fred can't resist needling Ginger about singing at the Paradise Ballroom:

FRED: As you said, marriage would have ruined your career.
GINGER: Well, I found out I was wrong.
FRED: Maybe you're right. If you'd've married me you wouldn't be working in a chop suey joint like this.
GINGER: Well, I don't see any admiral stripes on you.
FRED: Ha-ha. I like to go incognito just to mingle with the boys.

The fact is, Ginger explains, "they're not interested in a girl dancing alone. Unless she's got a fan." "Well, a fan doesn't cost much," is Fred's practical-minded reply.

In a later scene, discussing a man-hungry ex-chorus girl, now a wealthy divorcee, Fred asks Ginger, "What's she like?" And Ginger replies, "Anything in a uniform."

127

The clowning rehearsal dance to
"I'm Putting All My Eggs in One Basket."

128

Lucille Ball, though viewed only briefly, had one of the better lines in the picture. As she and the other girls arrive on deck of the schooner to rehearse the benefit show, they are looked over admiringly by the bashful sailors. One particularly burly gob (played by ex-prizefighter Frank Moran) is emboldened to approach Lucille. "Hello," he says in a voice of gravel, "how was heaven when you left?" To which Lucille deadpans: "Tell me, little boy, did you get a whistle or a baseball bat with that suit?"

Filming of *Follow the Fleet* began under Mark Sandrich's direction on November 1, 1936, though Astaire had started rehearsing two months before. Again, as in *Top Hat*, the main mishap involved a dress. This time it was the one Ginger wore for the "Let's Face the Music and Dance" sequence. As Astaire wrote in his autobiography, "The dress had heavy beaded sleeves that hung from the wrists, which I hadn't bargained for. When Ginger did a quick turn, the sleeves, which must have weighed a few pounds each, would fly—necessitating a quick dodge by me." As the cameras began to roll, however, Fred forgot to duck, and he received a flying sleeve smack on the jaw and partly in the eye. The team did twenty takes of the dance until about eight o'clock at night, and when it was all over they decided to go back to the very first one. Somehow, the cameras had failed to record Fred's sleeve-induced injury.

In addition to briefly exhibiting future luminaries Betty Grable and Lucille Ball, the movie also marked the screen debut of Tony Martin as a barely visible singing gob (nineteen years later he would have one of the leads in Metro's much altered remake of *Hit the Deck*). Apart from the pleasures of the dance routines, one of the film's most delectable moments was the sight

"There may be trouble ahead . . ."

of Fred sitting on the deck near his bunk, dancing his fingers on the keys of a typewriter, and using his right big toe to push back the carriage.

Since *Follow the Fleet* followed *Top Hat* it was fair game for reviewers to compare the two. Although Richard Watts, Jr., of the *New York Herald Tribune*, felt the story both weak and intrusive, he maintained that "the score and the dancing are at least up to the enchantment of *Top Hat*." The *New York Post* appraiser, Thornton Delehanty, however, held that the film "does not come within hailing distance of the glamorous and shining *Top Hat*," even though it does "reaffirm the endlessly amazing talent of Fred Astaire." On the other hand, Eileen Creelman, writing in the *New York Sun*, found it "as elaborate and more entertaining than the popular *Top Hat*." Avoiding direct comparison, *The New York Times'* Frank S. Nugent took the broader view: "Even though it is not the best of the series, it is still good enough to take the head of this year's class in song and dance entertainment. The screen's premier team taps as gayly, waltzes as beautifully, and disagrees as merrily as ever."

No matter the disagreements in the press, the public was of one mind: *Follow the Fleet* was another fleet-footed smash.

Victor Moore, Fred Astaire and director George Stevens.

SWING TIME

CAST

John "Lucky" Garnett	Fred Astaire
Penelope "Penny" Carrol	Ginger Rogers
"Pop" Cardetti	Victor Moore
Mabel Anderson	Helen Broderick
Gordon	Eric Blore
Margaret Watson	Betty Furness
Ricardo Romero	Georges Metaxa
Judge Watson	Landers Stevens
"Dice" Raymond	John Harrington
Al Simpson	Pierre Watkin
Schmidt (tailor)	Abe Reynolds
Eric Facannistrom (drunk)	Gerald Hamer
Policeman	Edgar Dearing
Red	Frank Jenks
Other Dancers	Jack Goode, Donald Kerr, Ted O'Shea, Frank Edmunds, Bill Brand
Minister	Ferdinand Munier
Announcer	Joey Ray
Hotel Desk Clerk	Ralph Byrd
Lucky's Butler	Floyd Shackleford

Producer: Pandro S. Berman for RKO Radio Pictures. Director: George Stevens. Lyrics: Dorothy Fields. Music: Jerome Kern. Screenplay: Howard Lindsay & Allan Scott, from story, "Portrait of John Garnett," by Erwin Gelsey. Dance director: Hermes Pan. Art director: Van Nest Polglase. Costumes: Bernard Newman. Settings & costumes for "Bojangles" number: John Harkrider. Music director: Nathaniel Shilkret. Orchestrations: Robert Russell Bennett. Cameraman: David Abel. Editor: Henry Berman. Release date: August 26, 1936. Running time: 103 minutes.

MUSICAL NUMBERS: "It's Not in the Cards"—brief dance by Astaire, troupe/ "Pick Yourself Up"—Astaire & Rogers; dance by Astaire & Rogers, Moore & Broderick/ "The Way You Look Tonight" —Astaire; reprised briefly by Metaxa/ "Waltz in Swing Time"—dance by Astaire & Rogers/ "A Fine Romance"—Rogers & Astaire/ "Bojangles of Harlem"—night club chorus; dance by Astaire, chorus/ "Never Gonna Dance"—Astaire; dance by Astaire & Rogers.

The success of *Follow the Fleet* made it apparent that the public would flock to see Fred Astaire in almost any line of work just so long as he remembered to bring along his dancing shoes—and at least one suit of tails. If his fans could accept Fred as a gob they could even accept him as a gambler—which happened to be the role he played in his next film, *Swing Time*.

Not a hood gambler, of course. Nothing more than a personable hoofer with an insatiable appetite for cards, dice, and other games of chance. ("My talent is gambling," he says early in the movie. "Hoofing is all right but there's no future in it.") The story concocted by Allan Scott (he was co-author of six Astaire-Rogers films) and Howard Lindsay (he had directed *Gay Divorce* on the stage) was obligingly loose enough to provide sufficient room for the expected song and dance specialties for Fred and Ginger, here playing a dance team that scales the glittering heights of Manhattan's most elegant nightclub. And since *Follow the Fleet* had been conspicuously bereft of the type of comedians that had distinguished *The Gay Divorcee* and *Top Hat*, the authors obligingly remedied the situation by writing in parts for two of the faithful: sharp-tongued Helen Broderick (Ginger's best friend again) and the huffily unctuous Eric Blore (in the oddly truncated role of a dance-school manager). New to the company was cherubic Victor Moore, as Fred's sidekick, whose biggest howl came when, after mouthing an insult to a policeman, he innocently explains that all he said was, "Look out for the great big ditch." In a slight departure from the norm, the film also gave the stars two other—more or less—serious romantic involvements: Fred's initial love was his hometown sweetheart, Betty Furness (she had been an extra in *Flying Down to Rio*), and Ginger was ardently pursued by Georges Metaxa, playing a smoother version of Erik Rhodes' Latin-lover caricature in *Top Hat*.

Though the appropriately gossamer fable did its best to keep out of the

Fred cleans up in a crap game while waiting for his trousers to come back from the tailor.

Now penniless, Fred and Victor hop a freight to New York.

Fred's first meeting with Ginger.
Edgar Dearing is the cop.

134

way of the singing and dancing, it nevertheless put a severe strain upon audience credulity. At the beginning of *Swing Time*, the boys in Fred's vaudeville dance act, fearful of losing their meal ticket, hatch a plot to prevent his marriage. They actually convince him —are you ready?—that since fashion now dictates cuffs must be worn on striped trousers for morning dress, Fred simply cannot be seen at his wedding in cuffless pants. So the trusting soul sends his pants to a tailor for cuffing, thereby missing his own nuptuals. (The writers liked this little ploy so much that at the end of the film they even had Fred successfully pull the same trick on Metaxa to prevent his marrying Ginger.)

The movie also made much of the fact that, according to an agreement with his stood-up fiancée's father, Fred is honor-bound to marry the local belle just as soon as he amasses $25,000. Actually, his would-be father-in-law had never specified any amount, only that Fred must first be successful if he ever is to get another chance to win Betty Furness's hand. Perhaps the most incongruous situation of all was the Fred and Ginger audition for a night-club engagement. Scheduled to dance at the Silver Sandal, they are at first thwarted by bandleader Metaxa's refusal to play for them (he's in love with Ginger and he's jealous), and then by the club owner's admission that he has lost the band to the Club Raymond in a card game. Nothing daunted, Fred goes to the Club Raymond, wins back the orchestra at cards, and gets to perform the audition

"No one could teach you how to dance in a thousand years."

But Fred picks himself up,
dusts himself off, and
they start all over again.

136

with Ginger. But where do they perform? Right there, at the Club Raymond, even though the proprietor of the Silver Sandal is nowhere in sight. Thanks apparently to some form of telepathic contact, they get the job.

But logical plot developments counted for little in the world of Astaire and Rogers. The foundation of that world was, of course, the songs and what the team did with them. And for *Swing Time*, Fred and Ginger were the beneficiaries of a superior collection provided by the *Roberta* collaborators, lyricist Dorothy Fields and composer Jerome Kern.

Surprisingly, though the film opens on a performance of Fred's dance act in a vaudeville theatre, we view it only fleetingly from the rear of the orchestra and from the right wing of the stage. The song that accompanies the troupe's dancing, "It's Not in the Cards," is neither sung nor identified; from then on it is used merely as background music for the subsequent backstage scenes.

The first actual song is set up early in the movie when Lucky Garnett (the Fred character), after arriving via freight train in New York, follows Penny Carrol (the Ginger character) into the dance studio where she teaches. Receptionist Mabel Anderson (Helen Broderick) asks him, "Have you any preference as to the type of instructress you'd like?"

"Yes, I have," replies Lucky. "I'd like one that comes to about here. And if she had red hair that would be a great help. And a cute little nose."

To which Mabel deadpans: "She might be able to teach you to move your feet."

Lucky does get Penny as an instructress, but he purposely dances as clumsily as he can. When the exasperated Penny tells him, "I can't teach you anything," Lucky pleads, "Please, teacher,

Fred checks in at the apartment hotel where Ginger lives. Ralph Byrd (later the movies' Dick Tracy) is the clerk.

Ginger and friend Helen Broderick unexpectedly discover Fred losing at piquet to drunk Gerald Hamer.

Picketing Ginger's apartment.

"The Way You Look Tonight."

teach me something,/ Nice teacher, teach me something. . . ." And suddenly the plea has turned into the bubbly polka, "Pick Yourself Up," during which Lucky acts out the words by oafishly falling all over himself. Just as Penny advises her incredibly inept pupil that he'll never be able to dance, she is overheard by the studio manager (Eric Blore in an oddly truncated role) and is fired on the spot. Lucky, however, saves Penny's job by giving a breathtaking demonstration of just how much this red-headed, cute-nosed, instructress has taught him in only one lesson.

Less integrally presented was the silken melody, "The Way You Look Tonight." Penny has refused to see Lucky for a week because he had failed to show up for their audition. Seems the poor chap had been unable to secure the required formal attire and had spent the evening playing piquet in a vain attempt to win the tails off a drunk's back. After being picketed by Lucky and his roly-poly friend, Pop Cardetti (Victor Moore), Penny, while still in the bathroom washing her hair, finally lets Lucky come into her hotel suite. Once inside, though he has only a quick glimpse of Penny, he saunters over to the piano and extolls her warm smile, her soft cheeks, her tender words, and her nose-wrinkling laugh. As the song ends, Penny emerges from the bathroom thoroughly transfixed by the adoring sentiment—and then rushes right back in embarrassment when she realizes that her hair is still lathered with shampoo. ("The Way You Look Tonight" was the third song to win an Oscar, and the second from a Fred-and-Ginger movie.)

Despite the absence of a dance routine, one of the brightest of all Astaire-Rogers numbers occurs at a deserted resort where Penny, Lucky, Mabel and Pop have bundled themselves off to for a wintry outing. By this time, the Lucky-Penny team has become a top night club attraction and the two talk about how they met and what has happened to them:

"Waltz in Swing Time."

LUCKY: It's quite an experience.

PENNY: It's more than an experience. It's sorta like a . . . a romance. (*On cue, "A Fine Romance" is heard in the background.*) Isn't it?

LUCKY: Yes. As we say in French, *"La Belle Romance."*

PENNY: A swell romance.

But just as they are about to kiss, Lucky is reminded by Pop of his pledge not to get romantic because, after all, he still is engaged to the girl back home. So he freezes up, and the rebuffed Penny sighs and sings, "A fine romance, with no kisses,/ A fine romance, my friend this is . . ." In the course of the song, she accuses Lucky of, among other things, being as cold as yesterday's mashed potatoes, calmer than the seals in the Arctic Ocean, and as hard to land as the *Ile de France.* When, a few moments later, Pop, in a naively tactless way, tells Penny about Lucky's fiancée, it is now her turn to be cold. And just as Lucky has impetuously decided to toss caution to the wind! "Now where were we when Pop interrupted us?" he asks. "As I remember it, you called me aloof."

"No," replies Penny. "It was a laugh."

With emotions now reversed, it's Lucky's turn to express exasperation with "A Fine Romance" that has no thrills, clinches or pinches.

Toward the end of the film, Penny agrees to marry bandleader Ricardo Romero (Georges Metaxa) because of Lucky's unlucky gambling and also because Lucky's fiancée (Betty Furness) has suddenly shown up. (Here, scriptwriter Howard Lindsay, recalling the words he had put into Victor Moore's mouth in a similar situation in the Broadway musical, *Anything Goes,* gave Moore almost the identical lines as he pledges to stick by the disconsolate Fred.) The final leave-taking for Lucky and Penny—before the inevitable reconciliation—occurs in the deserted night club:

PENNY: Does she dance very beautifully?

LUCKY: Who?

PENNY: The girl you're in love with.

LUCKY: Yes . . . very.

"A fine romance, with no kisses . . .

PENNY: The girl you're engaged to. The girl you're going to marry.

LUCKY: Oh, I don't know. I've danced with you. I'm never gonna dance again. (*And, appropriately, he glides into the song, "Never Gonna Dance."*) "Thouuuuuugh, I'm left without a penny the wolf was discreet/ He left me my feet . . ."

At the conclusion of the song (note the play on the word "penny"), Lucky coaxes Penny onto the dance floor. Separately but together, trying desperately to keep their feelings in check, they walk and waltz until unable to control their emotions, they cling desperately to each other as they twirl and glide on dancing levels both below and above two arched stairways.

For the film's finale, a slightly hysterical wedding scene with everyone laughing uncontrollably, lyricist Fields came up with a set of lyrics to "A Fine Romance" in which each of the principals was given a line appropriate to the situation. At the end, Fred warbles the song to Ginger, Ginger sings "The Way You Look Tonight" in counterpoint, and all Manhattan is at their feet.

Swing Time contained two non-plotted musical numbers offered as night club dance specialties. One was the audition, "Waltz in Swing Time" ("Constructed and Arranged by R. Russell Bennett," according to the sheet music) which was performed so airily and ecstatically by Fred in tuxedo and floppy *La Bohème* bow tie, and Ginger in billowing white ruffles. The other was Fred's "Bojangles of Harlem," the only routine he ever did in blackface. (Dorothy Fields has recalled that Jerome Kern, more accustomed to creating songs of romance than of rhythm, had a particularly difficult time getting the right beat for the number. To provide rhythmic inspiration, Astaire showed up one afternoon at the composer's Beverly Wilshire Hotel suite and spent hours improvising tap routines all over the room.) For this high-stepping tribute to the great dancer Bill "Bojangles" Robinson, the curtains part to reveal an enormous Negro head topped by a derby, which soon turns into the sole of a papier maché shoe. After another shoe sole comes into view, the audience then sees a pair of elongated false legs leading back to a reclining, derby-topped Fred Astaire. The black-faced chorus girls swiftly and painlessly amputate the legs and feet and sing their spirited paean to the dancing Pied Piper who has the whole town at his heels, leaving their flats, missing their meals. Fred joins the girls in the tap number, then does a solo with three huge shadows projected on the walls behind him.

Early in 1936, RKO announced that Fred Astaire and Ginger Rogers would appear together in a movie to be called *I Won't Dance*. By March the title had been changed to *Never Gonna Dance*. Then, fearful lest the public take it too literally, the studio changed the name again to *Swing Time*. Fred devoted almost eight weeks to preparing the dance routines, about one week shy of the actual time it took to shoot the movie. The two largest sets recreated two resplendent nightclubs, both the work of designer John Harkrider: the two-level Silver Sandal, with the orchestra under a platform above the dance floor and which seated 360, and the nautically flavored Club Raymond, which had a quilted ceiling and could seat 300. The film, which was directed by George Stevens was completed in August and opened at the Radio City Music Hall later that month.

The appeal of the scintillating Dorothy Fields–Jerome Kern, score should have been apparent to everyone from the start. Not, however, to Frank S. Nugent of *The New York Times*. "The picture is good, of course," he wrote. "But after *Top Hat, Follow the Fleet* and the rest, it is a disappointment. Blame it primarily on the music. Jerome Kern has shadowboxed with

144

"Oh! Bojangles of Harlem,
you dance such hot stuff! . . ."

"Never gonna dance, never gonna dance,
Only gonna love you . . ."

146

Fred and Betty Furness happily discover
they are no longer engaged.

Now it's Georges Metaxa's turn to be late for his wedding.

swing when he should have been trying to pick up a few companion pieces to 'Smoke Gets in Your Eyes' and 'I Won't Dance.' Maybe we have no ear for music (do we hear cries of 'No! No!'?), but right now we could not even whistle a bar of 'A Fine Romance,' and that's about the catchiest and brightest melody in the show." Ah, well.

Howard Barnes in the *New York Herald Tribune* also felt let down, but his criticism was directed at the story. "It is high time," said he, "that Fred Astaire and Ginger Rogers were relieved of the necessity of going through a lot of romantic nonsense. The vast success of *Swing Time* is more of a tribute to them than to the material of their latest song and dance carnival. They have never performed with more exquisite finish." Other comments on the team: "The team treads its measure in irresistible form and fashion"

—Regina Crewe, *New York Journal* . . . "Some of the most joyous dancing that Astaire and Rogers have ever offered to an enraptured public"—Eileen Creelman, *New York Sun* . . . "Fred Astaire doesn't dance. He floats—and just as waftily when the luscious Ginger is in his arms as when she's absent" —Irene Thirer, *New York Post*.

Soon after the movie's Radio City opening, *The Hollywood Reporter* named Fred and Ginger the nation's number one box-office attraction. But following initially successful weeks, the new film turned out to be a shade less popular than had the team's previous outings. Fred and Ginger, realizing that they couldn't continue together indefinitely, agreed that this was a good time to start planning separate careers again. The studio also agreed —there would definitely be at least a temporary parting following their next scheduled picture.

Together at last—with Manhattan at their feet.

Standing behind Fred, Ginger and composer George Gershwin are
dance director Hermes Pan, director Mark Sandrich, lyricist
Ira Gershwin, and music director Nathaniel Shilkret.

SHALL WE DANCE

CAST

Peter P. "Pete" Peters (alias Petrov)	Fred Astaire
Linda Keene (née Linda Thompson)	Ginger Rogers
Jeffrey Baird	Edward Everett Horton
Cecil Flintridge	Eric Blore
Arthur Miller	Jerome Cowan
Denise, Lady Tarrington	Ketti Gallian
Jim Montgomery	William Brisbane
Harriet Hoctor	Harriet Hoctor
Ship Passenger	Ann Shoemaker
Evans (bandleader)	Ben Alexander
Tai	Emma Young
Linda's Dancing Partner	Pete Theodore
Ballet Masters	Marek Windheim, Rolfe Sedan
Policeman in Park	Charles Coleman
Process Server	Frank Moran

Producer: Pandro S. Berman for RKO Radio Pictures. Director: Mark Sandrich. Lyrics: Ira Gershwin. Music: George Gershwin. Screenplay: Allan Scott & Ernest Pagano, adapted by P. J. Wolfson from story, "Watch Your Step," by Lee Loeb & Harold Buchman. Dance directors: Hermes Pan, Harry Losee. Art director: Van Nest Polglase. Costumes: Irene. Music Director: Nathaniel Shilkret. Orchestrations: Robert Russell Bennett. Cameraman: David Abel. Editor: William Hamilton. Release date: April 30, 1937. Running time: 116 minutes.

MUSICAL NUMBERS: "(I've Got) Beginner's Luck"—dance by Astaire/ "Slap that Bass"—uncredited singer, Fred Astaire; dance by Astaire/ "Walking the Dog"—background/ "(I've Got) Beginner's Luck"—Astaire/ "They All Laughed"—Rogers; dance by Astaire & Rogers/ "Let's Call the Whole Thing Off"—Astaire & Rogers; dance by Astaire & Rogers/ "They Can't Take That Away from Me"—Astaire; reprised as dance by Astaire & Hoctor/ "Shall We Dance"—Astaire; dance by Astaire & Rogers, chorus. Unused: "Hi-Ho!, "Wake Up, Brother, and Dance."

151

With *Shall We Dance,* Fred Astaire and Ginger Rogers returned to the world of the elegant and the affluent. Apparently no longer concerned about proving Fred a regular guy by casting him as a hoofing sailor or a gambling hoofer, RKO now dared to allow him play the role of not just a successful dancer but a successful ballet dancer— although we quickly discover him to be a regular guy who is anxious to combine ballroom and tap dancing with his arabesques and entrechats.

It was actually the last time out for the team to enjoy the ambience of improbable luxury, first in Paris, then on a palatial ocean liner (where staterooms have sliding glass doors opening on the deck), and finally in a glittering, ultrasmart New York hotel. Gone was even a hint of struggle for success or of financial concern, as there had been in *Follow the Fleet* and *Swing Time.* Spats there were, of course, with some of the most confused misunderstandings since *Top Hat,* but the tone throughout was always one of glossiest make-believe.

Once again, the story was blissfully illogical. But never before had Fred and Ginger appeared in a tale that for all its veneer of sophistication was so naively straitlaced. As usual, our hero has no romantic desires other than marriage—except that in this case Fred decides to marry musical-comedy star Ginger even before they meet. On board the liner taking the couple from Le Havre to New York, everyone mistakes them for man and wife, and the rest of the film is devoted to their frustrated attempts to disprove their marital condition. Eventually, they come to the conclusion that the only way people will believe them is to get married in order to get a divorce.

Because of all this confusion, the bumptious hotel floor manager (Eric Blore) takes it upon himself to unlock and lock the door connecting Fred's and Ginger's adjoining suites at each fresh report that the pair is either married or unmarried. In fact, the whole situation is so shocking that the ballet impressario (Edward Everett Horton)

Impressario Edward Everett Horton observing ballet
Masters Rolfe Sedan and Marek Windheim.

Fred sails on the *Queen Anne* just to be near Ginger.

reports the dreadful news that the Metropolitan has cancelled Fred's appearance because of his "scandalous behavior" with Ginger.

But perhaps Hollywood's excessive Puritanism was never more glaringly revealed than in the scheme hatched by Ginger's producer (Jerome Cowan) to convince everybody, once and for all, that unmarried Fred and Ginger are really married (somehow this is supposed to keep Ginger in show business even though she has threatened to quit). Finding a wax dummy that had been made in Ginger's likeness for an unproduced show, the producer and his accomplice stealthily creep into Fred's bedroom while Fred is sleeping and photograph the dummy, clad in a negligee, sitting on his bed. When the picture appears in the newspapers the next morning, everyone not only believes the dummy to be the real Ginger, but accepts the photograph as proof positive of the couple's marriage!

While much about *Shall We Dance* may strike a viewer today as simple-minded, many of its comedy sequences remain highly risible. There is still fun watching a drunken Edward Everett Horton, at the ship's bar, reply to the question "What does your watch say?" by answering "Tick-tick tick-tick tick-tick. . . ." Or a befuddled Horton, clad only in his underwear in his stateroom, suddenly become alarmed that the ship is on fire and dash madly on deck wearing a top hat, and—thanks to the solicitude of Astaire and Cowan—clutching a blanket, an alarm clock, a hot-water bottle, a basket of fruit, a tennis racket, and a golf bag. Or the scene at Fred and Ginger's hurried wedding in New Jersey in which Fred asks the judge, "What are the grounds for divorce in this state?" and the judge, peering over the tops of his rimless spectacles, rasps the one word, "Marriage." Or Eric Blore's agonizing vaudeville bit at the police station when he telephones Horton for help only to get all tangled up trying to spell the name of the Susquehanna Street Jail. (One memorable line: after

"Slap that Bass."

Blore has frantically told him that he has been arrested, Horton brusquely snaps, "That's all right. We don't need you.")

Shall We Dance, it should also be noted, was not the first story to offer Fred Astaire the chance to be a ballet dancer. A few years before, Richard Rodgers and Lorenz Hart had submitted an outline to him about a music teacher who composes and performs a work that is presented by a classical ballet company. Fred, however, turned it down because it gave him no opportunity to wear his trademark attire of top hat, white tie and tails. Rewritten for the Broadway stage and with Ray Bolger in the Astaire-intended role, *On Your Toes* began its successful run about a year before *Shall We Dance* was released.

Work on the film, called at various stages *Stepping Toes, Stepping Stones, Watch Your Step,* and *Stepping High,* began early in December, 1936. For the first time in his screen career, Fred

Astaire was reunited with Ira and George Gershwin, who had previously supplied the songs for Astaire's stage musicals, *Lady, Be Good!* and *Funny Face.* When it was decided to settle on *Shall We Dance* (without the question mark) as the movie's title, producer Pandro Berman also commissioned the brothers to come up with an appropriate title song. The additional song forced the elimination of a number called "Wake Up, Brother, and Dance," which had originally been written for the same spot. (The melody of *that* song turned up, though with some variation, years later under the title of "Sophia" in Billy Wilder's film, *Wake Up, Stupid.*)

The most difficult scene, choreographically, was the dance on roller skates following the duet, "Let's Call the Whole Thing Off." Astaire and Rogers spent a total of thirty-two hours in preparation for the routine, and skated an estimated eighty miles during the four days it required to

154

shoot this one sequence. Total number of takes: thirty. Total dancing time on the screen: less than two and a half minutes.

Following the May 14, 1937, opening at the Radio City Music Hall in New York, the press provided a veritable echolalia of praise for Fred and Ginger. In the *Brooklyn Daily Eagle,* Winston Burdette wrote: "Mr. Astaire is in top form for the occasion, registering as brisk and incisive a triumph as ever in the past," while Howard Barnes, in the *New York Herald Tribune,* greeted him with: "The greatest dancer on the screen is at top form in a brisk and pleasant entertainment." According to Rose Pelswick of the *New York Journal,* "The film is, of course, at its best when the nimble Mr. Astaire and the graceful Miss Rogers go into their dances," and in the words of *The New York Times'* Frank S. Nugent: "It has the nimble hoofing of a chap with quicksilver in his feet and of a graceful young woman who has learned to follow him with assurance."

As with all Fred Astaire–Ginger Rogers movies, much was expected of the score, and the brothers Gershwin did not disappoint. It was they, in fact, who provided the idea for the opening scene in *Shall We Dance.* Since the setting is Paris, Pete Peters (Fred Astaire) is first seen strolling down a tree-lined boulevard. Spotting a picture of Linda Keene (Ginger Rogers) on a kiosk poster advertising a stage revue, he falls immediately and completely in love, and breaks out in the song, "Hi-Ho!" This sparks a dance through the streets where every billboard carries a likeness of Linda and every passerby must be made aware of her charms. It was a bright, inventive mood-setter for the entire film. Unfortunately, however, the scene was never shot. The estimated cost of $55,000 to build the sets made the whole thing prohibitive.

The eight remaining pieces were all

Dancing to ''They All Laughed.''

156

vintage Gershwin. On the transatlantic voyage, Pete ducks a ballet rehearsal to catch the Negro crewmen singing and polishing the ship's engine room. After the verse is sung by an uncredited soloist, Pete jumps up and does the song's refrain. Then he bounds all over the seemingly ship-size, gleamingly white room synchronizing his taps to the pounding pistons and chugging engines.

Also while aboard ship, Pete literally dogs Linda's footsteps by following her as she walks her pooch on the kennel deck (to the accompaniment of a piquant little piece called "Walking the Dog"). Later that night, Pete finally gets a chance to talk to Linda as they lean against the ship's rail:

PETE: Isn't it wonderful being here tonight like this, still on the same boat?
LINDA: Oh, I seldom change boats in mid-ocean.
PETE: I mean, look how lucky I am. The first time I find myself on a boat with somebody like you it turns out to be . . . you. (*And he sails right into the verse to "Beginner's Luck".*)

Curiously, it isn't until *Shall We Dance* is almost half over that the two stars are finally joined on a dance floor. The locale is the Sky Room of an unnamed New York hotel (whose exterior looks exactly like the Waldorf-Astoria), where Linda, in response to applause, sings the bouncy catalogue of ridiculed creativity, "They All Laughed." Unknown to either Linda or Pete, the band leader (Ben Alexander) then announces that they will dance together. At first Pete performs some exaggerated ballet leaps around Linda as she stands there not knowing exactly what to do. Her answer comes in the form of a tap step, and he accepts the challenge with his own taps. Presently, the two are tapping and swirling together around the floor, and cap a breathtaking finish by leaping onto a piano.

Though Linda and Pete are obviously drawn to each other, the plot, of

"Let's Call the Whole Thing Off"
—on roller skates.

158

course, must discover ways to keep them out of each other's arms when they are not dancing. Such as the confusion caused by the publicity that the two are married. As a result, Linda and Pete must sneak out of the hotel to avoid seeing the reporters who are swarming all over the lobby. Cleverly wearing dark glasses to avoid detection, they spend the day in Central Park and end at the roller skating rink.

LINDA: How much longer do we have to stay out here?

PETE: Oh, the reporters will probably leave by dark. I guess it would look kinda funny if we denied the marriage now, wouldn't it?

LINDA: I don't know what to do.

PETE: I don't know eye-ther.

LINDA: The word is ee-ther.

PETE: All right. The word is ee-ther. No use squabbling. That will get nye-ther of us anyplace.

LINDA: The word is nee-ther.

PETE (singing): "Things have come to a pretty pass—/ Our romance is growing flat,/ For you like this and the other,/ While I go for this and that. . . ."

Once the two phoneticians end their bickering duet, "Let's Call the Whole Thing Off," they perform—and why not?—a gliding, tapping dance routine on roller skates. During the number, they seem almost about to—but never quite—fall down. That is, until following a round-and-round chase, they crash headlong into a grassy lawn.

After their trip to New Jersey to get married in order to get a divorce, Linda and Pete take a glum ride on the ferryboat back to Manhattan:

LINDA: I didn't know getting married was so depressing. I'm sorry now I asked you.

PETE: Oh, that's all right. I'll get over it.

LINDA: Oh, of course.

PETE (singing): "Our romance won't end on a sorrowful note,/ Though by tomorrow you're gone;/ The song is ended but as the song writer wrote,/ 'The melody lingers on'. . . ."

159

The film's finale, with Fred dancing with Harriet
Hoctor to "They Can't Take That Away from Me"...

As he continues singing "They Can't Take That Away from Me" (note, incidentally, the reference to Irving Berlin in the verse), Pete recalls with affection some of the things he can never forget, such as the way Linda wears her hat, sips her tea, holds her knife, etc. While the mood of this exquisite ballad certainly fits the mood of the scene, the captious may notice that, so far, the two have not really had any sort of a romance that would leave any sort of memories.

For the first time since *Top Hat,* Fred and Ginger had a big production number to end the picture. But in addition to being a spectacular way to bring down the curtain, the sequence also served two purposes: it functioned as the culmination of Pete's ambition to combine ballet with ballroom and tap dancing, and it also provided the means through which Linda returns to Pete.

The finale is performed on a circular stage atop the hotel. Pete is first seen in white satin shirt and black pants performing a graceful *pas de deux* with ballet dancer Harriet Hoctor, surrounded by the corps de ballet. Soon they are replaced by a group of modern dancers all wearing masks made in Linda's image. (This was Pete's idea because after a spat with Linda he had vowed, "If I can't dance with one Linda, I'll dance with dozens.") Pete joins them now clad in white tie and tails. Following a solo by Miss Hoctor, he sings the compellingly urgent invitation, "Shall We Dance," as the girls reappear wearing their Linda masks. There is one addition to the group: the real Linda, who having already seen the masked girls, now realizes that Pete loves only her. Pete dances up to each girl in turn but Linda's "Otchi Tchornya" turns him around. They rush into each other's arms, dance joyously, and bring the movie to a happy, self-satisfied ending:

They all said we'd never get together—
They laughed at us and how!
But ho, ho, ho—
Who's got the last laugh now?

. . . then with Ginger—and dozens of
"Gingers"—to "Shall We Dance?"

On the set with Burns and Allen.

162

A DAMSEL IN DISTRESS

CAST

Jerry Halliday	Fred Astaire
George Burns	George Burns
Gracie Allen	Gracie Allen
Lady Alyce Marshmorton	Joan Fontaine
Keggs	Reginald Gardiner (sung by Mario Berini)
Reggie	Ray Noble
Lady Caroline Marshmorton	Constance Collier
Lord John Marshmorton	Montagu Love
Albert	Harry Watson
Madrigal Singers	Jan Duggan, Mary Dean, Pearl Amatore, Betty Rone

Producer: Pandro S. Berman for RKO Radio Pictures. Director: George Stevens. Lyrics: Ira Gershwin. Music: George Gershwin. Screenplay: P. G. Wodehouse, Ernest Pagano, S. K. Lauren, from novel by P. G. Wodehouse, & play by P. G. Wodehouse & Ian Hay. Dance director: Hermes Pan. Art director: Van Nest Polglase. Music director: Victor Baravalle. Orchestrations: Robert Russell Bennett, Ray Noble, George Bassman. Cameraman: Joseph H. August. Editor: Henry Berman. Release date: November 20, 1937. Running time: 100 minutes.

MUSICAL NUMBERS: "I Can't Be Bothered Now"—Astaire; dance by Astaire/ "The Jolly Tar and the Milkmaid"—Astaire, Duggan, Dean, Amatore, Rone, Madrigal Singers/ "Put Me to the Test"—dance by Astaire, Burns & Allen/ "Stiff Upper Lip"—Allen; dance by Astaire, Burns & Allen, fairgoers/ "Sing of Spring"—Madrigal Singers/ "Things Are Looking Up"—Astaire; stroll by Astaire & Fontaine/ "A Foggy Day"—Astaire/ "Nice Work If You Can Get It"—Duggan, Dean, Amatore, Astaire; reprised as drum solo & dance by Astaire/ "Ah, che a voi perdoni Iddio" (Flotow, *from Marta*)—Gardiner (sung by Berini).

As dowager Constance Collier indicates silence, Fred joins
Madrigal Singers Jan Duggan and Mary Dean to sing "The Jolly
Tar and the Milkmaid."

One thing was certain. Although both Fred Astaire and Ginger Rogers agreed to a temporary separation following *Shall We Dance,* there was no intention of a permanent dissolution. But Ginger had been chafing under the constant references to her as Astaire's talented partner . . . or as Astaire's apt pupil . . . or being able to keep up with Astaire. She had long hoped to establish herself as a dramatic actress, but ever since *Flying Down to Rio,* the public's image of her was primarily as Fred Astaire's twinkle-toed co-star (even though, in between her seven Astaire movies, she had managed to appear in nine non-musical films).

Ginger's ambition, however, might never have impressed the RKO brass had it not been for the fact that box-office receipts of both *Swing Time* and *Shall We Dance* had fallen below the previous Astaire-Rogers attractions. Yes, a trial separation was definitely

in order: Fred would get himself a new leading lady for one film and Ginger would get her chance to appear more frequently unreliant on her dancing talent. Or her partner.

For Fred's first Gingerless movie, producer Pandro Berman chose a P. G. Wodehouse novel dating from 1919, which the author (in collaboration with Ian Hay) had converted into a London play nine years later. It was called *A Damsel in Distress* and was concerned with a composer of West End revues who goes to the aid of the fair Lady Maud at Totleigh Castle. For the movie, also co-authored by Wodehouse, the composer was changed to an American dancer appearing in London (whose last name was alternately pronounced "Halliday" and "Holliday"), Lady Maud became Lady Alyce, and there were changes and additions among the supporting characters. (There were also similarities to the 1932 film musical, *Love Me To-*

"Put Me to the Test"—
dancing with George and Gracie.

night, in which commoner Maurice Chevalier came to the romantic rescue of Princess Jeanette MacDonald in an imposing French castle.)

In his role as the dancer, Fred Astaire returned to the same basic part he had played in *The Gay Divorcée* and *Top Hat* (as in the latter, his first name was again Jerry). Once more, he falls in love at first sight, appears to be unconcerned about his career (except for being angry at his press agent for selling him to the public as a heart-breaker), leaves London to be with his beloved, gets into mishaps and misunderstandings, and ends up skipping gaily off to be married. RKO, however, made sure that there would be none of the regulars on view to remind audiences of any Fred-plus-Ginger movies. The studio, in fact, went to Paramount to borrow the comedy team of George Burns and Gracie Allen to play Fred's press agent and secretary. The pivotal role of the scheming butler at the castle went, not to Eric Blore, but to Reginald Gardiner—who, by coincidence, had appeared in the 1928 stage version as Lady Maud's brother. For the film, the silly-ass brother part was altered to that of a silly-ass suitor—named Reggie—and given to Ray Noble.

But who would be Fred's leading lady? There was some talk of Ruby Keeler until it dawned on the hierarchs that the character had to be British. Then Jessie Matthews, the reigning queen of English movie musicals, was sought, but that, too, didn't work out. Finally, RKO settled on Joan de Beauvoir de Havilland, the younger sister of actress Olivia de Havilland, who had adopted the professional name of Joan Fontaine. There was one problem: Miss Fontain couldn't dance. But even that was turned into an advantage. With true Hollywood logic, the studio rationalized that this would somehow leave her immune to comparisons with Ginger Rogers. Most important, though

165

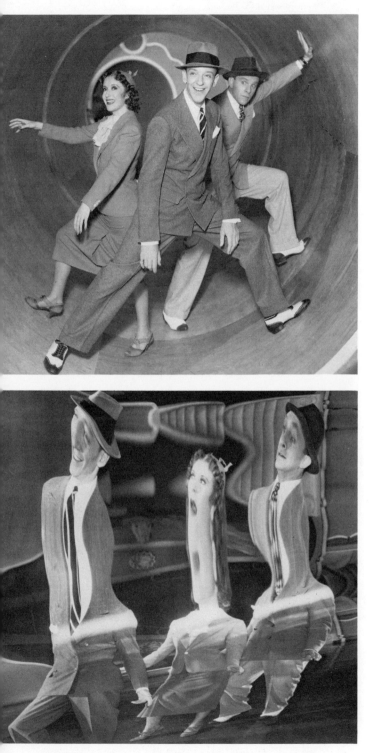

In the fun house of the amusement park.

born in Tokyo, she could easily pass as a titled lady living in an English castle.

For the director, producer Berman again tapped George Stevens (he'd already done *Swing Time*), and for the score, George and Ira Gershwin, writing their second-in-a-row Fred Astaire movie. In all, there were seven songs (eight, counting the instrumental "Put Me to the Test"). "Nice Work If You Can Get It" was musically derived from a nine-bar theme George had written some seven years before, and lyrically derived from a cartoon Ira recalled having seen in *Punch*. It showed two Cockney charwomen discussing a mutual friend who 'ad become an 'ore," and one of them remarks, " 'At's nice work if you can get it." In the film the song was presented almost as a joke by a trio of harpies (joined by Astaire), and later reprised for Fred's explosive drum dance that concluded the picture. The atmospheric "A Foggy Day (in London Town)" was sung not in the city of its title but, rather incongruously, by Fred Astaire in white tie and tails perched on a wooden fence on the castle grounds. The scene remains a pictorial gem: the fog enveloping Fred as he strolls through the grounds puffing a cigarette, with the moonbeams creating shimmering, lacy patterns through the trees.

Also of British inspiration were two folkish pieces, "The Jolly Tar and the Milkmaid," in the manner of an eighteenth-century ballad, and "Sing of Spring," a contrapuntal exercise originally called "Back to Bach." Though Ira's initial research authenticated "Stiff Upper Lip" as a genuine Britishism —and therefore appropriate in the company of "pip-pip," "toodle-oo," and "stout fella"—he later found, to his slight embarrassment, that the phrase was actually American in origin. This was Gracie's one vocal solo, which she sang to Fred and George Burns after sliding down into a funhouse at an English fair. They then proceed to tap out a dance on treadmills, a spinning disk (on which they revive the old Fred and Adele Astaire runaround trademark), and a revolving barrel, ending up cavorting in front of a series of distorted mirrors. (A bit earlier, the trio danced to an unpublished Gershwin song called "Put Me to the Test." Since the lyric went unsung, Ira Gershwin later used it—along with the title—for a number he wrote for the film, *Cover Girl*. Only this time the melody, which was quite similar to the Gershwin piece, was credited to Jerome Kern.)

"I Can't Be Bothered Now" and "Things Are Looking Up," though unconcerned about British identification, were perfect expressions for the scenes in which they were presented. The former was Fred's exuberant, single-minded ode to dancing, performed in a London street aswirl with traffic; the latter revealed his emotions upon hearing Joan Fontaine admit that he was the man she loved. Strolling and skipping through the English countryside (actually a hill near Malibu, California), Fred serenades his lady with references to four-leaf clovers covering the landscape and sunbeams beaming just because of her. And they really do.

As might be expected with Burns and Allen in co-starring roles, *A Damsel in Distress* was generous with their special brand of dimwitted humor. In a London hotel-room scene, press agent George angrily greets secretary Gracie arriving two hours late for work. Gracie, however, has little to fear since it was her father who had backed Jerry Halliday's first show:

GEORGE: If it weren't for your father, you wouldn't be working for me for two weeks. You wouldn't be working for me for two days. Not even for two minutes.

GRACIE: Well, a girl couldn't ask for shorter hours than that.

GEORGE: Did you type that letter I dictated last night?

"Things are looking up" for Fred
now that Joan Fontaine admits she loves him.

168

"A foggy day in London town . . ."

GRACIE: Well, no. I didn't have time to, so I mailed them my notebook. I hope they can read my shorthand.

GEORGE: You mailed your notebook? You know, Gracie, I'm beginning to think there's nothing up here. (*He taps his forehead.*)

GRACIE: Aw, George, you're self-conscious. (*The telephone rings and Gracie answers it.*) It's a Hawaiian.

GEORGE: A Hawaiian?

GRACIE: Well, he must be. He said he's Brown from the *Morning Sun.*

Later, when Jerry Halliday receives a note supposedly from Lady Alyce asking him to see her at Totleigh Castle, George consults the encyclopedia:

GEORGE (*reading*): "Since the 15th Century, Totleigh Castle has been the seat of the Earl . . ."

GRACIE: Oh, George, you'll have to do something about that Brooklyn accent. You mean "oyul."

GEORGE: I mean "earl." "Oil" and "earl" are two different things. Your daddy doesn't go to bed oilly, does he?

GRACIE: He did when he worked for the gas station.

GEORGE: Listen, Gracie. In England there are several titles for the nobility. Lords. Dukes. Earls.

GRACIE: Ho-ho, that's my daddy. If he ever gets his dukes on the earl company's money, Lord help them. I made that up myself.

169

When they get to the Tunnel of Love at the fair, Gracie is surprised to find herself seated next to Reggie (Ray Noble). She begins their awkward attempt at conversation by asking if he had seen the newspapers that morning.

"No, did you see them?"

"No, but I wish this was yesterday. Although I didn't see the papers yesterday morning either. Did you see the papers yesterday morning?"

"No."

"I never see the papers. But they're nice to talk about."

"Yes, they're so true to life."

"Oh, well, aren't we all?"

Despite the pleasures of Fred Astaire's dancing and singing, the Gershwin score, the Burns and Allen humor, and the pictorial beauty of some of the scenes, it was clear that *A Damsel in Distress* did lack one major ingredient. "According to Regina Crewe in the *New York Journal*, "the missing link between a smash Astaire hit and just good film fun is— Ginger Rogers." "An Astaire picture isn't quite itself without Ginger," opined Kate Cameron in the *New York Daily News.* "It's a good solo," voiced Eileen Creelman in the *New York Sun,* "but not as good as a duet with Ginger." Astaire's performance, however, received its customary praise: "Fred Astaire loves and laughs and dances with a blithe, lithe grace and graciousness that adds greatly to the gaiety of the occasion" . . . "Fred Astaire is at his nimble and most engaging best" . . . "The casual, bright lines and situations are right up Fred's alley and he makes the most of them." In *The New York Times*, Frank S. Nugent summed it all up with: "On the whole fresh, glib and agreeably presented. . . . What more can one ask of in an Astaire show? Miss Rogers? Don't be a pig, Willy!"

In truth, what Fred Astaire lacked in *A Damsel in Distress* was not specifically Ginger Rogers. It was simply a partner to dance with. Was he, as some claimed, a dancer in distress? Perhaps not, but this was one omission that would never again be repeated in a Fred Astaire musical.

The drum dance to "Nice Work if You Can Get It."

Ginger and Fred with Irving Berlin.

Celebrating Ginger's 27th birthday. Dance director Hermes Pan is
at far left and director Mark Sandrich is at far right.

CAREFREE

CAST

Tony Flagg	Fred Astaire
Amanda Cooper	Ginger Rogers
Stephen Arden	Ralph Bellamy
Cora Cooper	Luella Gear
Connors	Jack Carson
Judge Joseph Travers	Clarence Kolb
Roland Hunter	Franklin Pangborn
Dr. Powers	Walter Kingsford
Miss Adams (Tony's secretary)	Kay Sutton
Hattie (Amanda's maid)	Hattie McDaniel
Elevator Starter	Paul Guilfoyle
Henry (headwaiter)	Richard Lane
Policeman	Edward Gargan
Doorman	Charles Coleman

Producer: Pandro S. Berman for RKO Radio Pictures. Director: Mark Sandrich. Lyrics & Music: Irving Berlin. Screenplay: Ernest Pagano & Allan Scott, adapted by Dudley Nichols & Hagar Wilde from story by Marian Ainslee & Guy Endore. Dance director: Hermes Pan. Art director: Van Nest Polglase. Costumes: Howard Greer, Edward Stevenson. Music director: Victor Baravalle. Cameraman: Robert de Grasse. Editor: William Hamilton. Release date: August 30, 1938. Running time: 83 minutes.

MUSICAL NUMBERS: "Since They Turned Loch Lomond into Swing"—harmonica playing, golf-club swinging & dance by Astaire/ "The Night Is Filled with Music"—dance orchestra/ "I Used to Be Color Blind"—Astaire; dance by Astaire & Rogers/ "The Yam"—Rogers; dance by Astaire & Rogers/ "Change Partners"—Astaire; dance by Astaire & Rogers.

Of the ten movie musicals Fred Astaire appeared in with Ginger Rogers, *Carefree* holds the dubious distinction of being the one most people have forgotten. It was even considered forgettable in its day. Still, coming right after *A Damsel in Distress,* it was a welcome confirmation that Astaire was at his best when he could not only beat out rhythmic taps but also glide ardently around a dance floor with someone lovely and lissome in his arms.

Between *Shall We Dance,* her last film with Astaire, and *Carefree,* Ginger Rogers had co-starred in *Stage Door* with Katharine Hepburn, *Having Wonderful Time* with Douglas Fairbanks, Jr., and *Vivacious Lady* with James Stewart, three films that clearly established her position as a delectable nonsinging and nondancing screen comedienne. Possibly because of this, *Carefree* turned out to be more Ginger's movie than Fred's, allowing her full opportunity in which to display her comic range. Actually, the picture was something of a departure from the Astaire-Rogers mold in other ways, too. For the first time in his film career, Fred was neither dancer nor musician, but a psychiatrist with a practice apparently limited to the skeet-shooting country-club set. (Early in the film, however, Fred does admit to Ginger: "I wanted to be a dancer. Psychiatry showed me I was wrong.")

In *Carefree,* it was Ginger who played the professional entertainer, a radio singer, though on screen her singing and dancing were restricted to entertaining her fellow guests at the fashionable Medwick Country Club.

Attendant Jack Carson and Dr. Astaire help sober up Ralph Bellamy.

"Back here is a jungle full of the most noble and horrible things." "I don't doubt that."

The golf dance.

"I Used to Be Color Blind."

It was this country-club locale, in fact, that endowed the picture with more of the trappings of believable affluence rather than the implausible elegance associated with the team's previous endeavors. As for the story, it offered Fred as something of a psychiatric John Alden with whom Ginger—in a truly radical departure—fell in love *before* he fell in love with her.

With its emphasis on plot and comedy, *Carefree* devoted relatively scant attention to song—a rather perplexing situation particularly since it was Irving Berlin who provided the score. Only three songs—"I Used to Be Color Blind," "Change Partners" and "The Yam"—were actually sung, with two others used merely as background music. The willowy "The Night Is Filled with Music" was wasted as a dance-band tune and "Since They Turned Loch Lomond into Swing" was not even identified as the melodic accompaniment to Astaire's brilliantly executed golf dance.

It was this golf dance that required the greatest amount of preparation as it coordinated harmonica playing, tap dancing, and golf-club swinging. Although the final footage showed sixteen actual swings, Astaire had to slam out almost a thousand tee and iron shots during his ten-day, eight-hour-a-day rehearsal period. It then took two and a half days to film the sequence, which lasted less than three minutes on the screen.

Astaire and Rogers danced to all of the songs that they sang in *Carefree*. The first, "I Used to Be Color Blind" (the lyric had been inspired by producer Pandro Berman's original plan to shoot the scene in Technicolor), was performed during Ginger's dream after she had consumed a specially prepared dream-inducing dinner se-

Demonstrating "The Yam" step.

178

lected by Dr. Astaire. Amid a sylvan setting, Fred—in morning coat, striped trousers, and spats—leads Ginger though a languorous, slow-motion dance over a bed of lily pads, which culminates in the first solid, honest-to-goodness Fred-and-Ginger clinch. Thus it is through her dream that the confused girl realizes it's her psychiatrist, not her fiancé, whom she loves.

Ginger performs "The Yam" at a country-club formal, first as a vocal solo, then, in company with Fred, as a spectacular if hard-to-follow demonstration. It's a strutting, strolling, swinging affair, featuring a double time step executed with heels together and feet apart, and it soon sweeps other partygoers onto the dance floor. As if unable to confine themselves to just one room, Fred, Ginger and their dancing entourage, propelled by the sheer momentum of the number, exuberantly burst out into the clubhouse, then out onto the patio, and, finally, back again into the dining room. (The song's recurrent theme, "Any Yam today?" was later used by Berlin for the trumpet-call opening of his wartime exhortation, "Any Bonds Today?")

The third song, "Change Partners," was particularly well integrated in the story—all the more surprising since Berlin had written it a few years before in anticipation of Fred Astaire's expected change of dancing partner. In *Carefree,* even though Fred knows

"Won't you change partners? . . ."

Fred's alter ego convinces him he is in love with Ginger.

180

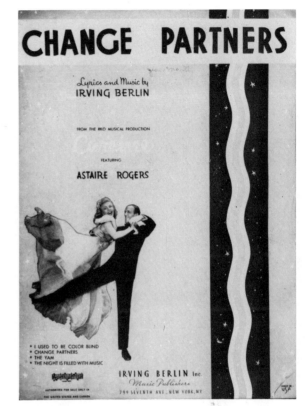

Ginger, in a hypnotic trance, thinks she [is] him and loves Ralph Bellamy.

The "Change Partners" dance,
with a hypnotized Ginger.

Ginger is roused from her trance by Ralph Bellamy,
Luella Gear and Clarence Kolb.

183

To make Ginger come to her senses,
Fred must knock her unconscious.

''Repeat after me, 'Tony loves Amanda.' ''

184

Ginger, shiner and all, walks down the aisle with her true love.

he shouldn't, he can't help revealing his emotions in song while Ginger is taking a spin around the dance floor with fiancé Ralph Bellamy. Following the lyric's instructions, he arranges to have her partner called to the telephone in order to be alone with her on the patio. Once she has been put into a trance by a few of Fred's hypnotic hand-passes, Ginger, pliant of body but blank of stare, joins the dancing Mesmer in another graceful variant of Astaire's wooing-and-winning routine.

The newspaper reviewers, happy to welcome back the screen's most illustrious dancing team, greeted the couple with such phrases as "Fred has never been more charming, Ginger never more winsome" . . . "the dances are as entrancing as anything they have ever done before" . . . "finds Mr. Astaire and Miss Rogers at their gayest and most proficient." The story, however, struck some as both too frail and too cumbersome, though most enjoyed the scenes that involved Ginger—while under hypnosis—going berserk through a city street, insulting her radio sponsor, and even trying to shoot Fred. Eventually, all ends to almost everyone's satisfaction when, aided by a punch in the eye, Ginger comes to her senses and—shiner and all—walks down the wedding aisle with Dr. Astaire.

In the cast of *Carefree* was Luella Gear (she had had the Alice Brady part in the original stage production of *The Gay Divorcee*), making her screen debut as Ginger's aunt. She also had the best line. When pompous Clarence Kolb asks her to dance, she answers politely, "Joe, you know I don't dance at your age." The usual balance of a friend for Ginger and a friend for Fred was maintained in the movie, though Fred's pal, Ralph Bellamy, ended up as his rival. Hattie McDaniel was in the film in the miniscule, unbilled role of Ginger's maid; the following year she won the Academy Award for her performance in *Gone with the Wind*.

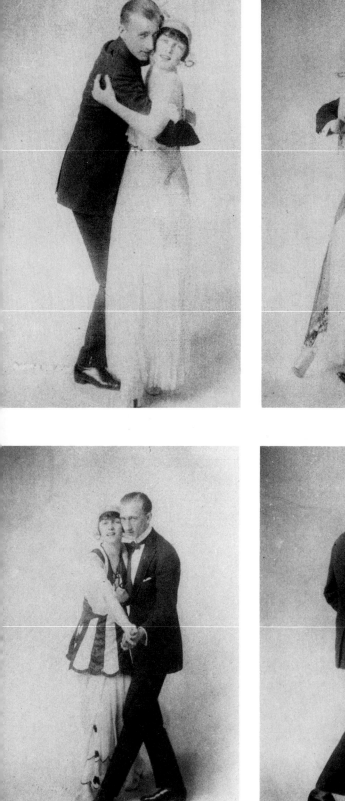

Vernon and Irene Castle.

186

THE STORY OF VERNON AND IRENE CASTLE

CAST

Vernon Castle (né Vernon Blyth)	Fred Astaire
Irene Foote Castle	Ginger Rogers
Maggie Sutton	Edna May Oliver
Walter	Walter Brennan
Lew Fields	Lew Fields
Aubel (French producer)	Etienne Girardot
Annie Foote	Janet Beecher
Emile Aubel (French co-producer)	Rolfe Sedan
Parisian Artist	Leonid Kinskey
Dr. Hubert Foote	Robert Strange
Louis Barraya	Clarence Derwent
Claire Ford	Frances Mercer
Grand Duke	Victor Varconi
Ft. Worth Hotel Manager	Donald McBride
Peters (student pilot)	Douglas Walton
Charlie	Sonny Lamont
Actor in "Patria"	Roy D'Arcy
Train Conductor	Dick Elliott
Irene's Friend	Marjorie Bell (Marge Champion)

Producer: George Haight for RKO Radio Pictures. Director: H. C. Potter. Screenplay: Richard Sherman, adapted by Oscar Hammerstein, 2nd, & Dorothy Yost from book, *My Husband,* by Irene Castle. Dance director: Hermes Pan. Art director: Van Nest Polglase. Costumes: Irene Castle, Walter Plunkett. Music director: Victor Baravalle. Orchestrations: Roy Webb, Robert Russell Bennett. Cameraman: Robert de Grasse. Editor: William Hamilton. Release date: March 31, 1939. Running time: 90 minutes.

MUSICAL NUMBERS: "Oh, You Beautiful Doll" (Brown-Ayer)—male chorus/ "Glow-Worm" (Robinson-Lincke)—female chorus/ "By the Beautiful Sea" (Atteridge-Carroll)—male chorus/ "Row, Row, Row" (Jerome-Monaco)—male chorus/ "Yama Yama Man" (Davis-Hoschna)—Rogers/ "Come, Josephine in My Flying Machine" (Bryan-Fisher)—chorus/ "By the Light of the Silvery Moon" (Madden-Edwards)—dance by Astaire/ "Cuddle Up a Little Closer, Lovey Mine" (Harbach-Hoschna)—chorus/ "Only When You're In My Arms" (Kalmar-Ruby, Conrad)—Astaire/ "Waiting for the Robert E. Lee" (Gilbert-Muir)—dance by Astaire & Rogers/ "The Darktown Strutters' Ball" (Brooks)—uncredited French singer/ "Too Much Mustard" (Macklin)—dance by Astaire & Rogers/ "Rose Room" (Williams-Hickman)—dance by Astaire & Rogers/ "Très Jolie" (Waldteufel)—dance by Astaire & Rogers/ "When They Were Dancing Around" (McCarthy-Monaco)—dance by Astaire & Rogers/ "Little Brown Jug" (Winner)—dance by Astaire & Rogers/ "Dengozo" (Nazareth)—dance by Astaire & Rogers/ medley including "You're Here and I'm Here" (Smith-Kern), "Chicago" (Fisher), "Hello, Frisco, Hello" (Buck-Hirsch), "Way Down Yonder in New Orleans" (Creamer-Layton), "Take Me Back to New York Town" (Sterling-VonTilzer)—dance by Astaire & Rogers/ "It's a Long Way to Tipperary" (Judge-Williams)—male chorus/ "Hello, Hello, Who's Your Lady Friend?" (David-Lee)—Astaire, soldiers; dance by Astaire, soldiers/ "Keep the Home Fires Burning" (Ford-Novello)—orchestra/ "Smiles" (Callahan-Roberts)—orchestra/ medley including "Destiny Waltz" (Baynes), "Night of Gladness" (Ancliffe), "Missouri Waltz" (Royce-Logan)—dance by Astaire & Rogers/ "Over There" (Cohan)—background.

They danced professionally for only a scant three years. But so influential were Vernon and Irene Castle that, all by themselves, they were responsible for the phenomenal growth of ballroom dancing in the United States. They toured the continent, appeared on Broadway, conducted dance studios, performed at their own night spots, and introduced and popularized such ballroom innovations as the Maxixe, the Turkey Trot, the Castle Walk, and the tango. Moreover, in addition to leading the way on the dance floor, Irene was also a trend-setter in fashion and in hair style.

It was certainly logical then that the story of their lives be depicted on the screen by the one team that most closely matched them in both fame and influence—Fred Astaire and Ginger Rogers. By taking the roles, however, this most contemporary of dance teams found themselves in a film that was far removed from their customary image of lighthearted modernity. Nevertheless, everyone connected with the enterprise deliberately set out to reproduce the spirit and the atmosphere of the early years of the century; though their technique was their own, Astaire and Rogers strikingly caught the style and flair of another dancing couple of another age. (It should be noted here that this was not the first screen biography of the dancing Castles. In 1914, they had appeared in one themselves, though the film, *The Whirl of Life,* showed little concern for the facts.)

In attempting to tell the story as faithfully as dramatic license would allow, RKO bought not only the rights to Mrs. Castle's memoirs, but also the services of the lady herself to act as "technical advisor." But there was trouble right from the start. Although never specific about her reasons, the strong-willed Irene Castle had always taken exception to Miss Rogers playing her part on the screen. Once she

Vernon Castle (Fred Astaire) rescues a puppy and meets its owner and his future wife, Irene Foote (Ginger Rogers).

Irene auditions her specialty number, "Yama Yama Man," for Vernon.

188

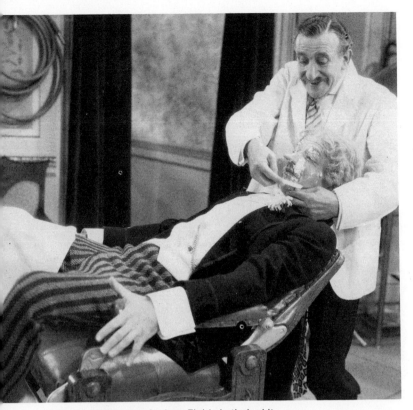

Vernon plays stooge for Lew Fields in their skit,
"The Barber and the Customer."

Vernon is obviously smitten with Irene, but faithful
retainer Walter (Walter Brennan) is dubious about his intentions.

was assigned the role, Ginger was confronted with Mrs. Castle's firm objections to her wardrobe and to her refusal to darken her blonde tresses to the shade favored by the lady she was depicting. In an interview following the movie's opening, the former first lady of the dance was quoted as saying, "I'm sure the studio would rather I had been dead. They even waited two years for me to kick off, I suspect, after I had sold them the story. But when they found that I was indestructible, they went ahead and made it."

Actually, RKO was more than fair to Mrs. Castle. The studio gave her a salary of forty-thousand dollars and even offered her the role of her own mother (this struck her as being rather unnatural, so they got Janet Beecher). In all, Mrs. Castle remained in Hollywood seven months, though she appeared on the set no more than ten times.

In a further effort to convey biographical accuracy, Lew Fields, the famed "Dutch" comic with whom Vernon Castle appeared in five Broadway musicals, was signed to play himself in the film. Fields, formerly of the team of Weber and Fields, was also the father of *Roberta* and *Swing Time* lyricist, Dorothy Fields.

Shooting of the movie took almost three months. All of the songs sung and danced to in the film were of the period, except for one new ballad, "Only When You're in My Arms" (whose lyricist, Bert Kalmar, was later portrayed by Fred Astaire in the movie, *Three Little Words*). Unfortunately, the song sounded so unmistakably late thirties that it distracted slightly from the authenticity of flavor that the movie otherwise so scrupulously maintained. Occasionally, though unperceptibly, even the "authentic" songs were a few years off. "By the Beautiful Sea," written in 1914, was sung in a scene occurring in 1911, and

190

The audition for Lew Fields, dancing
to "Waiting for the Robert E. Lee."

though "The Darktown Strutters' Ball" dated from 1917, it was sung—in French!—in a Paris night club in 1912. But these lapses counted for little. The film was universally accepted as an endearing, nostalgic document that faithfully recaptured the lives and times of the nation's foremost exponents of ballroom dancing.

There were two unforgettable scenes, both in Paris. After Vernon has discovered that the producers of a new musical had not hired the Castles to dance but only wanted Vernon as a slapstick comic, he returns dejectedly to his tiny garret and explains the situation to Irene. They have no prospects and no money and even owe the producers for their advance. They speak in hushed, choked monotones until, unable to express his emotions verbally, Vernon whispers, "Dance with me." As they dance, all their love and need for each other come through as, clinging tenderly, they glide silently around the room. The other scene comes soon afterward: their first appearance at the Café de Paris. To the infectious ragtime beat of "Too Much Mustard," Vernon, in white tie and tails, and Irene, in a lacy Dutch cap and ankle-length gown, flit lambently, ecstatically over the dance floor in the first public display of the Castle Walk. It is a moment of such communicative exuberance and style that the movie audience cannot help but share in the excitement of discovery.

For Fred Astaire, playing Vernon Castle was an opportunity to impersonate a dancer who, as Astaire wrote in his autobiography, had been "a tremendous influence on my career. Not that Adele and I copied the Castles completely but we did appropriate some of their ballroom steps for our vaudeville act." There had even been a closer professional association. In 1922, after Vernon's death, Fred and Adele were called in to stage Irene's solo dance act.

One of the movie's big problems was the title. Rejecting names such as *Castles in the Air* or *The Dancing Castles,* producer George Haight and director H. C. (Henry Codman) Potter settled for the slightly cumbersome handle, *The Story of Vernon and Irene Castle.* Their reasoning was sound, if unimaginative: the name was intended to serve notice that the treatment would be as faithful to the subjects as possible, avoiding excessive distortions or romanticizing. To lovers of Astaire-Rogers movies, however, it was quite a jolt not to see the pair at the close of the film tripping out of a hotel room or skipping down the wedding aisle. Vernon Castle died in a plane crash in Texas on February 15, 1918, and that's exactly the way the movie ended.

Because of its somewhat dichotomous quality, the picture received a mixed press. As Frank S. Nugent put it in *The New York Times:* "Rogers and Astaire have been so closely identified with light comedy in the past that finding them otherwise employed is practically as disconcerting as it would be if Walt Disney were to throw Mickey Mouse to the lions and let Minnie be devoured by a non-regurgitative giant." Similar if less strongly worded views were expressed by Howard Barnes in the *New York Herald Tribune* ("the first part of the film is the best . . . the latter episodes

In Paris, an advance against salary from a father-and-son producing team (Etienne Girardot and Rolfe Sedan).

In a garret with no job and no money. But Irene does have a new lacy Dutch cap.

are out of key") and John Mosher in *The New Yorker* ("Until tragedy has the impertinence to intrude upon this gay musical comedy stage, everything is graceful, just as it should be"). But the movie did have its champions. Such as *Time:* "To say that Fred Astaire and Ginger Rogers are well fitted to fill the Castles' dancing slippers is an understatement. Astaire and Rogers symbolize their era just as completely as the Castles symbolized theirs." And *Newsweek:* "Rogers and Astaire brilliantly recreate the famous couple's inspired contributions to the dance world. The result is not only a refreshing musical but a haunting screen biography."

These things in the film were true: In the summer of 1910, while appearing in a Broadway musical with Lew Fields, Vernon Castle met Irene Foote on a beach in New Rochelle. They fell in love and were married. Their first success came after they had gone to Paris—with Irene's faithful servant Walter—to appear in a French musical. Their fame, however, was won in a night club, and they went on to become the toast of Paris. They achieved even greater renown when they returned to the United States and introduced new steps and new fashions during a whirlwind tour of the country. When war broke out, Vernon enlisted in the Royal Air Corps and saw service in France. He later became a

194

Vernon in a Royal Air Corps uniform
for a benefit show. Edna May Oliver is
their agent, Maggie Sutton.

Introducing such specialties as
"The Castle Walk," "The Castle Polka,"
"The Castle Tango" and "The Castle Waltz."

195

flight instructor, first in Canada and later in Fort Worth, Texas. While there, in an effort to avoid hitting a student-piloted plane, he deliberately crashed his own plane and was instantly killed.

Still, many of the events in the lives of Vernon and Irene Castle were altered and rearranged. Irene first met Vernon through a mutual friend, not as a result of his saving a drowning puppy. Vernon was then appearing with Lew Fields in *The Summer Widowers,* not *The Hen Pecks,* which didn't open until eight months later. Vernon arranged to have Irene audition for Fields before, not after, their marriage; she even had a part in *The Summer Widowers* during the last few weeks of its run. Vernon and Irene Castle were married May 28, 1911; when *The Hen Pecks* reopened in August, following its summer layoff, Irene was in the cast. The film, however, showed Irene and her friends at a performance of *The Hen Pecks* soon after her first meeting with Vernon, and then berating him for wasting his dancing talent by being a stooge for Fields. Actually, it was Vernon's decision alone to change from a comic to a dancer.

Vernon and Irene went to London, not Paris, on their honeymoon. The Paris engagement came about in 1912 when they were both hired—not just

The last dance at the Café de Paris.

196

Vernon—to appear in a much-postponed variety show appropriately titled *Enfin . . . une Revue,* not a French version of *The Hen Pecks.* Contrary to the film, which had Vernon walk out on the show before the opening, the couple not only appeared in the revue but also added a dance routine. They did, however, leave it after two weeks. The film correctly had them accompanied by the tenaciously loyal man-of-all-work named Walter. But the real Walter Ash didn't look a thing like Walter Brennan—who played the part—because he was a black man.

The Castles' debut at the Café de Paris did not result from the efforts of an American agent named Maggie Sutton (their agent's name was Elisabeth Marbury, and the team did not meet her until early the following year in New York). They got the job through a French agent who had seen their act in the revue. The Castle Walk did not originate in Paris so they could not have danced it on their first night at the café. The step was first tried out in New York on March 16, 1913, at a birthday party for actress Elsie Janis.

There was nothing in the career of the Castles to prompt the motion picture to show the team quickly tiring of performing and wishing nothing more than a home in the country and time to travel. Their whirlwind tour— thirty-two cities in twenty-eight days —occurred during the month of May, 1914, and was followed by a summer-long series of professional engagements in Europe. They first became aware of the beginning of the World

Dreaming of Vernon after his death in a plane crash.

198

War while on a train from Paris to Deauville, not a train heading for New York after their American tour.

As the movie correctly showed, Vernon was anxious to enlist immediately in the Royal Air Corps. Nevertheless, the team returned to New York from France to appear in their biggest stage success, Irving Berlin's *Watch Your Step* (unmentioned in the film). Far from cutting down on their activities once they opened on Broadway, the Castles continued to maintain an unbelievably busy schedule, running their dance studio by day and performing at their night spots after the show. It was during the Boston engagement of *Watch Your Step* that Vernon enlisted in the Air Corps, not following a British War Relief Show (which never took place).

Irene Castle did manage to meet her husband while he was stationed overseas, but it was at the Savoy Hotel in London, not the Café de Paris in Paris. By the time Vernon returned to America, Irene had already finished acting in the movie *Patria,* and went to Canada—not Fort Worth—to visit him. Mrs. Castle, was married four times after Vernon's death. She died on January 25, 1969, at the age of seventy-five.

With *The Story of Vernon and Irene Castle,* Fred's Ginger years came to an end (though a decade later the team was reunited for *The Barkleys of Broadway*). In the years to come, Fred Astaire would be matched with some of the screen's most exciting dancing ladies. But never again would he be so closely identified with a partner as he was during those top-hatted days when he and Ginger Rogers were tapping and twirling their way through the most stylish, lighthearted musicals ever to dance out of Hollywood.

Rehearsing with Eleanor Powell.

BROADWAY MELODY OF 1940

CAST

Johnny Brett	Fred Astaire
Clare Bennett (née Brigit Callahan)	Eleanor Powell
King Shaw	George Murphy
Bob Casey	Frank Morgan
Bert Matthews	Ian Hunter
Amy Blake	Florence Rice
Emmy Lou Lee	Lynne Carver
Pearl de Longe	Ann Morriss
Juggler	Trixie Firschke
Masked Singer	Douglas McPhail
Audition Singer	Charlotte Arren
Silhouette Artist	Herman Bing
George (theatre manager)	Jack Mulhall
Receptionist	Barbara Jo Allen (Vera Vague)
Soda Jerk	Irving Bacon
Dance Hall Manager	Joseph Crehan
Dance Hall Worker	James Flavin
Dan (unemployed actor)	Joe Yule
Grady (press agent)	Hal K. Dawson
Miss Martin (bride)	Gladys Blake
Mr. Jones (groom)	George Chandler
Emmy Lou's Friend	William Tannen
Singing Quartet	The Music Maids

Producer: Jack Cummings for Metro-Goldwyn-Mayer. Director: Norman Taurog. Lyrics & Music: Cole Porter. Screenplay: Leon Gordon & George Oppenheimer, from story by Jack McGowan & Dore Schary. Dance director: Bobby Connolly. Art director: Cedric Gibbons. Costumes: Adrian, Valles. Music director: Alfred Newman. Orchestrations: Edward Powell, Leo Arnaud, Charles Henderson. Music supervisor: Roger Edens. Cameraman: Oliver T. Marsh, Joseph Ruttenberg. Editor: Blanche Sewell. Release date: February 14, 1940. Running time: 102 minutes.

MUSICAL NUMBERS: "Please Don't Monkey with Broadway"—Astaire & Murphy; dance by Astaire & Murphy/ "I Am the Captain"—Powell, sailors; dance by Powell, sailors/ "Between You and Me"—Murphy; dance by Powell & Murphy/ "I've Got My Eyes on You"—Astaire; piano playing & dance by Astaire/ "Jukebox Dance"—Astaire & Powell/ "I Concentrate on You"—McPhail; dance by Astaire & Powell/ "Begin the Beguine"—uncredited singers Music Maids; dance by Astaire & Powell, chorus. Unused: "I Happen to Be in Love," "I'm So in Love with You."

The movie that inaugurated the second phase of Fred Astaire's Hollywood career brought the dancer right back to Metro-Goldwyn-Mayer, the studio where he had made his very first picture six years before. The big news about *Broadway Melody of 1940* was that the screen's greatest male tap dancer was being teamed with the screen's greatest female tap dancer, Eleanor Powell. After a moderately successful Broadway career, Miss Powell, like Fred Astaire, found even wider opportunity in films and had soon become Metro's top heel-and-toe attraction. In addition to pairing Fred with a new girl, the movie also gave him a male dancing partner for the first time in his career. For this role the studio cast the readily available George Murphy, by then a Hollywood veteran of some fifteen pictures. Murphy's Broadway appearances, incidentally, had included *Roberta,* in which he introduced "Let's Begin," the song Astaire later sang in the film version.

Broadway Melody of 1940 was the fourth and final edition in M-G-M's series of musical main stem sagas. The undated *Broadway Melody* No. 1, which was released early in 1929, had the distinction of being the very first musical written directly for the screen, as well as the Academy Award winner as the best film of the year. In 1936, doubtlessly influenced by Warner Brothers' successful *Gold Diggers* series, Metro launched a rival series, using the *Broadway Melody* tag affixed to the year of the picture's creation. Eleanor Powell tapped away in both the 1936 and the 1938 exhibits, with George Murphy as her partner in the second. Now, two years later, the studio not only put Powell and Murphy back in another *Broadway Melody,* it also added the premier song-and-dance man of them all.

Fred introduces bridegroom George Chandler to bride Gladys Blake just before their marriage at the Dawnland Ballroom.

"... But please, please, I beg on my knees, don't monkey with old Broadway."

202

Eleanor Powell tapping out the "I Am the Captain" number.

203

The movie was filmed during the fall of 1939, shortly after the outbreak of World War II. The unsettled conditions at the time forced producer Jack Cummings to scrap plans to have the picture shot in Technicolor, though in all other respects it was one of the company's most lavish enterprises. The setting for the "Begin the Beguine" finale alone cost $120,000 to construct, and the studio's press department pridefully pointed out that it was more expensive than the "Pretty Girl Is Like a Melody" number in *The Great Zieg-feld*. The scene used a sixty-foot square, multipaneled mirror mounted on a revolving track, which swung it around to change backgrounds for the dance. For the "Between You and Me" sequence, a steeply banked ramp was constructed that was intended to be used for a grand sliding finish. When Eleanor Powell and George Murphy voiced concern because of the apparent danger, the film's technical expert, Arnold Gillespie, sought to allay their fears by sliding down the ramp himself. He ended up with a broken leg.

The story dreamed up for this ultimate *Broadway Melody* was written by George Oppenheimer (who, since 1955, has been the drama critic of the Long Island daily, *Newsday*) and Leon Gordon (author of the play *White Cargo*). Except for *Dancing Lady,* it was the first Fred Astaire movie concerned with the trials of mounting a mammoth Broadway revue and as such represented a distinct departure from the airy confections Fred had appeared in with Ginger Rogers. Like *Dancing Lady,* it began with one of the film's co-stars down on his luck, and ended with his replacing another dancer in the top spot. But this time it was Fred Astaire who got the big break, not Joan Crawford. The movie, however, dealt less with the creation of the show than with the problems arising when the wrong dancer—George Murphy—is selected as Eleanor's partner instead of Fred.

It must be admitted that the mistaken identity ploy used to bring about this mixup was worthy of a *Top Hat*. In the film, Frank Morgan played Bob

Fred is stopped at the producer's office by receptionist Barbara Jo Allen (later known as Vera Vague).

Secretary Florence Rice and her boss, Broadway producer Frank Morgan.

Morgan's partner, Ian Hunter,
agrees to audition George Murphy
as Eleanor's leading man.

Casey, a bumbling Broadway producer with a penchant for lending the same ermine cape to each girl he takes out (this running gag was inspired by the actual practice of an eccentric theatrical agent named Louis "Doc" Shurr). One night on the prowl for talent, Casey catches the Johnny Brett–King Shaw (or Fred Astaire–George Murphy) dance act at a dime-a-dance ballroom. He becomes wildly enthusiastic about Johnny (though it is hard to fathom how anyone, on the basis of the act, could have preferred one dancer so strongly over the other). But instead of going backstage to see him, Casey asks an employee to call "that young man who was just dancing here. You know, the one on the end there." When the message is conveyed that "a gent wants to see you guys," Johnny suspects that it's a bill collector demanding money for King Shaw's unpaid dress suit and goes out to see Casey. But the producer neither praises him nor introduces himself. He merely asks, "Hey, young man, where have you been hiding?", and demands

to know Johnny's name. Now thoroughly convinced that Casey is a bill collector, Johnny says his name is King Shaw, thus making sure the expected summons will be served on the wrong man. It takes the entire picture to straighten things out.

In his prior starring films, Fred Astaire was fortunate to introduce songs by such giants of popular music as Youmans, Berlin, Fields and Kern, the Gershwin brothers, and—by way of the retained "Night and Day" from *Gay Divorce*—Cole Porter. Now Porter was writing his first original score for a Fred Astaire movie. Surprisingly, of the six songs in the score, Astaire was given only one vocal solo, "I've Got My Eyes on You," and one duet, "Please Don't Monkey with Broadway."

Primarily the movie turned out to be what Astaire has called "an allout dance festival"—even though audiences had to wait more than an hour for Astaire and Powell to take their first steps together. Before that, there were duets for Astaire and Murphy, Powell and Murphy, and solos by Astaire and Powell. The film's ending found all three happily dancing together.

One of the tenets of each *Broadway Melody* movie seems to have been that it feature a new musical paean to the glories of Broadway. "Broadway Melody" came from *The Broadway Melody,* "Broadway Rhythm" from the the 1936 edition, and "Your Broadway and My Broadway" from the one in 1938—and all three were written by Arthur Freed and Nacio Herb Brown. For the current extravaganza, Cole Porter spurned sentiment in favor of a breezy, tongue-in-cheek tribute, "Please Don't Monkey with Broadway," which was used for the Astaire-Murphy vaudeville turn at the Dawnland Ballroom early in the picture. Following their vocal rendition, the top-hatted partners went into a clowning dance routine involving a kick in the pants and a duel with canes.

To introduce Miss Powell, the movie first shows her, grinning broadly, in a crow's-nest setting high above the stage during a performance of a nautical

205

"I've Got My Eyes on You."

206

Stepping out to a boogie-woogie beat.

Broadway musical. After sliding down the ship's mast, Captain Eleanor establishes her authority with the number "I Am the Captain" (a "Rocked in the Cradle of the Deep" takeoff of undisclosed authorship) and a striking rata-tap-tap display. The specialty ends with the lady being tossed about by her jolly tars. The previously mentioned "Between You and Me" was Murphy's oh-so-elegant song and dance audition with Powell. While most of the numbers were performed as part of theatrical productions, Fred's "I've Got My Eyes on You" was done on a deserted stage following a rehearsal. Spotting Eleanor's likeness on the cover of the sheet music propped against a piano, Fred plays the melody and sings the words to the photograph, and then dances with the sheet music as if he were actually holding the girl in his arms. Unknown to Fred, Eleanor is taking this all in, and bursts into applause at the end ("That was swell, Johnny, swell!"). Now she knows two things: he is in love with her and he is a far better dancer than George Murphy.

From the theatre, Fred and Eleanor go to a deserted outdoor restaurant for their first dance together. In a setting reminiscent of the "Isn't This a Lovely Day?" number from *Top Hat,* they perform a seemingly spontaneous routine that evolves naturally out of the kind of shop talk two dancers might be expected to engage in. As they discuss a new step, Eleanor rises to demonstrate it and Fred follows. A waiter puts a nickel in a jukebox, which blares out a boogie-woogie beat. Emboldened and inspired by the challenge

209

and joy of dancing with each other, the tapping couple improvise a succession of increasingly intricate patterns. At the end, in a state of mutual exhilaration, they stroll off the dance floor giggling happily as Fred lets out an appreciative, "Wellll . . ."

The two other dances Astaire performed with Powell were seen as part of their rather gargantuan Broadway show. The smoky "I Concentrate on You" is a balletic Harlequin number that Murphy was to have done, but he's passed out cold after getting drunk. So it's Fred who dons his eye-mask and diamond-patch tights (a perfect fit) and bounds onstage to prance about with Columbine Eleanor. After watching him for almost a minute, Eleanor suddenly realizes that she has been joined by an unscheduled partner. "Johnny," she whispers anxiously, "what's the matter with King?" "Don't worry, I'll tell you later," comes the reassuring reply.

Astaire and Powell get together again for the show's—and the film's —finale, "Begin the Beguine." Following a sultry vocal, the two appear dancing on a mirrored floor sur-

"When they begin the beguine . . ."

210

rounded by mirrored stars and palm trees. Their elegant tapping to the throbbing melody (originally written for the 1935 Broadway musical, *Jubilee*) is abruptly terminated by a change of pace and scenery, as a vocal quartet —patterned after the Andrews Sisters —emerge to mangle the song through some contemporary scat singing. Led by a wailing clarinet (*à la* Artie Shaw), Fred and Eleanor reappear in sportier garb to resume tapping—for a spell without orchestral accompaniment— and build the number to its jubilant finish.

As Astaire wrote in his autobiography, "On my list I count it thoroughly worth while if only for the opportunity of working with Eleanor, who certainly rates as one of the all-time great dancing girls. . . . She really knocks out a tap step in a class by herself." While audiences were happy to see Astaire in partnership with so accomplished a dancer, it was apparent that the two were not quite right for each other, either stylistically or physically. At any rate, Fred Astaire was never again to dance professionally with Eleanor Powell. Or George Murphy.

211

Kicking up their heels on the set: Charles Butterworth,
Fred Astaire, Paulette Goddard, Burgess Meredith.

Trumpeter Jack Cathcart (light dinner jacket) gives a lesson in
horn-blowing to Burgess Meredith and Fred Astaire,
while dance director Hermes Pan listens.

212

SECOND CHORUS

CAST

Danny O'Neill	Fred Astaire
	(trumpet-playing by Bobby Hackett)
Ellen Miller	Paulette Goddard
Artie Shaw	Artie Shaw
J. Lester Chisholm	Charles Butterworth
Hank Taylor	Burgess Meredith
	(trumpet-playing by Billy Butterfield)
Stu (Ellen's friend)	Frank Melton
Mr. Dunn	Jimmy Conlin
Hotel Clerk	Dan Brodie

Producer: Boris Morros for Paramount Pictures. Director: H. C. Potter. Lyrics: Johnny Mercer. Music: Artie Shaw, Bernard Hanighen, Hal Borne. Screenplay: Elaine Ryan & Ian McClellan Hunter, from story by Fred Cavett. Dance director: Hermes Pan. Art director: Boris Leven. Music director: Ed Paul. Orchestrations: Ed Paul, Artie Shaw, Gregory Stone, Johnny Guarnieri. Cameraman: Theodore Sparkuhl. Editor: Jack Daniels. Release date: December 3, 1940. Running time: 84 minutes.

MUSICAL NUMBERS: "(I Ain't Hep to That Step but I'll) Dig It" (Mercer-Borne)—Astaire; dance by Astaire & Goddard/ "Sweet Sue" (Will Harris-Victor Young)—Hackett, Butterfield, orchestra/ "Love of My Life" (Mercer-Shaw)—Astaire, Shaw Orchestra/ "I'm Yours" (E. Y. Harburg-Johnny Green)—Hackett, Butterfield, Shaw Orchestra/ "Concerto for Clarinet" ("Swing Concerto") (Shaw)—Shaw Orchestra/ "Poor Mr. Chisholm" ("Hoe Down the Bayou") (Mercer-Hanighen)—Astaire; reprised as dance by Astaire, with Shaw Orchestra. Unused: "Me and the Ghost Upstairs" (Mercer-Hanighen).

Artie Shaw and his Orchestra.

FRED'S BEST YET
'CAUSE HE'S GOT PAULETTE

Making due allowance for Hollywood hyperbole, the advertising slogan devised for *Second Chorus* carried studio puffery well beyond its customary egregious limits. Fred's Best Yet was, by common consent, Fred's Worst Ever.

Astaire even admitted as much in a 1968 interview. This is not, however, to deny the valid reasons that prompted him to appear in the film. Primarily, Fred saw it as a chance to break away from his glitter and glamour image by playing the part of an undergraduate trumpeter-band leader who keeps flunking his final exams in order to remain in college. But the main appeal of *Second Chorus* was that, for the first time, the dancer would get the

chance to appear with what he called "a real swingin' outfit." Said outfit was that of Artie Shaw, who at the time was second only to Benny Goodman as young America's favorite clarinetist (*Broadway Melody of 1940* had even included a brief imitation of Shaw's style during the "Begin the Beguine" number). The idea of matching taps to licks proved irresistible, particularly since Fred planned to cap the movie by conducting the orchestra and dancing at the same time.

Added to these reasons was the opportunity to appear opposite the beauteous Paulette Goddard, who, though hardly eligible for the Ginger Rogers or Eleanor Powell dancing class, was certainly many grades higher than Joan Fontaine. For comedy, *Second Chorus* was fortunate to have in

Collection agent Jimmy Conlin and secretary Paulette Goddard are horrified when college chums Burgess Meredith and Fred Astaire offer Conlin a two-dollar bribe.

Paulette, now the manager of Fred's dance band, proves highly efficient in lining up engagements.

Charles Butterworth an estimable addition to the company of bubble-headed funnymen—Edward Everett Horton, Victor Moore, Frank Morgan, and Robert Benchley—who producers apparently felt were necessary to offset Fred's debonair personality. Also in the film—as Astaire's professional and romantic rival—was Burgess Meredith, in something of a departure from his customary dramatic roles. (Off screen, Meredith eventually did win out romantically, albeit briefly. Four years later he married Miss Goddard.)

Originally, the story bought by producer Boris Morros for this Paramount release was to have been about two jazz trumpeters and their attempts to land jobs in the Artie Shaw Orchestra. There was no provision for dancing nor was there to be much comedy. Once Astaire was signed, however, the original script was scrapped and a new wave of writers was called in. Not, unfortunately, until after filming had already begun. Starting almost from scratch, the scenario was virtually banged out one page ahead of the camera. And it showed.

Second Chorus had only three songs, all with lyrics by Johnny Mercer. The first, "Dig It," evolved almost conversationally with Fred and Paulette improvising rhyming couplets full of jive jargon that led into the refrain. The theme of the song—"I ain't hep to that step but I'll dig it"—may well have described Miss Goddard's attitude toward her assignment. No trained dancer, she applied herself vigorously to an intensive cram course and performed the number with great flair and high spirits. The lone ballad, "The Love of My Life" (Artie Shaw wrote the music), was ardently sung by Fred to Paulette just before his audition with Shaw's band. He later reprised it —with Russian doubletalk—at a Russian café and followed it up with an

"I Ain't Hep to that Step but I'll Dig It."

216

agile *prisiadka*. The rather pretentious finale at Artie Shaw's jazz concert found Astaire in white tie and tails conducting and tapping as the orchestra played "Hoe Down the Bayou" or "Poor Mr. Chisholm," or whatever it was called. Of possible interest to jazz buffs is that Bobby Hackett played trumpet for Astaire and Billy Butterfield did the same for Meredith.

Although *Second Chorus* managed to garner some favorable press notices ("In all of 1941 there won't be four musicals as enjoyable as this"—Winston, *New York Post*), many reviewers found themselves wistfully recalling the dear departed Ginger Rogers days at RKO. "Paulette Goddard is no Ginger Rogers," was the irrefutable observation of William Boehnel in the *New York World-Telegram*, "nor has the film any of the charm, slickness or inventiveness which marked the early Astaire-Rogers attractions." Though less inclined to comparatives, Bosley Crowther was of similar mind in *The New York Times*: "Fred Astaire is still badly in need of a new dancing partner. He is even more desperately in need of a producer, writers and a director who will again stir up something smart, sleek and joyous for him to do."

This was a low point all right. *Broadway Melody of 1940,* despite its many pleasures, had never really made it to the hit class. And now there was the infinitely weaker *Second Chorus*. What's more, when Astaire finished the assignment, he was, for the first time, without any plans for a new project.

Then what happened? Then what happened was that Fred Astaire got a smashing new girl to dance with and three movie blockbusters in a row.

Fred and Burgess bid Paulette bye-bye at the railroad station.

Fred ruins Burgess's audition with the Artie Shaw Orchestra by knocking him off his chair. That's trumpeter Billy Butterfield (who doubled for Meredith) at the far right.

Fred dances and conducts the augmented Artie Shaw Orchestra.

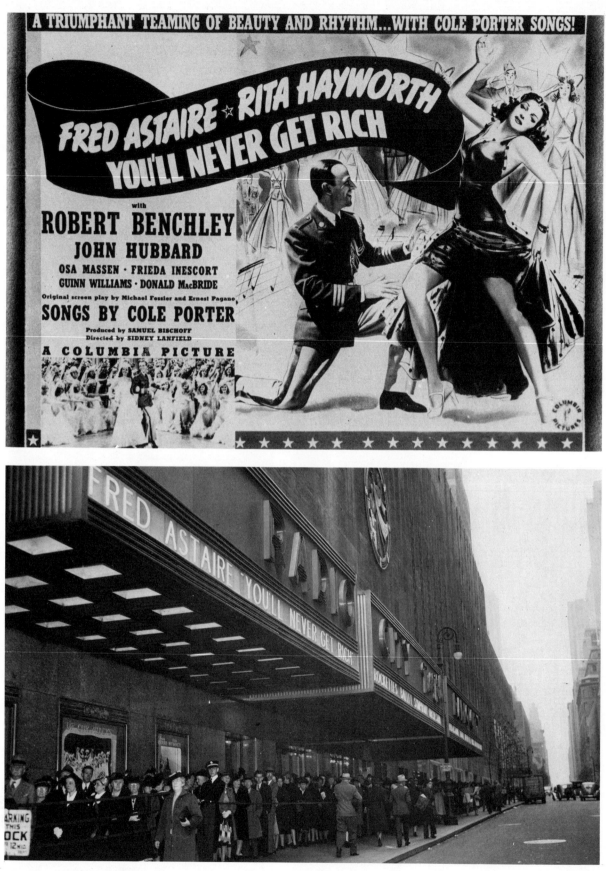

The line outside the Radio City Music Hall.

YOU'LL NEVER GET RICH

CAST

Robert Curtis	Fred Astaire
Sheila Winthrop	Rita Hayworth
Martin Cortland	Robert Benchley
Tom Barton	John Hubbard
Sonya	Osa Massen
Julia Cortland	Frieda Inescort
Kewpie Blain	Guinn Williams
Top Sergeant	Donald McBride
Swivel Tongue	Cliff Nazarro
Mrs. Barton	Ann Shoemaker
Aunt Louise	Marjorie Gateson
Col. Shiller	Boyd Davis
Army Doctor	Robert McWade
Singer	Martha Tilton
Guardhouse Inmates	Delta Rhythm Boys, also Chico Hamilton (drums), Buddy Colette (clarinet), A. Grant (guitar), Joe Comfort (jug), Red Mack (trumpet)

Producer: Samuel Bischoff for Columbia Pictures. Director: Sidney Lanfield. Lyrics & Music: Cole Porter. Screenplay: Michael Fessier & Ernest Pagano. Dance director: Robert Alton. Art director: Lionel Banks. Costumes: Irene. Music director: Morris Stoloff. Orchestrations: Leo Shuken. Cameraman: Philip Tannura. Editor: Otto Meyer. Release date: September 25, 1941. Running time: 88 minutes.

MUSICAL NUMBERS: "The Boogie Barcarolle"—dance by Astaire & Hayworth, chorus/ "Dream Dancing"—orchestra/ "Shootin' the Works for Uncle Sam"—Astaire, chorus; dance by Astaire, chorus/ "Since I Kissed My Baby Goodbye"—Delta Rhythm Boys; dance by Astaire/ "A-stairable Rag"—dance by Astaire, with jazz group including Hamilton, Colette, Grant, Comfort, Mack/ "So Near and Yet So Far"—Astaire; dance by Astaire & Hayworth/ "Wedding Cake Walk"—Tilton; dance by Astaire & Hayworth, chorus.

When wife Frieda Inescort finds out that Robert Benchley
has given Rita Hayworth a diamond bracelet,
Benchley tries to make it look like a gift from Fred.

In September 1941, exactly two years after the outbreak of World War II, Hitler's Nazi troops controlled all of non-Communist Europe and were deep into Russian territory. In Asia, Japan was extending its dominance of the mainland following its seizure of French Indochina early in the year. In the United States, where a state of unlimited national emergency had existed since May, the first peacetime draft in the nation's history was calling up thousands of men to train for a conflict many felt was inevitable. It was against this background that, on this wartime anniversary month, Columbia Pictures answered the universal desire for escapist films by releasing its most lavish musical, *You'll Never Get Rich*.

Of even more significance, however, was the effect that the movie had on the careers of its two stars, Fred Astaire and Rita Hayworth.

Prior to the new film, Miss Hayworth's abilities as a dancer had been kept pretty much of a secret. Everyone could see that she was beautiful,

but few movies had given her the opportunity to act, much less demonstrate that she had been a thoroughly trained professional dancer ever since she was thirteen. Miss Hayworth, née Margarita Carmen Cansino, was in fact, the daughter of Spanish dancer Eduardo Cansino, a vaudeville headliner who had once toured on the same Orpheum Circuit with the young Fred and Adele Astaire. When she was signed to a Columbia contract in 1937, Margarita Cansino became Rita Hayworth and her flaming beauty quickly attracted notice. However, she was largely limited to nondancing roles in loan-out movies made by other studios (most notably as the girl who vamped James Cagney in Warner's *Strawberry Blonde* and the girl who vamped Tyrone Power in 20th Century-Fox's *Blood and Sand*). Watching Rita win fame elsewhere, Columbia's head man, Harry Cohn, now decided that she was ready for the star buildup at Columbia. Her next assignment: *You'll Never Get Rich*.

By selecting Fred Astaire as Rita's

"Shootin' the Works for Uncle Sam."

The "A-stairable Rag" dance, backed by Buddy Colette (clarinet), A. Grant (guitar), Chico Hamilton (drums), Red Mack (trumpet), and Joe Comfort (jug).

co-star, Cohn felt reassured that his newest stellar attraction would have the most skilled and prestigious partner on the dance floor. He was also careful to take out additional insurance: Cole Porter to write the score and Robert Benchley as chief funnyman. For the story, a backstage plot was grafted onto a tale dealing with the up-to-the-minute theme of rookie life in an army camp. Fred's role was that of a successful Broadway dance director who gets drafted. After serving his basic training time—mostly in the guardhouse—he ends up with the luscious Rita for an onstage wedding in front of an army tank.

Since most of the action in *You'll Never Get Rich* (originally titled *He's My Uncle*) was to take place in an army base, the studio took pains to make sure that the locale would look as authentic as possible. Director Sidney Lanfield and his technical crew spent five days at Camp Haan, near Riverdale, amassing all the data needed to reconstruct an entire camp. It then took only six days to put together the film's Camp Weston, located on an eighteen-acre plot about three miles outside Hollywood. Everything was built in strict accordance with military specifications—everything, that is, except for the guardhouse, which had to be considerably enlarged to accommodate Astaire's tap routines.

In Rita Hayworth, Fred Astaire found a partner who, in his own words, "danced with trained perfection and individuality." But she did present a few problems. One was height. Standing 5′9½″, Fred was apprehensive that Rita, with heels, would look too tall. So Rita, who was 5′6″, didn't wear high heels. Then, too, Astaire was beginning to be a bit concerned about age. He was forty-two when he made the picture and Rita was twenty-two, and he was afraid of the public's resistance to them as a dancing and romancing team.

No one, it turned out, could care less. Wrote Henry T. Murdock in the *Philadelphia Inquirer*: "The spectacle

"So Near and Yet So Far."

of Fred Astaire—who didn't graduate yesterday from high school—ripping off intricate, athletic and artistic routines is an inspiration for all others who didn't graduate from high school yesterday. So, one might add, is Miss Hayworth." In the *New York Daily News*, Wanda Hale welcomed the team with: "Astaire is back in his rightful place as the ace dancing comedian of the screen. Rita Hayworth was made to order for him." From Robert W. Dana of the *New York Herald Tribune*: "Filmdom's master of grace and taps, who has been in somewhat of a decline since the cycle of films with Ginger Rogers, finds a gifted partner in Rita Hayworth." In Dallas, the *Morning News'* John Rosenfield was completely bowled over: "Miss Hayworth is a blitz, a bombshell and a wow. All this beauty in motion is teamed with Fred Astaire, no beauty, but surely one of the most exhilarating hoofers in creation . . . a romantic and dancing partnership of compelling appeal." The ultimate accolade, however, came from *Time* magazine. It put Rita's picture on the front cover and stated unequivacably: "It was news throughout the United States that the best tap dancer in the world, Fred Astaire, had a new dancing partner . . . there could be no doubt that she was the best partner he had ever had."

While Cole Porter's songs for *You'll Never Get Rich* were not considered up to his level for *Broadway Melody of 1940*, they might have enjoyed some life of their own had it not been for the hassle between ASCAP and the broadcasters which kept most current songs off the air. The movie had seven numbers in all, though only four were sung. Two were performed in a New York setting: in an early Broadway rehearsal scene, Fred joins Rita in the lively "Boogie Barcarolle," and in the mammoth cavern of Grand Central Station he bids his chorus cuties a cheery farewell to the tune of "Shootin' the Works for Uncle Sam."

Once at Camp Weston, Fred is forever being bawled out for making "patty-cake" with his feet during close-order drill, and it isn't long before he is clapped in the guardhouse for accidentally punching his sergeant. But it's really a lucky break because the Delta Rhythm Boys are also there serving time. In fact, their crooning of the bluesy "Since I Kissed My Baby Goodbye" so inspires Fred that he breaks out into what *Time* called "one of his oldtime paroxysms of unabashed American buck and wing." Fred, however, is no sooner out of the guardhouse than he's in again for impersonating an officer. This time it's a visit from Rita that sparks an equally exultant routine, backed by a newly incarcerated jazz group. (Only in the movies, of course, could an army post in 1941 have a non-segregated guardhouse.)

Despite the merry musical goings-on in the guardhouse, Fred is not allowed to spend all of his time there, and is summoned to stage and appear in a servicemen's show—with, of course, Rita. In a scene from the show, he dons formal attire to woo her in song and dance to the compelling, beguine-flavored "So Near and Yet So Far" (which Porter had based on the main theme from "Kate the Great," a song cut from his 1934 Broadway musical, *Anything Goes*). The finale of the entertainment, a slightly macabre bit with an army tank perched menacingly atop a huge wedding cake, finds the stage aswarm with some eighty dancing boys and girls for the "Wedding Cake Walk" (sung by Martha Tilton).

Apart from its musical and dancing pleasures, *You'll Never Get Rich* gave Robert Benchley one of the best parts he ever had in a feature-length film. Benchley, as Martin Cortland, a would-be philandering Broadway producer, is first seen in his limousine stopping in front of Cartier on Fifth Avenue because, as his chauffeur reminds him, this is his fifteenth wedding anniversary. In the store he selects an expensive diamond bracelet and is about to leave when the salesman asks if there might be anything else. "No, thank you," he replies absent-mindedly. Then he remembers: "Oh, yes, yes. I want to get something for my wife, too."

And so he does: a seven-dollar Chinese back-scratcher. The bracelet, however, is intended as a gift for Sheila Winthrop (Rita Hayworth), a dancer in the chorus (though she, pure thing, is unaware of the gentleman's intentions). While visiting Martin in his office, the producer's haughty wife, Julia (Frieda Inescort), accidently discovers the bracelet in his coat pocket. Martin fumbles his way through an explanation:

JULIA: Now you've lost your imagination. You're getting commonplace

The "Wedding Cake Walk"—with a tank on top of the cake.

and I'm getting bored with you.

MARTIN: Bored? With me? Is it my fault you reached into the wrong pocket? (*She eyes him suspiciously.*) You don't believe me then?

JULIA: Oh, of course, I do, darling. That's because I know you so well. I'm just wondering how your story will sound to twelve *strange* men. (*And she sweeps out of the room.*)

MARTIN (*mumbling to himself*): Twelve strange men? Twelve strange men? She's batty. What's twelve strange men got to do with this? Football

team? Eleven men. Baseball team, nine. Symphony orchestra, a hundred men. Twelve men . . . (*The light dawns.*) A jury!!

Shaken by the divorce threat (because all of his property is in his wife's name), Martin appeals to Robert Curtis (Fred Astaire), his director and friend, to help him out of the jam by romancing Sheila and letting it be known that the bracelet was *his* present, not Martin's:

MARTIN: Turn on the old charm. Fascinate her. Throw stardust in her eyes. Do anything so long as you make my wife believe I was telling the truth when I was lying to her.

ROBERT: Is that all?

MARTIN: Well, if you get a chance, you might put in a good word for me with Sheila.

Robert does help out the hapless producer—but then finds himself threatened by Sheila's fiancé. Rushing into Cortland's office, Robert tells Martin of his fears:

ROBERT: Look, Martin, you've got to get me out of this mess.

MARTIN: It serves you right for getting mixed up with a designing woman.

ROBERT: It serves *me* right? *You* caused it all!

MARTIN: Don't try to implicate me in your sordid affairs. I'm a married man.

ROBERT: That fellow's gonna shoot me!

MARTIN: Well, if he shoots you, I'll fire Sheila.

Fred Astaire's comment on *You'll Never Get Rich*: "I enjoyed making it because of Rita and the fact that it was one of the first films with a World War II service background. . . . It was quite a satisfactory show in its way."

Astaire had other reasons to be satisfied at the time. He was already committed to make a second musical with Rita Hayworth. And in between these two plush assignments, he was going to appear in a picture with Bing Crosby for Paramount. It was something based on an idea by Irving Berlin. . . .

229

230

HOLIDAY INN

CAST

Jim Hardy	Bing Crosby
Ted Hanover	Fred Astaire
Linda Mason	Marjorie Reynolds (sung by Martha Mears)
Lila Dixon	Virginia Dale
Danny Reed	Walter Abel
Mamie	Louise Beavers
Francois (headwaiter)	Marek Windheim
Gus (driver)	Irving Bacon
Assistant Headwaiter	Jacques Vanaire
Cigarette Girl	Judith Gibson
Vanderbilt	Shelby Bacon
Daphne	Joan Arnold
Parker	John Gallaudet
Dunbar (film director)	James Bell
Flower Shop Owner	Jacques Belasco
Band Leader	Harry Barris
Pop (studio doorman)	Robert Homans
Band at Holiday Inn	Bob Crosby's Bob Cats

Producer: Mark Sandrich for Paramount Pictures. Director: Mark Sandrich. Lyrics & Music: Irving Berlin. Screenplay: Claude Binyon, adapted by Elmer Rice from an idea by Irving Berlin. Dance director: Danny Dare. Assistant: Babe Pierce. Art directors: Hans Dreier, Roland Anderson. Costumes: Edith Head. Music director: Robert Emmett Dolan. Cameraman: David Abel. Editor: Ellsworth Hoagland. Release date: June 15, 1942. Running time: 100 minutes.

MUSICAL NUMBERS: "I'll Capture Your Heart Singing"—Crosby, Astaire, Dale/ "Lazy"—Crosby/ "You're Easy to Dance With"—Astaire, male chorus; dance by Astaire & Dale; reprised as dance by Astaire & Reynolds/ "White Christmas"—Crosby, Reynolds/ "Happy Holiday"—Crosby, Reynolds, chorus/ "Holiday Inn"—Crosby, Reynolds/ "Let's Start the New Year Right"—Crosby/ "Abraham"—Crosby, Beavers, Reynolds, chorus/ "Be Careful, It's My Heart"—Crosby; dance by Astaire & Reynolds/ "I Can't Tell a Lie"—Astaire; dance by Astaire & Reynolds, with Bob Cats/ "Easter Parade"—Crosby/ "Let's Say It with Firecrackers"—chorus; dance by Astaire/ "Song of Freedom"—Crosby, chorus/ "Plenty to Be Thankful For"—Crosby. Background: "Oh, How I Hate to Get Up in the Morning." Unused: "It's a Great Country."

During the Broadway season of 1933-34, the sassiest, classiest revue in New York was *As Thousands Cheer,* an ingeniously devised musical in which every Moss Hart sketch and every Irving Berlin song was based either on headline news or sections of a newspaper. For the first-act finale, however, the show turned away from topicality to offer—as the Rotogravure Section—an old-fashioned, canorous Easter Parade on Fifth Avenue. A few years later, Messrs. Hart and Berlin attempted another musical revue with a theme. This time, expanding on the "Easter Parade" sequence, they planned an entire entertainment inspired by American holidays. It would contain some satirical fun, a dash of lighthearted patriotism, and a full calendar of red-letter Berlin songs, each one cued to a specific observance.

But the revue never materialized. Sometime in 1941, Berlin accidentally met Mark Sandrich, who had directed five of the nine Astaire-Rogers films at RKO and who was now both producer as well as director at Paramount. When the songwriter proposed his holidays musical idea as a movie for Bing Crosby, Sandrich was highly receptive. First, however, there had to be a story line, and the two came up with a rough outline concerning an easygoing chap who quits his song-and-dance partnership to work only on holidays. As the plot developed, it seemed like a natural for Fred Astaire to play Crosby's ex-partner, but when his name was proposed the studio heads balked. There was, after all, a war going on, and Paramount, like all other film companies, was extremely budget conscious. Crosby plus Astaire would simply make the project too expensive.

Berlin and Sandrich, however, refused to yield. So strongly, in fact, did they feel that Sandrich even threatened to abandon the production if they couldn't get Fred Astaire. That did it. *Holiday Inn* became the first of two

Bing and Fred woo Virginia Dale with "I'll Capture Your Heart Singing."

232

musicals to co-star the screen's number one male singer with the screen's number one male dancer.

For leading ladies, Sandrich, now under increasingly heavy pressure to cut down on expenses, chose two relatively unknown actresses. The romantic lead was given to Marjorie Reynolds, whose talents had been wasted on a string of low-budget westerns and horror films, and the sort-of other woman lead went to Virginia Dale, until recently a member of a night club dance act known as the Paxton Sisters.

Since the film was being made at Paramount where Crosby was then the reigning king of musicals, the singer's role was more prominent and sympathetic than Astaire's. For the first time, in fact, Fred was cast as something of a light heavy, and, of course, loses the girl. Bing played one of his familiar screen roles: the casual fellow whose idea of true contentment is to turn his back on worldly attainments and spend his time doing just as he pleases. He

breaks up his successful nightclub act with Fred and Virginia so that he might hie himself off to a farm, and among other things, loaf on holidays. ("What happens in show business," he asks, "when a holiday comes around? You give an extra performance. Not for me, brother.") Yet, after a year of farming—and a nervous breakdown—he completely reverses himself by turning the farm into a nightclub open *only* on holidays.

That both Astaire and Crosby managed to remain likable chaps throughout the film was more of a credit to their own personal charm than to the characters they portrayed. Fred thought nothing of trying any scheme —including moving right into the farm with Bing—to snare Marjorie Reynolds away from him and make her his dancing partner. (This resulted from the hard-to-swallow bit of having Fred vow, after only one dance with Marjorie while intoxicated, that he would never again dance with any other girl.) For his part, Bing is not

"You're Easy to Dance With." Fred and Virginia Dale.

234

"I'm dreaming of a white Christmas . . ."

235

above bribing a cabdriver to prevent Marjorie from showing up at Holiday Inn for a movie audition.

What made *Holiday Inn* the best-attended film hostelry of all were, of course, the songs and the way Crosby and Astaire put them over. There were nine for eight holidays (the Fourth of July got two), plus four unaffiliated numbers. Crosby sang ten of them, two were sung by Astaire, and one was a duet. In all, Astaire had six dances, including one in which he had fire-crackers for partners.

The story of *Holiday Inn* begins Christmas Eve and covers a period ending New Year's Eve two years later. The first song, "I'll Capture Your Heart Singing," is performed in a nightclub by the team of Crosby, Astaire, and Dale. In this challenge number, the boys woo the lady according to their specialties: Bing trills sweetly, Fred taps politely, and each even impersonates the other.

Once Bing breaks up the act by retiring to a farm, Fred and Virginia continue as a double. Bing visits them the following Christmas eve during their engagement at the swank Club Pierre. As part of their act, Fred, in white tie and tails, and Virginia, in a spangly short evening dress, truck on down to offer ample proof of Fred's jaunty claim, "You're Easy to Dance With."

Bing has definitely decided to open his farm as a holidays-only night club, and Marjorie Reynolds auditions for him the following day. First, she is serenaded by Bing singing "White Christmas," with chime accompani-

"Be Careful It's My Heart." Marjorie Reynolds becomes Fred's newest partner.

236

237

"I Can't Tell a Lie."

ment provided by Bing's tapping his pipe stem on the Christmas tree baubles. Marjorie (with the voice of her dubbing vocalist, Martha Mears) gets to sing it, too, and she also gets the job as the only other featured entertainer at Holiday Inn. With the Inn all spruced up for New Year's Eve, Bing and Marjorie welcome the guests with "Happy Holiday" and an invitation to "Come to Holiday Inn." An unexpected visitor that night is Fred, who, having been ditched by partner Virginia, gets roaring drunk and swings Marjorie around for some inebriated jitterbugging to "You're Easy to Dance With."

Lincoln's Birthday party at Holiday Inn features the song, "Abraham," sung by Bing as an old black preacher, his housekeeper Louise Beavers, and Marjorie in a Topsy outfit. Only two days later, it's time to open up again for Valentine's Day. The song here is the tender, "Be Careful, It's My Heart," which Bing sings to Marjorie at a rehearsal. It's during this number that Fred comes in, takes one look at Marjorie, and knows immediately that she is the girl he danced with New Year's Eve. Eight days later, Fred joins Marjorie in the Holiday Inn floor show to perform an elegant minuet, "I Can't Tell a Lie," in honor of George Washington's birthday. Jealous because he fears his former partner will cut him out with Marjorie, Bing gives Fred a hard time by making the accompanying Bob Crosby Bob Cats keep altering tempos and rhythms.

"Easter Parade," borrowed from *As Thousands Cheer,* is sung by Bing to Marjorie not on the Avenue, Fifth Avenue, but in a horse-drawn buggy on their way to a country church on Easter Sunday. (Actually, the melody of the song had been around since 1917 when Irving Berlin called it "Smile and Show Your Dimple.")

239

"Let's Say It with Firecrackers."

240

By the time the Fourth of July rolls around, Fred has become a regular Holiday Inn attraction. For this occasion, there are two songs: Bing's "Song of Freedom" ("For all people who cry out to be free"), backed by a montage of military might and a picture of General MacArthur, and Fred's "Say It with Firecrackers." The latter was a literally explosive dance performed by Astaire in white shirt and slacks, with contrasting star-filled ascot, scarf belt, and socks. Crosby once wrote that Astaire did this one number thirty-eight times before the camera until he was completely satisfied. In the routine, according to Astaire, "I had the stage wired to set off what looked like strings of firecrackers with visible flashes as I stepped on certain spots. It was a great satisfaction, that dance, being able to explode things expressing emphasis on beats here and there."

Before the year ends, Holiday Inn goes commercial when Bing allows a movie company to make a film about it. Fred and Marjorie are in the picture, but not Bing! And it's made in Hollywood, not at the real Holiday Inn. Bing's job is only to write the songs, including "Plenty to Be Thankful For" for Thanksgiving, while sulking on his farm. Eventually, he flies west and brings Marjorie—plus a reconciled Fred and Virginia—back to Holiday Inn. And the grand "Let's Start the New Year Right" finale.

Upon its release in June, 1942, *Holiday Inn* was greeted like a star-spangled present. It was "the best musical drama [*sic*] of the year" (*The New York Post*); "full of the most tuneful songs any movie score has had in years" (*New York World-Telegram*); "a clear occasion for hat-tossing" (*PM*); and "a reason for celebration not printed in red on the calendar" (*The New York Times*). As for the new team of groaner and hoofer, it was reported that "both Crosby and Astaire play their respective roles with nonchalance and good-natured

A lonely Thanksgiving with Louise Beavers.

humor, and honors divided" *(Newsweek)*, and also that "Crosby's easy, banter is just the right foil for Astaire's precision acrobatics, his wry offbeat humor" *(Time)*.

Marjorie Reynolds was also given a full measure of praise—plus the almost inevitable comparison to Ginger Rogers: "Miss Reynolds is the most lissome of the Astaire golliwogs since Ginger Rogers" *(PM)*; "Paramount doesn't pretend to have found another Ginger Rogers for Fred Astaire but in giving Miss Reynolds a chance the studio has tapped potential star material" *(Newsweek)*; "Miss Reynolds is as attractive a leading lady to come along for Fred Astaire since the departure of Ginger Rogers" *(Morning Telegraph)*; "In Marjorie Reynolds, a very fetching blonde young lady, Mr. Astaire has a new partner who can hold her own at all speeds" *(The New York Times)*. But Fred and Marjorie

would never again get the chance to dance together before the cameras.

In addition to serving as inspiration for the name of the largest chain of motels in the world (latest count: 1,483), *Holiday Inn* has also been kept very much before the public eye as a television perennial at Christmastime. But surely the most noteworthy phenomenon to emerge from this production has been the song, "White Christmas," which not only won an Academy Award, but may well be the most successful popular song of all time. As of January 1, 1973, the sale of sheet music alone amounted to 5,346,926 copies, and the sale of records—based on some four hundred versions—hit the staggering total of 89,779,673. Of these, it's still Bing Crosby's version on Decca—with over twenty-five million in sales—that easily outdistances the field to become the best selling best seller of all time.

Reunion New Year's Eve.

Composer Jerome Kern with Fred and Rita.

YOU WERE NEVER LOVELIER

CAST

Robert Davis	Fred Astaire
Maria Acuña	Rita Hayworth (sung by Nan Wynn)
Edouardo Acuña	Adolphe Menjou
Xavier Cugat	Xavier Cugat
Cecy Acuña	Leslie Brooks
Lita Acuña	Adele Mara
Maria Castro	Isabel Elsom
Fernando	Gus Schilling
Delfina Acuña	Barbara Brown
Juan Castro	Douglas Leavitt
Julia Acuña	Catherine Craig
Grandmother Acuña	Kathleen Howard
Louise (maid)	Mary Field
Tony	Larry Parks
Roddy	Stanley Brown
Singer	Lina Romay

Producer: Louis F. Edelman for Columbia Pictures. Director: William A. Seiter. Lyrics: Johnny Mercer. Music: Jerome Kern. Screenplay: Michael Fessier, Ernest Pagano & Delmar Daves, from story by Carlos Oliveri & Sixto Pondal Rios. Dance director: Val Raset. Art director: Lionel Banks. Costumes: Irene. Music director: Leigh Harline. Orchestrations: Leigh Harline, Conrad Salinger, Lyle "Spud" Murphy. Cameraman: Ted Tetzlaff. Editor: William Lyon. Release date: October 5, 1942. Running time: 98 minutes.

MUSICAL NUMBERS: "Chiu, Chiu" (Niconar Molinare) —Romay, chorus, Cugat Orchestra/ "Dearly Beloved"—Astaire, Cugat Orchestra; reprised by Hayworth (sung by Wynn), dance by Hayworth/ "Audition Dance"—dance by Astaire, Cugat Orchestra/ "I'm Old Fashioned"—Hayworth (sung by Wynn); dance by Astaire & Hayworth/ "Shorty George"—Astaire, Cugat Orchestra; dance by Astaire & Hayworth/ "Wedding in the Spring"— Romay, Cugat Orchestra/ "You Were Never Lovelier"—Astaire; dance by Astaire & Hayworth/ "These Orchids"—Delivery Boys. Unused: "On the Beam."

About a year after filming *You'll Never Get Rich*, Fred Astaire returned to the Columbia lot for *You Were Never Lovelier*, his second movie with Rita Hayworth. The new picture was also written by the same authors as the first, and the character Fred played was again named Robert (never, be it noted, Bob or Bobby).

But that's about as far as similarities went. The second "You-Never" movie had a totally different atmosphere, with a more romantic theme and score, and made little attempt to be up-to-date in situations or comedy. Yet the new picture did try to do its bit for Latin American relations—very much on everyone's mind at the time—just as the previous Astaire-Hayworth vehicle had sought to extoll the fun of service life. In fact, the story was based on an Argentinian movie—though, initially, the locale was to be switched from Buenos Aires to Rio de Janeiro, with the picture first called *Carnival in Rio*. When word got out, however, the Brazilian Minister of Press and Propaganda, fearful that Columbia would overrun the annual Rio fete with hoards of galloping gauchos, strongly protested the new setting. The studio quickly capitulated and the story was once again moved back to Buenos Aires. Actually, the innocuous new title and the gossamer fable that went with it were so lacking in anything identifiably Argentinian that the locale could have been almost anywhere.

Directing the film was William A. Seiter (he had also directed *Roberta*), and creating the score was the newly matched team of Johnny Mercer and Jerome Kern, both of whom—with different partners—had supplied songs for previous Fred Astaire musicals. By the time the movie was released, the ASCAP radio ban had ended, thus allowing the new score—unlike Cole Porter's for *You'll Never Get Rich*—to win deserved popularity.

Neither Fred nor Xavier Cugat has much luck getting past Adolphe Menjou's secretary Gus Schilling.

Menjou gives eldest daughter, Catherine Craig, in marriage. Bridesmaids are sisters Leslie Brooks, Adele Mara and Rita Hayworth.

246

Fred finally gets his audition for hotel owner Menjou.

In the movie, Fred played the part of Robert Davis, a New York night-club dancer, who goes to Buenos Aires to loaf and play the horses. After losing his money, however, he vainly seeks employment at the plush hotel owned by Edouardo Acuña (Adolphe Menjou). Acuña, who has just married off the eldest of his four daughters, aims to uphold the family tradition by making sure the other three marry according to age. Since Maria (Rita Hayworth), the next in line, has a personality more likely to freeze than to please, Acuña dreams up a plan to make her fall in love. He writes her anonymous mash notes accompanied by orchids, and Maria is not only swept off her feet but mistakenly thinks it's Robert Davis who is doing the sweeping. When the ruse is revealed, Robert wins the lady on his own by appearing under her window as Lochinvar, Maria's teen-age inamorato.

Fred's role was not too different from his customary screen portrayals, though the picture did have the negative distinction of keeping audiences waiting some thirty-five minutes before Astaire was permitted to dance. There were, however, teasing indications along the way. When Acuña's swishy secretary (Gus Schilling) asks what he wants to see Acuña about, Robert answers by doing a tap step. As he waits in the reception room, he idly taps while sitting down. After meeting an old friend, Xavier Cugat, whose orchestra is playing at the hotel, Robert impatiently drums his fingers while taking in a rehearsal.

Finally, the big moment arrives. Unable to contain himself any longer, Robert charges into Acuña's office and announces his firm determination to dance. "Now look," he tells the furious hotel owner, "this is a matter of pride with me. I don't like to dance, see. As a matter of fact I came down here to get away from it. Now you're gonna see me dance and like it!" With that he cocks his hat over one eye, kicks aside a rug, and does a wild, leaping tap routine all over the chairs and furniture. At one point he even jumps

"He's the one who's in love with me!"
"He is not!"

Papa Adolphe and daughter Rita obviously have different feelings about Fred.

248

on Acuña's desk and uses a cane to tap out a rhythm on Acuña's head (during one of the takes, Astaire's pounding was so strong it almost knocked Menjou out).

Apart from a brief theme lifted from Liszt's *Second Hungarian Rhapsody*, the music accompanying the dance was made up of a medley of Latin American tunes. The Mercer-Kern songs, however, were strictly Mercer-Kern, with no attempt at all to utilize south-of-the-border rhythms. The first song in the film, "Dearly Beloved," was introduced by Astaire, suitably enough, at a wedding reception. The title later became part of the movie's plot when Menjou uses it for the salutation of the love notes he pens to his daughter.

Once the impressionable Maria believes that Robert Davis is the ardent note-writer, he is invited to the Acuña mansion for dinner and shows up, naturally, in formal attire. Forced by Acuña to disillusion the adoring girl, Robert sits her on a bench in the garden and proceeds to belittle his profession and confess his proclivity for gambling—and also claim Fred Astaire's birthplace as his own. But Maria remains unswayable.

ROBERT: Look little lady, as they say in Brooklyn, I can't bat in your league. I'm a plain, ordinary guy from Omaha, Nebraska. Just an old-fashioned, everyday Middle Westerner. Why, my grandfather was a cattle-raiser.

MARIA: So was mine!

ROBERT: But you're streamlined. You're today. Sister, I was raised amongst the grasshoppers. I am strictly from corn.

This has no affect on Maria either. In the song, "I'm Old Fashioned," she confesses that she has no interest whatever in the latest fads and fancies. All she really cares about are the old-fashioned things—things like the moonlight, the sound of rain upon a window pane, and the starry song that April sings. As the song ends, Maria and Robert dance, combining tradi-

Rita drops in on Fred's rehearsal.

249

"High stepper
is Shorty George."

251

tional ballroom steps with Latin American steps, and end up gaily tapping up and down a flight of stairs.

After Robert has won a contract to dance at Acuña's hotel, Maria visits him during rehearsal:

ROBERT: We were just running over a little thing from Harlem. But I don't suppose you ever heard of Harlem down here.

MARIA: Isn't that where the zoot suit with the reet pleat comes from?

ROBERT (*admiringly*): Yeah.

MARIA: I'd like to hear it, may I?

ROBERT: Certainly. Oh, Cugie, let's have it.

And Robert sings the happy tale of "Shorty George" (something of a poor relation to "Bojangles of Harlem"), who is not only a high-stepper but also the inspiration for a new dance step ("You beat your feet until your feet is beat"). Once Robert has demonstrated the dance on his knees, Maria is on her feet spiritedly hoofing right along with him.

At the ball in honor of his wedding anniversary, Sr. Acuña announces a traditional song of his family. But since the dainty "Wedding in the Spring" has little of the Latin American about it, he explains everything by revealing that his family had originally come from Brittany. The party also provides the setting for the film's title song (similar in thought, if not in music, to Kern's and Fields' "Lovely to Look At" and "The Way You Look Tonight"). Again seated in the garden of the Acuña home, Robert tries to bid Maria good-bye. But he is dazzled by her beauty:

"You Were Never Lovelier"

ROBERT: Look, would you mind turning the other way, please?

MARIA: Why?

ROBERT: I can't concentrate when you look at me like that. *(She turns her head.)* I was only kidding. Oh, you're terrific! What's the use . . . *(And he glides into the liquid strains of "You Were Never Lovelier.")*

Throughout the movie, a clinging leitmotif is heard every time the love notes and the orchids are delivered to Maria. Once Maria discovers that it's papa who's been sending them, Robert decides to woo her with his own notes and flowers. He even supplies a quartet of delivery boys to serenade Maria by quoting—to the melody of the leitmotif—the messages he has written.

Though not long on humor, *You Were Never Lovelier* did give Adolphe Menjou two well-remembered lines. One occurs after Xavier Cugat, having been caught eavesdropping, feigns the excuse, "There's something in my eye." To which Menjou snaps, "A keyhole, no doubt." The other occurs just before the anniversary ball. Gazing adoringly at his wife, Menjou murmurs sweetly, "You are just as beautiful as ever, my dear. It just takes a little longer now."

You Were Never Lovelier scored an even lovelier success than *You'll Never Get Rich,* and received generally favorable notices in the nation's press. *Newsweek* claimed that it "comes closer than any of the latter-day Astaire shows to capturing the casual charm of the Astaire-Rogers musicals. . . . Although the story is hardly original, the dialogue is bright, the score tuneful and the players expert." *Time,* only slightly less charmed, maintained that it "does not quite live up to its title but presents fresh evidence that Fred Astaire is still a superb dancer and a deft light comedian, and that

254

Backed by Xavier Cugat's Orchestra,
Fred—at first disguised as Lochinvar—
finally wins the lovely Rita.

Rita Hayworth is still the most am-
brosial lady he has ever teamed up
with." "The older Fred gets the lighter
he dances," was the view of Archer
Winsten in the *New York Post*. "You
can't help looking for the invisible
wires enabling him to jig with such
youthful featheriness."

Alton Cook, of the *New York
World-Telegram,* took the occasion to
pen a personal tribute: "One thing you
can count on with Fred Astaire. You
won't catch him in a bad picture. You
can sit in on one of his and first thing
you know his adroit feet and nimble
spirit and mirth have switched the

place out of this world into his own
special region of fantasy, a musical-
comedy Shangri-La, where everyone
sings or dances pleasantly whenever
opportunity arises. You're a little too
happy for good use, coming out of a
Fred Astaire picture, happy enough so
you babble along like this. . . ."

But the final word belongs to Rita.
"I guess the only jewels in my life,"
she told a *Times* interviewer in 1970,
"were the pictures I made with Fred
Astaire. They are the only pictures of
mine I can watch today, Fred and me
dancing, without laughing hysterically.
And *Cover Girl*, too . . ."

With composer Harold Arlen.

256

THE SKY'S THE LIMIT

CAST

Fred Atwell (alias Fred Burton)	Fred Astaire
Joan Manion	Joan Leslie (sung by Sally Sweetland)
Phil Harriman	Robert Benchley
Reg Fenton	Robert Ryan
Mrs. Fisher	Elizabeth Patterson
Canteen Hostess	Marjorie Gateson
Jackson	Eric Blore
Harvey J. Sloan	Clarence Kolb
Dick Merlin	Richard Davies
Longshoreman	Paul Hurst
Mac (bartender)	Ed McNamara
Man Driving Car	Olin Howlin
Colonial Club Orchestra	Freddie Slack Orchestra

Producer: David Hempstead for RKO Radio Pictures. Director: Edward H. Griffith. Lyrics: Johnny Mercer. Music: Harold Arlen. Screenplay: Frank Fenton & Lynn Root from story "A Handful of Heaven." Dance director: Fred Astaire. Art directors: Albert S. D'Agostino, Carroll Clark. Costumes: Renie. Music director: Leigh Harline. Orchestrations: Leigh Harline, Roy Webb, Phil Green. Cameraman: Russell Metty. Editor: Roland Gross. Release date: July 13, 1943. Running time: 89 minutes.

MUSICAL NUMBERS: "My Shining Hour"—Leslie (sung by Sweetland), Slack Orchestra; reprised by Astaire; reprised as dance by Astaire & Leslie/ "A Lot in Common with You"—Leslie & Astaire; dance by Astaire & Leslie/ "One for My Baby (and One More for the Road)"—Astaire; dance by Astaire. Background: "Three Little Words" (Kalmar-Ruby), "Can't Get Out of This Mood" (Loesser-McHugh), "I Get the Neck of the Chicken" (Loesser-McHugh). Unused: "Hangin' on to You," "Harvey the Victory Garden Man."

257

"My Shining Hour." Joan Leslie, with Freddie Slack's Orchestra (including Barney Bigard on tenor sax).

In *Follow the Fleet* he had been a sailor. In *You'll Never Get Rich* he had been a World War II draftee. Now in *The Sky's the Limit* Fred Astaire was at last admitted to membership in a truly elite fighting unit, The Flying Tigers. Unfortunately, the movie was no match for such military distinction.

The Sky's the Limit must have seemed promising enough, with its tale of a war hero who skips a nationwide tour to head for New York City where under an assumed name, he tries to cram as much fun as possible into a brief period of time. Supplying the lyrics was Johnny Mercer, who had previously worked on Fred's

Second Chorus and *You Were Never Lovelier,* and providing the music was Harold Arlen, here creating his only score for a Fred Astaire film. Though no more than three songs were used, the team managed to come up with the remarkably high average of two resounding hits—"My Shining Hour" and "One for My Baby (and One More for the Road)." Fred was also fortunate in having an attractive co-star in eighteen-year-old Joan Leslie, fresh from her appearance opposite James Cagney in *Yankee Doodle Dandy*.

One of the movie's major problems was its inconsistency of mood. At one moment it seemed to be striving for

258

Fred's first meeting with photographer Joan Leslie
and magazine publisher Robert Benchley.

"I seem to have a lot
in common with you . . ."

In the Eyeful Magazine
darkroom with Joan Leslie.

259

lightness, the next it appeared to attempt something profound. It went from Fred's and Joan's dance-floor capers to a philosophical discussion about freedom, and from a funny, fumbling speech by Robert Benchley to the tear-stained face of a war widow—and from there to Fred's startling attack on the deficiencies in American bombers.

Joan Leslie, it was generally agreed, while no competition for a Rogers or a Hayworth, turned out to be a more than competent dance partner for Astaire. She had her opportunity in two numbers. At a servicemen's canteen, she is called upon to sing "A Lot in Common with You," a sprightly piece about two well-matched screwballs. Fred joins her in the duet much to Joan's annoyance (even though the lyric would have made it impossible for her to have done it solo), but they get chummier in the exuberant, playful tap routine that follows, ending with Fred and Joan leaping over each other. Later, in a more romantic setting, the two glide and twirl gracefully together all over a spacious penthouse terrace to the music of "My Shining Hour."

Fred's big solo comes toward the end of the picture. Despondent about returning to duty and unhappy after a row with Joan, he sits morosely at a South Seas–styled bar. He takes a gulp of his drink, smashes the glass against the wall, and swings around on his stool to face the bartender as he tells him to "Make it one for my baby and one more for the road." Fred continues the song at a second bar, and then returns to the lounge at the banquet hall where he had attended a formal dinner with Joan. At the bar he continues drinking—and smashes another glass. But drinking and singing about drinking and smashing glasses are no longer satisfactory outlets for his feelings. So he begins to tap, glumly and resolutely, right up on top of the bar, unleashing all of his pent-up frustra-

Arranging a rendezvous with
Benchley's valet, Eric Blore.

Dancing on a penthouse
terrace to "My Shining Hour."

261

tions in a sliding, slipping dance. As the tempo accelerates, he becomes a man obsessed as he kicks all the glasses lined up on the mirrored wall behind the bar. He leaps down and, as a final uncontrollable act, heaves a bar stool through the mirror.

Although the movie marked Fred Astaire's return to the RKO lot, he found the surroundings a good deal less sumptuous than they had been during his glossy heyday with Ginger Rogers. For one thing, they made the setting for a plush night spot also serve as the setting for a testimonial dinner being tendered an aircraft manufacturer. There was, however, one familiar face from the old days: Eric Blore, as Robert Benchley's valet, and he didn't even receive billing. A new contract player, Robert Ryan, did get billing, but he had little to do as Fred's Flying Tiger buddy.

Benchley had one characteristic bit, his rambling introduction at the testimonial dinner. After insisting that the honored guest needed no introduction, he proceeds to give him one: "The man that we have as guest of honor here tonight is the man I feel free to say who has made this company what it is today. The question now arises, what *is* this company today? I don't want to inject a serious note into the occasion but . . . ha-ha . . . what is anything today? Ahem. So much for the production end." Benchley then goes on to demonstrate something or other with charts. "Now here is a chart showing plastic production as compared . . . ahem . . . with metal production in the year. . . . *(He examines the chart carefully.)* The year doesn't seem to be shown here. Uh . . . So we'll say 1936, for fun, huh? In 1936, you'll see—or whatever year it was—that these things ran into fantastic figures. Uh . . . For instance

"Make it one for my baby and one more for the road . . ."

262

... ahem ... in 1936, two million four hundred and forty-five thousand as compared with three million three hundred and fifty thousand in some other year. Or twenty-five percent of 1936. And by 1936 is meant 1934. This is all per capita, mind you. . . ." And on and on. (This monologue was much in the same vein as "The Treasurer's Report," the humorist's classic routine, which he first performed professionally in Irving Berlin's 1923 *Music Box Revue*.)

Viewers of the movie today might also be amused at some of the inside references (though there seems to have been no special reason why Fred was called Fred and Joan Joan). Early in the film, Fred enrages Joan, playing a magazine photographer on assignment in a nightclub, by suddenly showing up in every group she is about to photograph. "I'm supposed to be taking pictures of celebrities," she wails. But Fred pleads: "Couldn't I be the fellow who never gets his name mentioned? The one they call a 'friend'? You know, 'Ginger Rogers and Friend.'" Later, in the duet, "A Lot in Common with You," the team ends the song with Joan asking, "Where's Cagney?" and Fred asking, "Where's Hayworth?" (rhymes with "horseplay worth" and "eggs that we lay worth").

The Sky's the Limit may have been more often grounded than airborne, but it does deserve a place in the book of negative records: it was the first movie in which Fred Astaire did not appear in white tie and tails.

263

Director Vincente Minnelli with wife, Judy Garland.

Fanny Brice in her dressing room with Lucille Ball.

ZIEGFELD FOLLIES

CAST

Fred Astaire	Lucille Ball
Lucille Bremer	Fanny Brice
Judy Garland	Kathryn Grayson
Lena Horne	Gene Kelly
James Melton	Victor Moore
Red Skelton	Esther Williams
William Powell	Edward Arnold
Marion Bell	Bunin's Puppets
Cyd Charisse	Hume Cronyn
William Frawley	Robert Lewis
Virginia O'Brien	Keenan Wynn
Grady Sutton	Rex Evans
Charles Coleman	Joseph Crehan
Harry Hayden	Eddie Dunn
William B. Davidson	Gary Owen
Harriet Lee	Rod Alexander

Producer: Arthur Freed for Metro-Goldwyn-Mayer. Director: Vincente Minnelli (also George Sidney, Robert Lewis, Lemuel Ayers, Roy Del Ruth). Lyrics: Ralph Freed, Earl Brent, Piave, Arthur Freed, Ralph Blane, Douglas Furber, Charles Ingle, Kay Thompson, Ira Gershwin. Music: Roger Edens, Giuseppe Verdi, Harry Warren, Hugh Martin, Philip Braham, Charles Ingle, George Gershwin. Sketches: Pete Barry, Harry Turgend, George White, David Freedman. Dance director: Robert Alton (also Eugene Loring, Charles Walters). Art directors: Cedric Gibbons, Merrill Pye, Jack Martin Smith. Costumes: Helen Rose, Irene Sharaff. Music director: Lennie Hayton. Orchestrations: Conrad Salinger, Wally Heglin. Musical adaptation: Roger Edens. Vocal arrangements: Kay Thompson. Cameramen: George Folsey, Charles Rosher. Editor: Albert Akst. Color by Technicolor. Release date: January 11, 1946. Running time: 110 minutes.

MUSICAL NUMBERS: "Ziegfeld Days" medley including "It's Delightful to Be Married," "Sunny," "I'm an Indian," "If You Knew Suzie"/ "Here's to the Girls" (R. Freed-Edens)—Astaire, male chorus; whip-cracking by Lucille Ball, dance by Charisse, chorus/ "Bring on the Wonderful Men" (Brent-Edens)—O'Brien/ "Libiamo ne' lieti calici" (Piave-Verdi)—Melton & Bell, chorus/ "This Heart of Mine" (A. Freed-Warren)—Astaire, chorus; dance by Astaire & Bremer/ "Love" (Blane-Martin)—Horne/ "Limehouse Blues" (Furber-Braham)—Lee; dance by Astaire & Bremer/ "Wot Cher" (Ingle)—busker chorus/ "Madame Crematon" (Thompson-Edens)—Garland, reporters; dance by Garland, reporters/ "The Babbitt and the Bromide" (I. Gershwin - G. Gershwin)—Astaire & Kelly; dance by Astaire & Kelly/ "There's Beauty Everywhere" (A. Freed-Warren)—Grayson. Unused: "If Swing Goes, I Go Too" (Astaire).

William Powell as a heavenly Ziegfeld.

Though seldom seen on Broadway any more, the revue was a once-vital and popular form of the American musical theatre. A revue may be lavish or intimate, satirical or slapstick, have a theme or a point of view—or not have a theme or a point of view. The only thing it must never have is a story or "book." It differs from vaudeville in that it is conceived as an entity, not merely as a tossed-together collection of assorted dancers, singers, jugglers, comics, and the like. Of all the impresarios who ever offered revue entertainment on the Main Stem, none had greater flair or was more closely identified with the form than impressario Florenz Ziegfeld.

From 1907 until his last revue in 1931, Ziegfeld presented twenty-two annual—or almost annual—*Ziegfeld Follies.* Dedicated to the glorification

of the American girl, these shows were distinguished by their adroit combination of lavish but tastefully artistic tableaux and some superlative performers. Among the many stars who won fame in Mr. Ziegfeld's *Follies* were Will Rogers, Fanny Brice, Eddie Cantor, Bert Williams, W. C. Fields, Marilyn Miller, Ann Pennington, Gallagher and Shean, and Charles Winninger. But not Fred Astaire.

Not until the M-G-M movie version anyway. In 1944, producer Arthur Freed conceived the idea for a screen edition of the *Ziegfeld Follies* that would adhere to the storyless tradition of the form. Now this was a particularly daring concept. Even though major studios during the early "talkie" days did offer star-filled, plotless spectacles (Universal's *The King of Jazz,* Paramount's *Paramount on*

266

"Here's to the Girls"—Cyd Charisse . . .

. . . and Lucille Ball.

Parade, M-G-M's *Hollywood Revue of 1929*, Warner's *The Show of Shows)*, it had long been established as gospel that a story line, no matter how tenuous, was essential for any constellatory musical extravaganza.

Following *The Sky's the Limit,* Fred Astaire signed a term contract at Metro-Goldwyn-Mayer, with *Ziegfeld Follies* scheduled as his first project. There were so many delays during the film's production, however, that Fred's second Metro picture, *Yolanda and the Thief,* was actually the first to be released. Primarily, the difficulty was that the shooting had to be flexible enough for the performers to fit in their mostly one-shot appearances between filming of other pictures. And of course, there was the problem of what to put into a movie that was un-structured by plot, since it was of ut-most importance that every number in the movie not only register on its own but also contribute to the total effect.

As a result, much footage was dis-carded. Jimmy Durante's two sketches, "Death and Taxes" and "The Pied Piper," had to be cut. Likewise excised were the Lena Horne–Avon Long "Liza" duet, two musical sequences featuring James Melton (one with Esther Williams), and a sketch with Fanny Brice as Baby Snooks. Two other casualties: Fred Astaire's solo of his own song, "If Swing Goes, I Go Too," and his dance in the finale with his newest partner, Lucille Bremer.

What remained were some new songs and dances and some old songs and sketches, with Vincente Minnelli responsible for directing most of the scenes. While the ingredients of the entertainment were self-contained, pro-ducer Arthur Freed still felt it neces-sary to tie the production together with a Prologue in which Ziegfeld is seen in an elegant penthouse version of Heaven. Since William Powell had already impersonated The Great Ziegfeld in Metro's epic biography, he was the logical choice to play the part. With hair Rinso white, he sips his champagne and, with the rather stilted aid of the Bunin Puppets, recalls some of the attractions of past *Follies* revues—the Anna Held Hour Glass Girls in the first edition, Marilyn Miller (though the accompanying music, "Sunny," was from the musical produced by Charles Dillingham), Fanny Brice, Will Rogers, and Eddie Cantor (singing "If You Knew Suzie," which Al Jolson had introduced in the non-Ziegfeld show, *Big Boy*).

But Ziegfeld's mind quickly turns to the present. What he wouldn't give to produce one more *Follies* with the great stars of today. And who would he get to introduce the whole thing? Why, Fred Astaire, of course. Right on cue, Fred shows up in top hat and cutaway to offer this tribute: "As long as there is a dance, a song, a musical show and it's good, somewhere around or in it is Ziegfeld. He never cared so much about villains, plots, stories. The *Follies* never had a story. The *Ziegfeld Follies* was itself the story of an era."

Then by way of introducing the girls —and paying his respects to both his first and his current dancing partner— Fred sails into . . . "So here's to the beautiful ladies, / Here's to the wonderful girls—/Adeles and Mollies, Lucilles and Pollys, / You'll find them all in the *Ziegfeld Follies*. . . ." Suddenly, the screen opens up in a dazzling display as the lovely ladies—all in pink—are rolled into view on a merry-go-round with live horses. Cyd Charisse dances on points, an imperious Lucille Ball stands atop a horse cracking a whip, and a slinky crew of black-clad feline females break out of cages to prance around her. A quick change of pace and Virginia O'Brien comes galloping onto the scene to offer the distaff version of Astaire's jaunty musical tribute.

Virginia O'Brien (riding the Lone Ranger's Silver) sings "Bring on the Wonderful Men."

Esther Williams in "A Water Ballet."

The "Number Please" sketch, with Grady Sutton and Keenan Wynn.

Victor Moore and Edward Arnold
in "Pay the Two Dollars."

With the format of the revue thus established, the next scene introduces "A Water Ballet," performed by Esther Williams, whom *Time* described as "the prettiest amphibian of them all, sliding and slithering through water lilies."

The frustrations of telephone service —surely a theme that has transcended time—is the subject of the sketch, "Number Please," based on a Fred Allen routine in the 1930 Broadway revue, *Three's a Crowd*. Keenan Wynn's inability to place a local call from a hotel lobby telephone becomes especially infuriating when he sees others swiftly put calls through to Chattanooga and South Africa. So Wynn dreams up a fantastic scheme:

WYNN: Operator, I would like to speak to . . . Oogoo in, er . . . Dumdum Proper, South Transylvania. No, I don't know the number and I don't know Mr. Oogoo's first name. All I know is Oogoo. Just. Plain. Oogoo.
OPERATOR: One moment, plee-yuzz.
VOICE: Hallo, Oogoo speaking.
WYNN *(baffled but game)*: Look, Oogoo, you won't remember me but we met at a preview of *Dorian Gray*.
VOICE: Ah, shewwr, shewwr.
WYNN: Look, Ooogoo, I wonder if you would do me a favor.
VOICE: Ah, shewwr. Any friend of a friend is a friend.
WYNN: Well, I'm glad you feel that way. Look, Oogoo, would you get me Plaza 5-5597?
OPERATOR: Sorry, your three minutes are up. That'll be $94.45.

When last seen, Wynn is eating the telephone.

Ziegfeld's musical taste did not include opera, but Freed put in an operatic sequence anyway. By a rather odd coincidence the duet chosen, "Libiamo ne' lieti calici" from *La Traviata,* had been sung eight years earlier by Helen Jepson and Charles Kullman in another screen *Follies,* the *Goldwyn Follies.* Now in Freed's *Follies* it featured James Melton, Marion Bell, and a roomful of chandeliers.

The sketch, "Pay the Two Dollars," was, ironically, first performed on Broadway in *George White's Scandals* of 1931, a revue sponsored by one of Ziegfeld's bitterest rivals. The leading roles, created by Willie and Eugene Howard, were performed in the movie by Victor Moore and Edward Arnold. Like the "Number Please" routine, it is a skit based on frustration, though one far more nightmarishly Kafkaesque. When Moore absentmindedly spits the end of his cigar on the floor of a subway car, lawyer Arnold forbids him to pay the two-dollar fine and insists on taking the matter to court. Despite Moore's pathetic bleat, "Pay the two dollars! Pay the two dollars!", Arnold continues to appeal the decision until Moore, broken and broke, is eventually freed. In the last scene, he is back again in a subway train with Arnold, bites the end of his cigar, and . . .

The first major dancing sequence takes place in the pantomine number, "This Heart of Mine." Outside a glitteringly formal embassy ball, Fred is seen with a wide crimson ribbon across his chest, a monocle in his left eye, and an elongated cigarette holder in his mouth. However, he quickly reveals himself to be a shady character by filching an invitation from a doddering old man and passing it off as his own. Once inside the ballroom, he spies the porcelain loveliness of auburn-tressed Princess Lucille Bremer and they dance together to the meltingly lyrical melody. During an embrace following the dance, Fred coolly removes the lady's bracelet but she, unperturbed, just as coolly offers her necklace to the

"This Heart of Mine."

Fanny Brice, Hume Cronyn and William Frawley in a scene from "The Sweepstakes Ticket."

270

Lena Horne: "Love can be a moment's madness . . ."

Red Skelton giving his pitch for Guzzler's Gin ("Get the college size. One bottle and you're in a class by yourself").

271

"Limehouse Blues" with Fred as a Chinese coolie,
Lucille Bremer as the lady he loves,
and Robert Lewis as the menace.

embarrassed Raffles. As he leaves dejectedly, he takes one final look at Lucille. She rushes into his arms and they dance gaily off together—presumably to become the slickest, sleekest thieving couple in the business.

The one sketch in the entire film to have originated in a *Ziegfeld Follies* was "The Sweepstakes Ticket"—but it was in a Shubert-sponsored edition that came along some four years after Ziegfeld's death. Fanny Brice, the sole member of the movie's cast to have appeared under the Ziegfeld banner, repeated her role of a New York housewife who wins the Irish Sweepstakes, only to find that her Milquetoast husband, Hume Cronyn, has given the ticket to landlord William Frawley as part of their rent money.

A tropical barroom scene next offers such atmospheric touches as a screeching cockatoo, curling cigarette smoke, beaded curtains, and brawling women —all to set off Lena Horne's smoldering, pulsating compilation of the many faces of "Love."

Red Skelton's monologue, "When Television Comes," was his famous Guzzler's Gin routine that he had been doing in vaudeville all over the country. As a television announcer, he not only extols the product ("No bad taste, no aftereffects, no upsetting the nerves, just a nice smooth drink"), he also keeps nipping away at the bottle. At the end, completely smashed, he passes out with the line, "With Guzzler's you don't need a chaser. Nothing can catch ya! Shmoooooooooth. . ."

The song "Limehouse Blues," first introduced in New York by Gertrude Lawrence in *André Charlot's Revue of 1924,* inspired director Minnelli and choreographer Robert Alton to create one of the most striking film ballets of all time. It also owed something to a

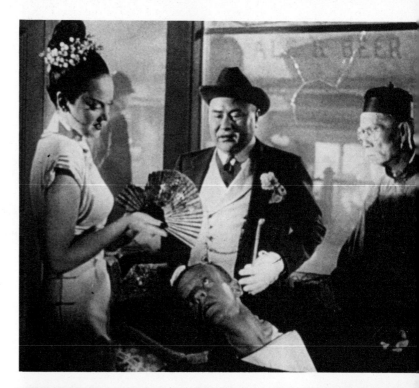

The death of the coolie in "Limehouse Blues."

274

The "Madame Crematon" number with Judy Garland.

ballet Astaire had performed in *The Band Wagon,* one of Broadway's legendary revues. In that version, set to the music of Arthur Schwartz's "Beggar Waltz," Fred played a beggar on the steps of the Vienna Opera House. He adores prima ballerina Tilly Losch, and dreams that he is onstage dancing with her. Once the dream ends, he is again on the steps and Fräulein Losch, taking pity, tosses him her purse. As a variation and enlargement on this theme, the movie's "Limehouse Blues" presents Astaire as a blank-faced Chinese coolie, first seen aimlessly strolling by opium smokers, buskers, sailors, street walkers, and swells who crowd the streets of London's Chinatown (the set—done primarily in browns and yellows—had previously been used for *The Picture of Dorian Gray*). The coolie sees and instantly falls in love with a beauteous Chinese girl (Lucille Bremer), who is being trailed by a rotund, sinister-looking Chinese merchant (played by Robert Lewis, who directed the "Number Please" sketch). After the coolie is mortally wounded during a "smash-and-grab," he dreams that he is pursued by demons until he emerges into the bright sunlight with the girl he loves. Both clad in scarlet, they perform an oriental dance in a chinoiserie setting, punctuating their movements with large fans that they hold in both hands. Once the vision is over, the scene returns to the dingy Limehouse setting. The coolie dies reaching for a fan, the girl has succumbed to the merchant, and the episode ends with Chinatown enshrouded in fog.

Greer Garson was originally supposed to have done "The Interview" number but friends, fearful of her grande-dame image, talked her out of it. It was then offered to Judy Garland, who spiced things up with a vocal takeoff of Miss Garson in her depiction of a movie star grandly granting an interview to the press. To the beat of a hand-clapping chorus of reporters,

275

she reveals that her next epic would be the life of Mme. Crematon, the inventor of the safety pin. (Miss Garson had been sought for the number because she had recently appeared in the role of Mme. Curie, the discoverer of radium.)

Back in 1927, one of the highlights of the Broadway musical *Funny Face* had been the duet, "The Babbitt and the Bromide," performed by Fred Astaire and his sister Adele. For *Ziegfeld Follies,* the Gershwin number provided the occasion for the only joint screen appearance of Hollywood's two leading male dancers, Astaire and Gene Kelly. Actually, the piece made more sense being sung by two men, since it describes how two "sub-sti-an-tial" solid citizens meet on the avenue one day, meet again ten years later, and meet for the third time in Heaven. At each encounter, they are unable to express themselves in any way other than such examples of bromidic bab-bittry as "Hello! Howa you? Howza folks? What's new?" The dance routines, so full of genuine gaiety and mutual admiration, were a rare cinematic treat.

For the film's far from grand finale, Kathryn Grayson sings "There's Beauty Everywhere," engulfed by huge soap bubbles and surrounded by diaphanously gowned Loreleis poised on rocklike formations. Although Fred and Lucille were supposed to be in

Gene Kelly and Fred Astaire in "The Babbitt and the Bromide."

276

this sequence too, the specially imported 6,000-gallon bubble tanks "overextended" themselves thus forcing the episode to be terminated after Miss Grayson's solo.

While honors could be bestowed on many in the movie's cast, it was obviously Fred Astaire—in his first Technicolor film—who provided the mainstay of the picture, appearing in four of the numbers (except for Miss Bremer, none of the other stars was in more than one). *Newsweek,* which referred to *Ziegfeld Follies* as a "mixed grabbag," singled out "The Babbitt and the Bromide" as the "dance for the archives," and John McCarten, in *The New Yorker,* felt "You may be willing to put up with a good deal of spectacular boredom just to watch Astaire and Kelly together." As for "Limehouse Blues," *Time* called it "magnificent," while Bosley Crowther in *The New York Times* hailed its "smooth, imaginative choreography." His verdict on the film itself: "A Technicolor revel, which has humor, magnificence and style."

But *Ziegfeld Follies* made not the slightest impact upon Hollywood in heralding a resurgence of totally plotless musicals. There hasn't been one produced since. Thus the movie remains not only a dazzling entertainment cornucopia but also a unique example of motion-picture experimentation on the grand scale.

277

On the set with director Vincente Minnelli (above)
and co-star Lucille Bremer (below).

YOLANDA AND THE THIEF

CAST

Johnny Riggs	Fred Astaire
Yolanda Aquaviva	Lucille Bremer (sung by Trudy Erwin)
Victor "Junior" Trout	Frank Morgan
Amarilla Aquaviva	Mildred Natwick
Duenna	Mary Nash
Mr. Candle	Leon Ames
Schoolteacher	Ludwig Stoessel
Mother Superior	Jane Green
Puppeteer	Remo Buffano
Padre	Francis Pierlot
Taxi Driver	Leon Belasco
Police Chief	Charles La Torre
Major Domo	Richard Visaroff

Producer: Arthur Freed for Metro-Goldwyn-Mayer. Director: Vincente Minnelli. Lyrics: Arthur Freed. Music: Harry Warren. Screenplay: Irving Brecher, from story by Jacques Thery & Ludwig Bemelmans. Associate producer: Roger Edens. Dance director: Eugene Loring. Art directors: Cedric Gibbons, Jack Martin Smith. Costumes: Irene Sharaff, Irene. Music director: Lennie Hayton. Orchestrations: Conrad Salinger. Cameraman: Charles Rosher. Editor: George White. Color by Technicolor. Release date: October 19, 1945. Running time: 108 minutes.

MUSICAL NUMBERS: "This Is a Day for Love"— school children/ "Angel"—Bremer (sung by Erwin)/ "Dream Ballet"—dance by Astaire & Bremer, dancers; including "Will You Marry Me?"— Bremer (sung by Erwin), chorus/ "Yolanda"— Astaire; dance by Astaire/ "Coffee Time"—chorus; dance by Astaire, Bremer, Patrians.

"Johnny, do you realize the penalty for impersonating an angel?"

The "Dream Ballet."

Yolanda and the Thief seems to be one of those rare minor films that have won the affection of a small coterie who willingly overlook flaws to appreciate favors. Such favors would include the movie's striking use of color and its rich scenic texture, an air of genial make-believe, a few funny moments, and the dances. Especially the dances.

In fact, so impressed was dance critic John Martin with the work of director Vincente Minnelli and choreographer Eugene Loring that he took the unusual step of praising their achievements in his *New York Times* column. "Whatever its failings as a movie," Martin wrote *"Yolanda and the Thief* contains two notably beautiful and imaginative dance numbers. . . . The larger and more impressive of the two is a dream ballet—which sounds forbiddingly commonplace but is exactly the reverse. Mr. Loring moves his figures through the sets with a vivid economy of design and an admirable relationship of groups to settings. The whole thing has a sense of space that is altogether rare. What is perhaps especially noteworthy is the harmony with which dream figures of fantastic character are blended with realistic figures, especially with the deliberately mundane figure of the thief as danced by Fred Astaire. Hence in the juxtaposition of the incongruous is a thoroughly successful use of one of the basic methods of surrealism, stripped of all implications of the macabre and the repugnant, but still completely effective."

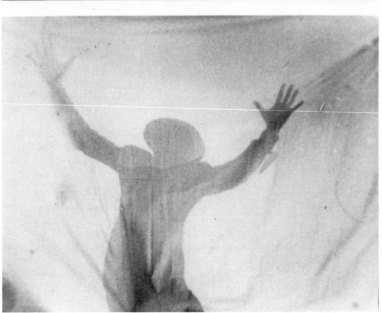

The "Dream Ballet" continued—

Leading up to this sixteen-minute "Dream Ballet" (that was its only identification) was a fairy tale involving Johnny Riggs (Fred Astaire) and Victor Trout, alternately and inexplicably known as Junior (Frank Morgan), a couple of amiable con men on the lam in a sleepy, mythical South American country called Patria (described by Johnny as a "cemetery with a train running through it"). The boys discover a likely quarry in Yolanda Aquaviva (Lucille Bremer), the wealthiest Patrian of them all, who has just assumed the responsibility of running her family's multiple business enterprises. Playing on a degree of gullibility amounting almost to mental retardation, the two crooks manage to pass Johnny off as Yolanda's guardian angel, who has come down to earth. The girl's unquestioning faith, however, touches Johnny; that night, after restlessly tossing in bed, he eventually manages to fall asleep. And dream.

Only the viewer, at first, is not quite sure it is a dream. Johnny, wearing a cream-colored suit, is seen ambling through the town of Esperado. When a stranger asks for an American cigarette, he gives him one and lights it— only to discover that the man has an unlimited number of arms and hands, each one holding an unlighted cigarette. Taking its cue from this rather menacing surrealistic touch, the entire locale itself suddenly assumes a Daliesque quality. Johnny comes across a group of girls washing clothes who dance with him to a percussive Latin rhythm, and end by entwining him in their sheets. Yolanda emerges in a billowy gown with coins attached to it; she and Johnny perform a close, clinging dance revealing their growing love. After Yolanda proposes to Johnny through the song "Will You Marry Me?" the scene becomes darker and the music more agitated as three jockeys simulate a horserace to remind

283

Fred with Lucille Bremer.

"When you have a nightmare you sure keep busy."

us of Johnny's unsavory past. After marrying Yolanda, Johnny tries desperately to escape with a chest bulging with her money. But repeating the entrapment of the early scene with the clothes-washing girls, he now becomes ensnared in Yolanda's veils and he cannot flee. He flails desperately—and awakens flailing desperately at his bedsheets.

The second major dance sequence—coming near the end of the film—was the more formalized "Coffee Time," performed at a carnival celebration. Here the street throng executes a gay, hopping and stomping dance, and is soon joined by Johnny and Yolanda for a dazzling display in part performed solely to the beat of the revelers' handclapping.

As Yolanda, Lucille Bremer was a willing if rather mechanical dancing partner. A product of Broadway and night club chorus lines, Miss Bremer was once dismissed by director Minnelli with the line, "She was a protégée of one of the studio bosses and was quite unsuitable."

What humor the picture possessed was reserved almost exclusively for the few appearances of Mildred Natwick as Yolanda's starched, scatterbrained Aunt Amarilla. Early in the film, welcoming her niece home after years in a convent, she shows her around the mansion all the while chattering on about the young girl's many possessions.

"You have the largest, most modern stables in the entire country," Amarilla tells Yolanda. "Do you like horses?"

"Oh, yes, I do," exclaims the girl.

"Fine," says her aunt. "We must buy a horse."

Then, turning to a servant, Amarilla commands, "Conchita, do my fingernails immediately and bring them to my room." As soon as everyone has left, she looks around quickly, hikes up her skirt, and slides down the bannister.

Since it was made after *Ziegfeld Follies* (though released before it), *Yolanda and the Thief* may well have been influenced by the Astaire-Bremer "This Heart of Mine" sequence in the previous picture. In both Fred played a thief who first sets out to rob highborn Lucille but then falls in love with her. They even had songs by the same writers: lyricist Arthur Freed (who produced both movies) and composer Harry Warren. Actually, *Yolanda*'s screenplay was derived from a short story by Ludwig Bemelmans, whose use of "paint-box" colors for his illustrations prompted Minnelli to employ the same color scheme for the film.

In Minnelli's words, *"Yolanda and the Thief* was a fantasy that just didn't perfectly come off." Yet in its boldly imaginative dance sequences it was— like the "Limehouse Blues" episode in *Ziegfeld Follies*—a pioneering effort in the realization of the screen's vast potential for ballet.

Fred and Frank Morgan spot their satchel being carried by the mysterious Leon Ames.

"Coffee Time."

288

BLUE SKIES

CAST

Johnny Adams	Bing Crosby
Jed Potter	Fred Astaire
Mary O'Dare Adams	Joan Caulfield
Tony	Billy DeWolfe
Nita Nova	Olga San Juan
Jeffrey (Jed's valet)	Jimmy Conlin
Cliff (pianist)	Cliff Nazarro
Mack (stage manager)	Frank Faylen
Drunk	Jack Norton
Detroit Stage Manager	Will Wright
Martha (nurse)	Victoria Horne
Mary Elizabeth Adams	Karolyn Grimes
Charles Dillingham	Roy Gordon

Producer: Sol C. Siegel for Paramount Pictures. Director: Stuart Heisler. Lyrics & Music: Irving Berlin. Screenplay: Arthur Sheekman, adapted by Allan Scott from idea by Irving Berlin. Dance director: Hermes Pan. Assistant: David Robel. Art directors: Hans Dreier, Hal Pereira. Costumes: Edith Head, Waldo Angelo. Music director: Robert Emmett Dolan. Vocal arrangements: Joseph J. Lilley. Cameraman: Charles Lang, Jr., William Snyder. Editor: LeRoy Stone. Color by Technicolor. Release date: September 26, 1946. Running time: 104 minutes.

MUSICAL NUMBERS: "A Pretty Girl Is Like a Melody" —male chorus; dance by Astaire/ "I've Got My Captain Working for Me Now"—Crosby, with DeWolfe/ "You'd Be Surprised"—San Juan/ "All By Myself"—Crosby/ "Serenade to an Old Fashioned Girl"—Caulfield, male quartet/ "Puttin' on the Ritz"—Astaire; dance by Astaire/ "(I'll See You in) C-U-B-A"—Crosby & San Juan/ "A Couple of Song and Dance Men"—Crosby & Astaire, with Nazarro, piano/ "You Keep Coming Back Like a Song"—Crosby, male chorus/ "Always"—chorus/ "Blue Skies"—Crosby/ "The Little Things in Life" —Crosby/ "Not for All the Rice in China"— Crosby/ "Russian Lullaby"—Crosby/ "Everybody Step"—Crosby; dance by chorus/ "How Deep Is the Ocean?"—female chorus, Crosby/ "(Running Around in Circles) Getting Nowhere"—Crosby/ "Heat Wave"—San Juan, chorus; dance by Astaire & San Juan, chorus/ "Any Bonds Today?"— Crosby/ "This Is the Army, Mr. Jones"—Crosby/ "White Christmas"—Crosby. Background: "Tell Me, Little Gypsy," "Nobody Knows," "Mandy," "Some Sunny Day," "When You Walked Out," "Because I Love You," "How Many Times?," "Lazy," "The Song Is Ended."

289

Dancing to "A Pretty Girl Is Like a Melody."

After the show, Fred takes Joan Caulfield to The Flapjack to meet old buddy Bing Crosby.

Bing and Billy DeWolfe entertain with "I've Got My Captain Working for Me Now."

Over at the Paramount lot during the Spring of 1946, producer-director Mark Sandrich was putting together a sequel to his vastly successful *Holiday Inn*. It was called *Blue Skies,* and once more he had an array of Irving Berlin songs through which to spin a tale of a crooner, a hoofer, and the girl they both loved. The crooner was again Bing Crosby, the girl was newcomer Joan Caulfield, and the hoofer was Paul Draper who, though new to Hollywood, had won renown in Broadway revues, night clubs, and concerts.

Now, while Draper was universally acknowledged to be an exceptionally brilliant stylist, particularly in his skill at combining classical and modern forms, he did have one problem as an actor. He had a slight stammer. Sandrich, however, was confident that with effort this could be overcome, and filming began on schedule.

Then tragedy struck. After the picture had been before the cameras about nine days, Sandrich, only forty-four, succumbed to a heart attack. When his duties were taken over by producer Sol C. Siegel and director Stuart Heisler, one of their first decisions was to replace Draper. Their logical choice: Fred Astaire.

The offer came at an opportune time. Having just completed the indifferently received *Yolanda and the Thief,* Astaire felt strongly that his next Metro assignment would have to be a major effort. But Arthur Freed had scheduled *The Belle of New York,* a frothy period piece that, to Astaire, had the same fatal drawback as *Yolanda:* it was a fantasy and fantasies usually spelled disaster at the box office. The call from Paramount was, if not a solution to Fred's dilemma, at least a postponement. However, on its own, it loomed as considerably more than that. *Holiday Inn* had been a hit, and Astaire was now being given a second chance to team up with Crosby and Berlin. Even the title, *Blue Skies,* looked like an omen. And it was.

No matter what Fred says about Bing, Joan is
too much in love to care.

Like its predecessor, *Blue Skies* was
based on a musical format: for *Holiday Inn* it had been to fit appropriate
songs to American holidays; for *Blue
Skies* it was to fit appropriate songs
to a variety of night clubs. But whereas
Holiday Inn had housed mostly new
pieces created by Berlin specifically
for the project, *Blue Skies* was studded
largely with well-known Berlin stan-
dards, with only four new numbers
written specifically for the film. In all,
twenty-five songs—including "White
Christmas," a *Holiday Inn* holdover—
were sung, or danced to, or played as
background music.

Even apart from boasting the same
songwriter and the same two male
stars, *Holiday Inn* and *Blue Skies* had
other points of similarity. Both depicted Crosby and Astaire as former
song-and-dance partners in love with
the same girl, and in both cases Crosby
got the girl (in *Blue Skies* he even got
her twice). In *Holiday Inn,* however,

Bing had played an easygoing sort who
settled down on a farm and opened his
night club only on holidays; in *Blue
Skies* he played an easygoing sort who
was unable to settle down any place
and kept buying and selling night clubs
all over the country. For some reason,
this was supposed to make him appear
irresponsible—even though he made a
success of each venture and his constantly changing business locales provided him with fun, variety, travel,
and the opportunity to sing some great
Irving Berlin songs. What more could
a loving wife want? Nevertheless, this
was the issue over which loving wife
Joan Caulfield left him—only to return at the end when he was apparently too old to do much of anything
except stay in one place.

But again, as in *Holiday Inn,* the
story of *Blue Skies* was little more
than a none-too-obtrusive peg on
which to hang a string of melodic
pleasures, this time beginning in 1919

"Puttin' on the Ritz."

293

With Cliff Nazarro at the piano,
Fred and Bing recall their vaudeville days
as ''A Couple of Song and Dance Men.''

297

and going right on through to 1946. The first song in the film, "A Pretty Girl Is Like a Melody," was presented as part of a lavish Broadway revue whose identity, curiously, went unrevealed. Well, maybe not so curiously. Since the show was the *Ziegfeld Follies* of 1919 and the song itself was something of a theme for all the *Follies,* Paramount's reticence was simply due to a disinclination to plug M-G-M's *Ziegfeld Follies,* released earlier the same year. *Blue Skies,* however, did make a fuss over impressario Charles Dillingham, whom Hollywood has somehow always considered the only other Broadway producer with prestige comparable to Ziegfeld's.

It was, of course, Bing's varied and constantly changing night clubs that provided the settings for most of the songs, either reflecting their immediate surroundings or the periods in which they were sung. In his first location, The Flapjack, Bing sings the universal expression of postwar wish-fulfillment, "I've Got My Captain Working for Me Now." The following year, with the advent of Prohibition—and the purchase of a new spot, The Hole in the Wall—Bing and Olga San Juan invite one and all down to "Cuba, where wine is flowing." At The Song Book, an open-air club near New York's Central Park, Bing appropriately introduces "You Keep Coming Back Like a Song," one of the new pieces written for the movie, which also serves as the Crosby-Caulfield love theme.

After his marriage to Joan, Bing warbles such well-matched selections as "The Little Things in Life" at The Little Spot, "Not for All the Rice in China" at the Chop Suey, and "Russian Lullaby" at the Balalaika. Then he buys the most glittering pleasure dome of all, The Top Hat, where the chorus struts and Bing sings —not the expected "Top Hat, White Tie and Tails"—but the equally scintillating "Everybody Step."

Faithful Fred still carries the torch for Joan.

Bing singing "You Keep Coming Back Like a Song" at The Song Book.

298

Billy DeWolfe's routine about
dear Mrs. Mergatroyd
getting soused in a cocktail lounge.

Fred and Olga San Juan in the "Heat Wave" number.

299

When World War II comes, Bing does his bit by singing "Any Bonds Today" during a war bond rally, "This Is the Army, Mr. Jones" at a training camp, and "White Christmas" for the troops in the South Seas (actually a more meaningful locale for the song than the farmhouse in *Holiday Inn*). For those situations calling for more intimate, personal expressions, Bing croons "All by Myself" to Joan on the night they meet, "Blue Skies" while caught in a rainstorm during a picnic, and a new song, "Getting Nowhere," as a lullaby to his daughter. The inevitable Crosby-Astaire duet inspired Irving Berlin to create a bit of cornball horseplay, "A Couple of Song and Dance Men," which has the boys cutting loose in a recreation of their old-time vaudeville act.

Paralleling Bing's career as a bouncing boniface is Fred's as a perennial Broadway leading man. In "Puttin' on the Ritz" (supposedly performed in a Dillingham show but actually taken from the 1929 movie of the same name), Fred recreates the quicksilver elegance of his "Top Hat, White Tie and Tails" routine. Appearing in top hat, ascot, cutaway, striped pants, and spats, he seems powerless to control the fulgurous movements of his flashing legs and, even before he has finished singing, breaks into a dance with his cane as both prop and partner. After scampering toward the rear of the stage, he kicks apart two inner curtains revealing a row of miniature Fred Astaires, all dressed alike and all tapping in unison behind their lifesize leader. Then, like the shadows in the "Bojangles" number in *Swing Time*, each "chorus Astaire" begins dancing individually, thus achieving what *Life*

"Heat Wave" continued—and Fred's fall.

called "possibly the most stupendous tap dance of all time."

Fred's other dance, the more elaborate and dramatic "Heat Wave" (in which, during a performance of a show, he falls off a bridge almost the height of the proscenium arch) was also a strikingly effective number, but "Puttin' on the Ritz" was the one that Astaire wanted to make especially memorable. In addition to being the final dance routine filmed for *Blue Skies,* it was also intended to serve as Fred's final performance as a dancer. During the shooting of the picture Astaire became determined to retire upon its completion. He was then forty-seven and had been dancing professionally for over forty years. He was finding it harder to come up with fresh ideas, and he was afraid that the public would soon tire of him. Besides, he wanted time to oversee the chain of dance studios he had recently started —and he wanted time to play golf and to breed racehorses. What better way to bid farewell than in a three-million-dollar epic musical that was certain to be a wopping success?

Events, of course, did make Astaire change his mind and return to moviemaking two years later. There were, in fact, fifteen screen appearances following *Blue Skies.* One that Astaire never made, however, was *White Christmas,* which was planned as the third collaboration for Messrs. Crosby, Astaire, and Berlin. Although signed to appear in the film later in 1953, Fred became ill and had to be replaced by Donald O'Connor. Then O'Connor took sick and was replaced by Danny Kaye. *White Christmas* ended up by being an even bigger box-office bonanza that *Blue Skies*—and *Blue Skies* took in the highest grosses of any movie Fred Astaire ever made.

Irving Berlin on the set with Judy and Fred.

EASTER PARADE

CAST

Hannah Brown	Judy Garland
Don Hewes	Fred Astaire
Jonathan "Johnny" Harrow, III	Peter Lawford
Nadine Hale	Ann Miller
Francois	Jules Munshin
Mike (bartender)	Clinton Sundberg
Singer	Richard Beavers
Essie (Nadine's maid)	Jeni LeGon
Al (Ziegfeld stage manager)	Dick Simmons
Boy in Toy Store	Jimmy Bates
Cab Driver	Jimmy Dodd
Policeman	Robert Emmett O'Connor
Marty (audition pianist)	Wilson Wood
Drugstore Clerk	Nolan Leary
Sam (valet)	Peter Chong
Specialty Dancers	Pat Jackson, Dee Turnell, Bobbie Priest
Cover Girls	Lynn & Jean Romer, Elaine Sterling, Lola Albright, Pat Walker, Pat Vaniver, Marjorie Jackson, Gail Langford, Shirley Ballard, Joi Lansing, Ruth Hall
Dog Act	Hector & His Pals
Woman at Bar	Benay Venuta

Producer: Arthur Freed for Metro-Goldwyn-Mayer. Director: Charles Walters. Lyrics & Music: Irving Berlin. Screenplay: Sidney Sheldon, Frances Goodrich & Albert Hackett. Associate producer: Roger Edens. Dance director: Robert Alton. Art directors: Cedric Gibbons, Jack Martin Smith. Costumes: Irene, Valles. Music director: Johnny Green. Orchestrations: Conrad Salinger, Van Cleave, Leo Arnaud. Vocal arrangements: Robert Tucker. Cameraman: Harry Stradling. Editor: Albert Akst. Color by Technicolor. Release date: June 1, 1948. Running time: 103 minutes.

MUSICAL NUMBERS: "Happy Easter"—Astaire, hat models, New Yorkers/ "Drum Crazy"—Astaire; drumming & dance by Astaire/ "It Only Happens When I Dance with You"—Astaire; dance by Astaire & Miller; reprised by Garland/ "Everybody's Doin' It"—dance by night club chorus, including Garland/ "I Want to Go Back to Michigan"—Garland/ "Beautiful Faces Need Beautiful Clothes"—dance by Astaire & Garland/ "A Fella with an Umbrella"—Lawford & Garland/ "I Love a Piano"—Garland; dance by Astaire & Garland/ "Snooky Ookums"—Astaire & Garland/ "Ragtime Violin"—Astaire; dance by Astaire & Garland/ "When the Midnight Choo-Choo Leaves for Alabam' "—Astaire & Garland; dance by Astaire & Garland/ "Shakin' the Blues Away"—Miller, chorus; dance by Miller/ "Steppin' Out with My Baby"—Astaire, chorus; dance by Astaire, with Turner, Jackson, Priest, chorus/ "A Couple of Swells"—Astaire & Garland/ "The Girl on the Magazine Cover"—Beavers, with Cover Girls, Miller, chorus/ "Better Luck Next Time"—Garland/ "Easter Parade"—Garland & Astaire, chorus. Background: "At the Devil's Ball," "This Is the Life," "Along Came Ruth," "Call Me Up Some Rainy Afternoon." Unused: "Mr. Monotony."

M-G-M brought him back.

And it seemed only right. Metro had been the first to introduce him to movie audiences, had starred him in his first post–Ginger Rogers musical, and had given him a term contract four years later. Now the studio again paged Fred Astaire.

The timing was perfect. At first, Astaire had every intention of staying permanently retired following *Blue Skies,* and he seemed to have enough to do to occupy his time. But after about a year away from the cameras, he began to feel restless. His dance studies were going well and did not require his personal supervision. And he couldn't spend all his time on the golf course or at the racetrack. In April 1947 he had even taken a step back into show business by making his first radio appearance in a nonmusical play, Philip Barry's *The Animal Kingdom,* produced by the Theatre Guild of the Air. Retirement just wasn't for Fred Astaire, not yet anyway.

Early in 1948, Metro was riding the crest of what many have dubbed the Golden Age of Hollywood Musicals. Primarily—but not exclusively—under the supervision of producer Arthur Freed and director Vincente Minnelli, the studio had been turning out a string of bright, imaginative screen musicals including *Meet Me in St. Louis, Anchors Aweigh, The Harvey Girls, Ziegfeld Follies,* and *The Pirate* (and would continue with *The Barkleys of Broadway, On the Town, An American in Paris, Singin' in the Rain, The Band Wagon,* and *Seven Brides for Seven Brothers*).

To distract young Jimmy Bates,
Fred performs his "Drum Crazy" routine.

Almost as soon as *The Pirate* was completed, producer Freed signed its co-stars Judy Garland and Gene Kelly, to appear together again in *Easter Parade,* a tale that was actually little more than a variation on Judy's and Gene's first film together, *For Me and My Gal.* But there was one major new element: Freed's plan was to build a period musical around a flock of old and new songs written by Irving Berlin —just as the composer's songs had provided the framework for both *Holiday Inn* and *Blue Skies.* (In *Holiday Inn* the action had covered a two-year period beginning Christmas Eve; in *Easter Parade* it would cover a one-year period beginning the day before Easter.) Rehearsals had already begun under the direction of Charles Walters (a former Broadway juvenile who had already directed Freed's production of *Good News*) when Kelly fell and broke his ankle. Since the shooting could not be postponed, a replacement was needed immediately. Astaire, having already decided to return to moviemaking if the opportunity ever arose, needed little persuasion to take over the part. Thus, at the age of forty-eight, and after a screen absence of about two years, Fred Astaire came back—and in triumph.

According to Arthur Freed, the picture got started simply because Irving Berlin was anxious to do a movie with Judy Garland. Judy provided a new type of partner for Astaire, with her rare singing-and-acting ability projecting an irresistible combination of stamina and vulnerability. And she could keep up with the master on the dance floor. But even though Judy received billing over Fred, the movie

Ann Miller breaks the news to Peter Lawford and Fred that she's leaving the act to star in a Broadway show.

So Fred drowns his sorrows at Luigi's. Clinton Sundberg is the sympathetic bartender.

"Miss Brown, what idiot ever told you you were a dancer?" "You did."

gave Astaire maximum footage for his footwork, not alone with his co-star but also with Ann Miller and of course, in solos. Moreover, there was greater emphasis than before in depicting him as a dominant personality as he played the role of a nimble-toed Pygmalion who transforms Galatea Judy Garland into a Broadway star.

Easter Parade opens with jaunty Don Hewes (Fred Astaire) bobbing down Fifth Avenue wishing one and all a "Happy Easter"—even though he's a day early. Don is on a gift-buying spree for his partner, Nadine Hale (Ann Miller), and at a toy store, puts on a spectacular "Drum Crazy" display of drumming and tapping just to pry loose a stuffed rabbit from a little boy.

At Nadine's apartment, Don is shocked to learn that Nadine is quitting their act to star in a Broadway musical. (The dear girl's unnatural failure to reveal that it's to be the next *Ziegfeld Follies* was due less to personal reticence than it was to a plot development later in the film.) Trying to romance his partner into changing her mind, Don coos in her ear, "This isn't just dancing, it's different. This is . . . us." Mere words, of course, are not enough. So he sings, "It only happens when I dance with you . . . ," and then coaxes Nadine to dance with him in her rather overstuffed room. But nothing works. Even best friend, Johnny Harrow (Peter Lawford), cannot budge the ambitious girl.

Hurt and angry, Don storms out of the apartment and into Luigi's tiny night spot, where he stations himself at the bar. Johnny, who has followed Don, urges him to go back to Nadine, but Don scoffs at the idea. He's taught her everything she knows and besides, says he—eyeing a row of prancing chorus girls—"I could teach any of those girls to do the same thing." Then to make good his Henry Higgins boast, Don wambles over to the girls as they rush off the dance floor and stops in front of Hannah Brown (Judy Garland):

"A Fella with an Umbrella."

308

"Fiddle up, fiddle up, on your violin . . ."

DON: Yeah, I think you'll do.

HANNAH: You think I'll do what?

DON: I'm looking for someone to dance with.

HANNAH: Wrong number.

DON: I need a new dancing partner. I don't know how much you're getting here but I'll give you a hundred dollars a week.

HANNAH: A hundred dol— . . . ? *(She goes along with the gag.)* That would never do for me.

DON: All right. A hundred and fifty.

HANNAH *(flatly)*: A hundred and fifty. Thank you very much. Now may I go?

DON: Sure. Just a minute. Here's my card. I'll get a rehearsal hall at Michael's. Know where it is?

HANNAH: Yes.

DON: All right. Tomorrow morning at ten. *(He walks away.)*

HANNAH *(still unbelieving)*: You'll wait for me.

Looking at Don's card, Hannah realizes that the offer wasn't a joke— and she has just enough time to get into her milkmaid apron to sing wistfully of the simple life in "Michigan, down on the farm."

The next day, even though it is Easter Sunday, Don has no trouble renting a hall and pianist. Hannah shows up, slightly flustered, and Don, who now regrets the whole deal, is impatient with her. But this is, after all, Easter, and the two go for a stroll along Fifth Avenue ("Oh, look!," cries Hannah, all bubbly. "The Easter Parade! Isn't it beautiful?"). Spotting the flamboyant cynosure, Nadine and her two Russian wolfhounds, Don makes an Easter Parade date with Hannah for next year, with the prediction: "One year from today no one is going to notice her when they look at you."

Unwilling to see that his Galatea has a personality of her own, Don makes Hannah wear clothes like Nadine and dance like Nadine. He even changes

309

"When the midnight choo-choo
leaves for Alabam'. . ."

her name to Juanita. And the result, in their first engagement, is a disaster.

Faithful Johnny Harrow arranges a restaurant reunion for Nadine and Don. Even before ordering lunch, however, Nadine accuses Don of allowing Hannah to imitate her. This lights a spark and Don dashes off, leaving Nadine to huff out of the restaurant all by herself. Francois, the waiter (Jules Munshin), stares at her haughtily. "Come again soon," he says through clenched teeth. "Bring your friends."

On her way to meet Don, Hannah ducks into a doorway to avoid a sudden downpour and strikes up a conversation with, of all people, Johnny Harrow, although she has no idea who he is. Snatching a huge umbrella from a pushcart, he offers to escort her:

HANNAH: In two minutes you've managed to find out that I'm not married, I'm not engaged, that I come from the country, and that I'm going to meet a man on business.
JOHNNY: Wasn't bad, was it?
HANNAH: Yeah, but you haven't told me a thing about yourself.
JOHNNY (singing): "I'm just a fella, a fella with an umbrella,/Looking for a girl who saved her love for a rainy day. . . ."

Hannah, obviously taken with the courtly, if brash, young man, joins him in song.

At Don's apartment, Don is very businesslike as he tells Hannah that from now on all the fancy dress and la-de-da business is out. She'll be just plain Hannah Brown, no more Juanita —or Nadine—stuff for her. First off, he has her try the raggy "I Love a Piano." Boy! That's the kind of number for her! As Hannah belts out the exuberant tribute, Don joins her in a spontaneous dance, all the while peppering her with words of encouragement. Quick lap dissolve. They're doing the number in vaudeville and

Ann Miller's "Shaking the Blues Away."

they're a hit. Quick lap dissolve. Another vaudeville stage and the team is panicking the audience with "Snooky Ookums." Quick lap dissolve and another smash vaudeville number, "The Ragtime Violin" ("Fiddle up, fiddle up—on your violin . . ."). Everything they do catches fire and the singing and dancing and clowning fairly tumble out.

Now they are ready for the biggest test of all: an audition for the next *Ziegfeld Follies*. Here Don and Hannah put all the chug-chugging razzmatazz into "When the Midnight Choo-Choo Leaves for Alabam'," and Ziegfeld is ready to put their names on a contract.

But to the surprise of all, this turns out to be the show in which Nadine Hale is to star (historic note: no performer was ever starred in a *Ziegfeld Follies*). Hannah somehow gets the notion that Don is still in love with his former partner and rushes out of the theatre in tears. But Don refuses to take second billing to Nadine and turns down the offer anyway.

At dinner, Johnny Harrow proposes marriage to Hannah, but she cannot accept. "You know," she tells Johnny, fighting back the tears, "I . . . I used to dream that when I'd fall in love with a man he'd send me flowers, sweep me off my feet, take me in his arms. It's nothing like that with Don. He doesn't know I'm alive half the

"Steppin' Out with My Baby."

313

time. When he sweeps me off my feet
it's during a dance number. And when
he sends me flowers it's because it's
good for business. Oh, he's taken me
in his arms, but there's never been less
than seven hundred people watching.
Oh, it's not his fault. It's mine. I . . .
when they passed out the wishes, I . . .
I wished for him."

It is the opening night of the *Zieg-feld Follies* of 1912. Nadine does her
electrifying tap version of "Shakin' the
Blues Away" (really from the 1927
Follies), and of course, scores a great
success. That doesn't bother Don one
bit since he's just received an offer
from producer Charles Dillingham
("He wants to build a show around
us"), and he and Hannah excitedly
check the calendar to discover that the
opening date, April 6, falls on the day
before Easter.

Don wants to celebrate ("Pick me
up at my apartment, huh?"), but when
Hannah arrives, he decides to stay
home to rehearse some new steps.
Hannah has finally had it, and she
accuses Don of being nothing but a
pair of dancing shoes. Shutting her
eyes, she challenges him to tell her
their color. He kisses her and answers—
correctly—"They're brown." Hannah
is so happy she even sings "It Only
Happens When I Dance with You,"
the song associated with Nadine. "Why
didn't you tell me I was in love with
you?" Don asks tenderly, and they
embrace.

At last, with the opening of the
Dillingham show, *Walking Up the
Avenue,* it is Hannah's and Don's turn
to shine. Don's first song, "Steppin'
Out with My Baby," is a cane-twirling,
high-strutting affair he performs in a
straw hat and white suit. In turn, he
dances with a lively blonde, a seduc-
tive brunette, and a spirited redhead,

314

"We're a couple of swells . . ."

followed by a series of machine-gun steps using his cane as a prop. Thanks to cinema sorcery, Don executes a string of dazzling slow-motion leaps in front of a dancing chorus whose movements remain at their regular speed.

The show's show-stopper, however, is the mocking, madcap duet, "A Couple of Swells." As a pair of seedy bums, the aristocratic Don and the mischievous Hannah prance about with elegant airs as they kid the pretensions of the upper classes. It's a delicious bit, offering a rowdy contrast to the more formal strolling up the avenue referred to in the movie's title song.

After scoring a resounding hit, Hannah and Don celebrate by taking in the late-night *Ziegfeld Follies* on the New Amsterdam Roof. (Actually, this series of supper-club entertainments was called *Ziegfeld's Midnight Frolic,* not *Follies,* and was not inaugurated until three years later.) In a production number reminiscent of the "Cover Girl" routine in the 1944 movie, *Cover Girl* (though the Berlin song, "The Girl on the Magazine Cover," dated from 1915), a stalwart baritone serenades eleven girls representing the major magazines of the period. Nadine, a tireless soul who is appearing in the midnight show in addition to the regular *Follies,* is so jealous of Don's success with Hannah that she invites him to dance with her to their theme song, "It Only Happens When I Dance with You." Right on cue, Hannah heads for the nearest exit.

Despite the slimness of the evidence,

315

Fred and Ann dancing to "It Only Happens when I Dance with You."

"... Because there ain't gonna be no next time for me."

"Innnn your Easter bonnet . . ."

poor Hannah is convinced that Don still loves Nadine. Returning to Luigi's, she sits at the bar and pours her heart out in the emotional lament, "Better Luck Next Time." The next morning, however, it doesn't take too much prodding on Johnny's part to get her to dash over to Don's apartment. It's Easter Sunday again, and upon her arrival Hannah presents Don with his gift, a beribboned top hat with a rabbit inside—thus providing an excuse for the girl rather than the boy to sing the familiar serenade, "Innnn your Easter bonnet . . ." Radiantly, the two now join the elegant strollers on Fifth Avenue.

Fred Astaire's return to films elicited a unanimously warm welcome in the nation's press. "The important thing is that Fred Astaire is back again with Irving Berlin calling the tunes," was the greeting in *Newsweek*. "He's as brilliant a dancer as ever and, if anything, a more accomplished comedian." *Pictorial Review* proclaimed the film "the most joyous of the year. Not since the halcyon days of Ginger Rogers has Fred Astaire danced with such style or punch." Both Howard Barnes in the *New York Herald Tribune* and Thomas M. Pryor in *The New York Times* used the identical phrase when they maintained that Astaire was dancing "at the top of his form." The gentleman from the *Times* also added the wish: "Let's hope that he'll never again talk of retiring."

He didn't. At least, not for the next six years.

Fred and Ginger with producer Arthur Freed.

THE BARKLEYS OF BROADWAY

CAST

Josh Barkley	Fred Astaire
Dinah Barkley	Ginger Rogers
Ezra Miller	Oscar Levant
Millie Belney	Billie Burke
Jacques Pierre Barredout	Jacques Francois
Shirlene May	Gale Robbins
Judge in Play	George Zucco
Bert Felsher	Clinton Sundberg
Pamela Driscoll	Inez Cooper
Gloria	Carol Brewster
Larry (press agent)	Wilson Wood
Genevieve	Joyce Matthews
Henrietta	Roberta Jackson
Cleo	Lorraine Crawford
Mary (Dinah's maid)	Margaret Bert
Perkins ("Look" writer)	Frank Ferguson
Clementine Villard	Mary Jo Ellis
Ladislaus Ladi	Hans Conried
Orchestra Leader	Lennie Hayton

Producer: Arthur Freed for Metro-Goldwyn-Mayer. Director: Charles Walters. Lyrics: Ira Gershwin. Music: Harry Warren. Screenplay Betty Comden & Adolph Green. Associate producer: Roger Edens. Dance directors: Robert Alton, Hermes Pan. Art directors: Cedric Gibbons, Edward Carfagno. Costumes: Irene, Valles. Music director: Lennie Hayton. Orchestrations: Lennie Hayton, Conrad Salinger. Vocal arrangements: Robert Tucker. Cameraman: Harry Stradling. Editor: Albert Akst. Color by Technicolor. Release date: April 11, 1949. Running time: 109 minutes.

MUSICAL NUMBERS: "Swing Trot"—dance by Astaire & Rogers/ *Sabre Dance* (Khatchaturian) —Levant, piano/ "You'd Be Hard to Replace" Astaire/ "Bouncin' the Blues"—dance by Astaire & Rogers/ "My One and Only Highland Fling"— Astaire & Rogers; dance by Astaire & Rogers/ "A Weekend in the Country"—Astaire, Rogers, Levant/ "Shoes with Wings On"—Astaire; dance by Astaire/ *Piano Concerto in B-flat Minor* excerpt (Tchaikovsky)—Levant, piano/ "They Can't Take That Away from Me" (I. Gershwin-George Gershwin)—Astaire; dance by Astaire & Rogers/ "Manhattan Downbeat"—Astaire, chorus; dance by Astaire & Rogers, chorus. Background: "Angel," "This Heart of Mine" (both Freed-Warren). Unused: "The Courtship of Elmer and Ella," "Natchez on the Mississipp'."

Opening night curtain calls, with Oscar Levant joining them below.

The Judy Garland–Fred Astaire click in *Easter Parade* could mean only one thing: a quick follow-up movie. Again in charge were the same producer (Arthur Freed), director (Charles Walters), and choreographer (Robert Alton). For the songs, Freed turned to his own occasional composing partner, Harry Warren, and brought him together with lyricist Ira Gershwin. To write the story, he signed the Broadway team of Betty Comden and Adolph Green, who had already been responsible for the screenplays of *Good News* and *On the Town*.

Although the new film could claim an original scenario, the saga of the bickering Barkleys looked very much like a continuation of the tale of the *Easter Parade* couple, Don Hewes and Hannah Brown—only brought up-to-date with the team now married. For just as Don had made good his vow to turn Hannah into the toast of Broadway within a year, so Josh Barkley is not above reminding wife Dinah just how much her success is dependent upon him.

320

"You couldn't walk across the stage without me," he tells her during an angry exchange early in the picture. "There isn't a gesture you do that I didn't teach you."

"That's a lie!"

"It took a lot of patience to put you where you are. I worked. I pulled things out of you! I molded you! Like Svengali did Trilby."

Or like Don did Hannah.

Rehearsals had already begun for *The Barkleys of Broadway* when it became apparent that there would be a serious problem. Judy Garland, who was ill at the time, had been promised a rest after *Easter Parade*, but was rushed into the new film almost immediately. As she once wrote: "By now I was just a mechanical hoop they were rolling around. I was sure I wasn't going to make it but it didn't matter. The rehearsals began and my migraine headaches got worse. I went for days without sleep but I kept on.

Then I started to be late to rehearsals and began missing days. Finally I was fired. They didn't even give me the courtesy of a call or a meeting or a discussion. They sent me a telegram."

Oscar Levant, who appeared in the movie, recalls the situation a bit differently: "I looked forward to working with Judy, but she never appeared on the set after we were ready to begin. Arthur Freed and Louis B. Mayer both went to her Hollywood hilltop home, but apparently no one could persuade her to show up. Finally, Ginger Rogers was engaged to take Judy's place and the picture proceeded. Then suddenly Judy appeared on the set. When she poised herself behind the camera it was too unnerving Chuck Walters finally asked her to leave. Judy refused. Chuck took her by the arm and led her out as she hurled imprecations about Ginger."

The substitution of Ginger for Judy, of course, necessitated some alterations

Gale Robbins is chosen as Ginger's understudy.

321

"Bouncin' the Blues."

Broguing through "My One and Only Highland Fling."

Playwright Jacques Francois insists only
Ginger can play Sarah Bernhardt.

Complications when Fred mistakenly
thinks Ginger is pregnant.

in the script, and particularly in the songs. One casualty: an elaborate minstrel sequence, "Natchez on the Mississip'," which Gershwin and Warren had written especially for Judy Garland. In its place, they revived "They Can't Take That Away from Me," the same haunting George and Ira Gershwin ballad Fred had sung to Ginger on the ferryboat in *Shall We Dance*. In *The Barkleys of Broadway* it served for an elegant dance the two perform at a benefit show.

One unusual touch was the sequence shown behind the film's credits. It had originally been Fred Astaire's notion to dance to a song he wanted titled "Swing Trot," which Gershwin and Warren wrote after all the other songs had been completed. But once the routine—part of a stage revue—was shot, nobody had any idea where to put it. According to Ira Gershwin: "Since the film was plentiful with other numbers and it would have been a pity to cut 'Swing Trot' entirely out, I believe it was Arthur Freed's idea to use a good deal of the number behind the titles, an innovative touch we all thought most interesting for the start of a film musical."

Most of the other numbers in the picture were also presented as part of stage productions. (Two exceptions: "You'd Be Hard to Replace," a song of reconciliation Fred sang to Ginger, and "A Weekend in the Country," which Astaire, Rogers and Levant did scampering over the countryside.) "My One and Only Highland Fling" was a Scottish song and dance which Fred and Ginger brogued their way through wearing kilts, tams, and dour expressions. For his part, lyricist Gershwin was careful to avoid rhyming "MacTavish" with "lavish," since that had already won immortality in an Ogden Nash verse, and instead offered "MacDougall" to go with "frugal."

The instrumental "Bouncin' the Blues" was performed by Astaire and

325

"When I've got shoe's with wings on . . ."

326

Rogers as part of a rehearsal. Backed by a group including such jazz men as clarinetist Gus Bivona and pianist Mel Powell, the team did a radiantly joyous routine that recalled the sparkling informality of "I'll Be Hard to Handle" in *Roberta* and "I'm Putting All My Eggs in One Basket" in *Follow the Fleet.*

"Shoes with Wings On," a rhythmic variation on the theme of dancing, was inspired by a picture of Mercury that the lyricist had seen in a copy of Bulfinch's *Mythology.* In the number, which Astaire choreographed with Hermes Pan's assistance, Fred plays a young man working in a shoe-repair shop. After a dancing customer has left a pair of white shoes on the counter, the shoes suddenly begin to tap by themselves (actually, it was Fred Astaire's disembodied feet doing the tapping). Fred puts on the shoes and—miraculously—begins to dance, while his offscreen voice is heard singing, "When I've got shoes with wings on/ The Winter's gone, the Spring's on. . . ." Presently, two other pairs

of shoes start tapping, then five. They form a circle around Fred and are joined by a pair of ballet slippers. In the climax to the dance, a bit reminiscent of the ending of his classic "Top Hat, White Tie and Tails" number, Fred tries shooting down the unstoppable tapping shoes with a broom. Nothing works, however, until he blasts away at them with pistols—and they all fall down on his head.

When last the audience sees the screen's most scintillating dancing couple, Fred and Ginger are onstage together clad in formal evening dress dancing joyously in front of a backdrop representing New York's Pulitzer Fountain as the chorus sings the lively paean: "Drive up any avenue,/ Swing down any street,/ There's no beat has that Manhattan Downbeat beat!"

The Barkleys of Broadway may have reunited Fred Astaire with his most frequent screen co-star, but it also gave him a different type of male buddy. Instead of the bumbling Hortons, Moores, Benchleys, and Morgans, or the bland Scotts, Bellamys, and Law-

327

fords, he now had the acerbic Oscar Levant to make typically Oscar Levant remarks. Such as the one to a young actress: "You know what I like about you, Gloria? You're free of the slavery of talent." Or, while strolling in the country with Fred and Ginger: "I hope you two have had enough of this good clean fun. Why don't we all go inside and take a sleeping pill?" Or, describing a pushy young actress: "You know, I find that girl completely resistible." Or his advice to Fred: "If at first you don't succeed, give up." Levant was also given the opportunity to perform Khatchaturian's *Sabre Dance,* and to race through Tchaikovsky's B-flat Minor Piano Concerto in six minutes, 52 seconds.

One of the intriguing aspects of *The Barkleys of Broadway* was that even though it was initially supposed to co-star Fred Astaire and Judy Garland, the story presented a dilemma similar to the one Ginger Rogers had faced during her years with Fred Astaire at RKO. Ginger was then desperately trying to break away from musicals and to concentrate not only on comedies but on dramas as well (she had even auditioned for the role of Queen Elizabeth in *Mary of Scotland* but lost out to Florence Eldridge). In *The Barkleys of Broadway,* goaded by an egotistical French playwright, she aspires to dramatic roles and eventually gets the chance to appear in a play as Sarah Bernhardt reciting the "Marseillaise." In French, too! (Miss Rogers might have been spared the critical opprobrium that greeted her reading had the authors stuck to the facts. For her entrance examination to the Paris Conservatoire, the scene depicted in the film, Mlle. Bernhardt had actually recited La Fontaine's fable, "Les Deux Pigeons." Her reading so impressed the judges that she was admitted by the time she got to the end of the second line.)

Though in the film, Ginger's performance is acclaimed, scenarists Comden and Green could never allow Dinah to desert the musical stage.

The dance to "They Can't Take That Away from Me."

Ginger reciting the "Marseillaise."

330

"Manhattan Downbeat," the film's finale.

JOSH: You don't know how great you are. I have an idea for a play.

DINAH: Darling, I don't want to do another play.

JOSH: No more dramas?

DINAH: No biographies.

JOSH: No messages?

DINAH: No worrying about the plot.

JOSH: No?

DINAH: No.

JOSH: Then we'll have nothing but fun set to music!

Just as *Easter Parade* had been an occasion for welcoming Fred Astaire back to movies, so *The Barkleys of Broadway* now became an occasion for welcoming Fred Astaire and Ginger Rogers back together. The press was bountiful in its praise—at least for the team. "The couple is as fresh and as slick as it was in the days of yore," wrote *New York Times'* critic Bosley Crowther. "Fred and Ginger still have that wonderful gaiety and bounce which derive from the singular equating of their personalities. They still have that gift of mutual timing in absolute unison, so that always they're clicking together, whether dancing or trifling with the plot, and of course they are both of them dancers whose talents have never been surpassed on the screen—at least Mr. Astaire's hasn't—and who never looked better with anyone else."

This "singular equating" theme was also picked up by other appraisers. "Like the Barkleys they impersonate, Fred and Ginger need each other more than they suspect," maintained John Rosenfield in the *Dallas Morning News*. In *The New Yorker*, John McCarten found the movie to be "distinguished chiefly by the fact that it brings Astaire and Rogers together once more." And *Time* magazine, which once proclaimed Rita Hayworth to be Fred's ideal partner, now declared flatly: "Ginger is still the best movie dancing partner that Astaire ever had."

But this was to be their final film appearance together. *The Barkleys of Broadway* had made it an even ten.

Mr. and Mrs. Harry Ruby visit Vera-Ellen and Fred Astaire on the set.

Debbie Reynolds and Helen Kane.

THREE LITTLE WORDS

CAST

Bert Kalmar	Fred Astaire
Harry Ruby	Red Skelton
Jessie Brown Kalmar	Vera-Ellen (sung by Anita Ellis)
Eileen Percy Ruby	Arlene Dahl
Charlie Kope	Keenan Wynn
Terry Lordel	Gale Robbins
Mrs. Carter DeHaven	Gloria DeHaven
Phil Regan	Phil Regan
Clanahan	Harry Shannon
Helen Kane	Debbie Reynolds (sung by Helen Kane)
Dan Healy	Carleton Carpenter
Al Masters	Paul Harvey
Al Schacht	George Metkovich
The Great Mendoza	Harry Mendoza
Philip Goodman	Pierre Watkin
Pianist at Party	Harry Barris
Barker	Sid Saylor
Marty	Alex Gerry
Baseball Player	Harry Ruby

Producer: Jack Cummings for Metro-Goldwyn-Mayer. Director: Richard Thorpe. Lyrics: Bert Kalmar. Music: Harry Ruby. Screenplay: George Wells, based on lives of Kalmar & Ruby. Dance director: Hermes Pan. Art directors: Cedric Gibbons, Urie McCleary. Costumes: Helen Rose. Music director: Andre Previn. Orchestrations: Leo Arnaud. Cameraman: Harry Jackson. Editor: Ben Lewis. Color by Technicolor. Release date: July 12, 1950. Running time: 103 minutes.

MUSICAL NUMBERS: "Where Did You Get That Girl?" (Kalmar-Harry Puck)—Astaire & Ellen (sung by Ellis); dance by Astaire & Ellen/ "She's Mine, All Mine"—barbershop quartet/ "Mr. and Mrs. Hoofer at Home"—dance by Astaire & Ellen/ "My Sunny Tennessee" (Kalmar-Ruby-Herman Ruby)—Astaire & Skelton/ "So Long-Oo-Long"—Astaire & Skelton/ "Who's Sorry Now?" (Kalmar-Ruby-Ted Snyder)—DeHaven/ "Come On, Papa" (Edgar Leslie-Ruby)—Ellen (sung by Ellis); dance by Ellen, chorus boys/ "Nevertheless"—Astaire & Ellen (sung by Ellis); dance by Astaire & Ellen/ "All Alone Monday"—Robbins/ "You Smiled at Me"—Dahl/ "I Wanna Be Loved by You" (Kalmar-Ruby-Herbert Stothart)—Astaire, Reynolds (sung by Kane)/ "Up in the Clouds"—chorus/ "Thinking of You"—Ellen (sung by Ellis); dance by Astaire & Ellen; reprised by Dahl/ "Hooray for Captain Spaulding" (incomplete)—Skelton & Astaire/ "I Love You So Much"—Dahl, male chorus/ "You Are My Lucky Star" (Arthur Freed-Nacio Herb Brown)—Regan/ "Three Little Words"—Astaire; reprised by Regan.

For a good many years, Hollywood dearly loved grinding out screen musicals based on the lives of popular songwriters. Because these movies were so crammed full of familiar melodies they had the special advantage of widespread public identification, plus providing studios with the opportunity to put on display their most vocally gifted contractees. As for the story lines that bridged the musical cues, they usually depicted the writers winning recognition through music inspired by their love for particularly inspirational women. Predictably, the films themselves were less memorable than the songs simply because it was difficult to evoke much excitement over a composer struggling through a thirty-two-bar piece of music that everyone immediately recognizes. Generally, too, these biographical treatments were sober affairs, all too careful to treat their heroes with a reverence that all but dehumanized them.

M-G-M, in particular, was noted for the lavishness of its "and-then-I-wrote" productions, as witness such offerings as *Till the Clouds Roll By* (Jerome Kern), *Words and Music* (Rodgers and Hart), and *Deep in My Heart* (Sigmund Romberg). Producer Jack Cummings, however, had a different concept when he secured the film rights to the lives of Bert Kalmar and Harry Ruby. *Three Little Words* boasted no parade of super stars coming in for one or two selections. It devoted little attention to the struggle for recognition along the road to Tin Pan Alley heights. It was simply a light, funny, warm, unpretentious period musical. And it had the offbeat casting of Fred Astaire as Bert Kalmar and Red Skelton as Harry Ruby. (Apart from playing himself in *Dancing Lady* and *Ziegfeld Follies,* this was Fred's second biographical movie. Coincidentally, in his first one, *The Story of Vernon and Irene Castle,* the only new song written for the film was co-authored by Bert Kalmar.)

"Where Did You Get that Girl?"

Since the public is generally unfamiliar with the lives of songwriters or even what they look like, it mattered little that neither Astaire nor Skelton bore much resemblance in either appearance or personality to the man he was portraying. Or that the exiguous plot played more than occasional hob with the facts.

The bare outline of the careers of Bert Kalmar and Harry Ruby went something like this: Bert was born in New York, February 16, 1884. As a child he appeared as a magician in tent shows; later he became a vaudeville comedian, writing lyrics both for his own act and others. Harry was born in New York, January 27, 1895. Although his early aspiration was to become a professional baseball player, he was also devoted to music and was self-taught in the piano. He began his professional career as a song plugger and, for a brief time, was part of an act known as Edwards and Ruby, the "Edwards" being Harry Cohn, who later became the head man at Columbia Pictures. Kalmar met Ruby in vaudeville and they were soon writing occasional songs together. When a knee injury forced Kalmar to retire as a performer, he became a full-time lyricist, and from 1920 on, wrote almost exclusively with Ruby. Among the team's Broadway musicals were *The Ramblers, The Five O'Clock Girl, Good Boy, Animal Crackers* (for the Marx Brothers), and *Top Speed* (Ginger Rogers' first show). In 1930, the writers joined the westward trek to Hollywood. There they wrote songs for Amos 'n Andy's *Check and Double Check* (whence came "Three Little Words") and *The Cuckoos* (another name for *The Ramblers*), and both songs and screenplays for two Marx Brothers classics, *Horse Feathers* and *Duck Soup,* and for Eddie Cantor's *The Kid from Spain.* Bert Kalmar died in 1947, just two days after signing the contract that granted Metro the screen rights to his life story.

Vera-Ellen and agent Keenan Wynn unexpectedly drop in on Fred after his magic act. Red Skelton is the none-too-helpful assistant.

"Mr. and Mrs. Hoofer at Home."

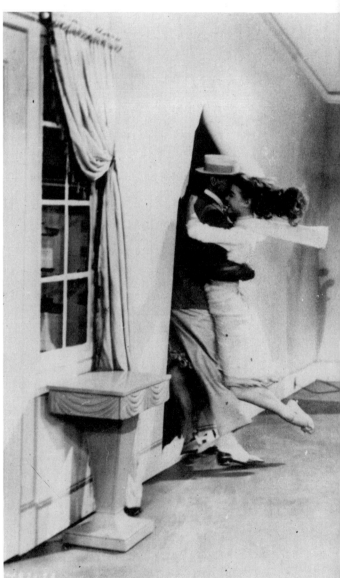

In the movie, Fred Astaire's Bert Kalmar is clearly established as the senior partner of the firm. Bert is the vaudeville headliner who picks the timid song-plugger, Harry Ruby, to be his collaborator. Bert marries his level-headed dancing partner, Jessie Brown, while Harry flits from one grasping female to another. And whenever Harry becomes too involved it's always Bert who extricates him—invariably by hustling him out of town to join his favorite baseball team, the Washington Senators, at its Florida training camp. One especially unusual aspect of Fred Astaire's role was that the part required him to injure his knee about a quarter of the way through the film, thus precluding any dazzling choreographic display for the rest of the picture. There is, however, one agonizing moment when Fred does attempt an intricate tap routine, only to fall with excruciating pain when he bends his knees.

Astaire's newest dancing mate, Vera-Ellen, had made her film debut about five years earlier in *Wonder Man*, starring Danny Kaye, and had more recently been seen opposite Gene Kelly in both *Words and Music* and *On the Town*. Astaire described Miss Ellen as "a brilliant dancing star," and Philip Hamburger in *The New Yorker* wrote that "Astaire has never had a more charming associate." Also prominent in the cast was Arlene Dahl as Eileen Percy, the actress whom Ruby eventually marries. (The film gallantly depicted Miss Percy as a more celebrated performer than she had been in real life. It even had her introduce the song, "I Love You So Much," in *The Cuckoos,* a movie in which she did not appear.)

Since *Three Little Words* was the story of two songwriters, it was of course mandatory that it include scenes showing exactly how they were inspired to create some of their memorable songs. The first such scene occurs in the office of a music publisher. Kalmar, hearing a tune being pounded out in the next room, likes it so much that he has the composer, Ruby, play it for him. But the lyric—"I can't forget the night we met/ On the shores of Araby . . ."—is something else:

Red and Fred sweating out a song.

BERT: You haven't got an Arabian song there. It's more like Dixie, a Dixie tune. Maybe Mississippi, Alabama, Tennessee . . . Sure, look . . . *(He tries it out on the piano.)* "DA da-da DA in Tennessee, da da-da da da da . . ."

HARRY: Gee, that's swell, Mr. Kalmar. Tennessee!

And that one turns out to be "My Sunny Tennessee."

Years later, while the team is in London with a show, Harry calls Bert and Jessie into his hotel room in the middle of the night.

HARRY: Remember those lyrics you wrote for Jessie? I think I got a tune for 'em.

JESSIE *(reading the lead sheet)*: "Thinking of You." You wrote it for me, Bert?

BERT: Yeah, yeah. I wanted to surprise you. But not at two o'clock in the morning.

As Harry plays, Jessie sings the song and follows it with a lighter-than-air dance with Bert.

But the big inspiration song is saved until the end of the picture. Bert and Harry, now in Hollywood, have had a falling out, but their wives conspire to bring them together again on a radio program built around their songs. Realizing that they must prepare something in advance, the men meet at Bert's home and Harry produces a tune he had been vainly trying to interest Bert in ever since they had first met. Soon, however, they start quarreling:

BERT: I wouldn't write that song with you if you begged me.

HARRY: Begged ya? I didn't even ask ya.

BERT: I guess you just can't help it, Harry. I feel sorry for you.

HARRY: Feel sorry for *me*? You must think I'm just a . . .

BERT: I could tell you what I think of you in just three little words. You're a dope!

Trying to dance again after his knee injury.

341

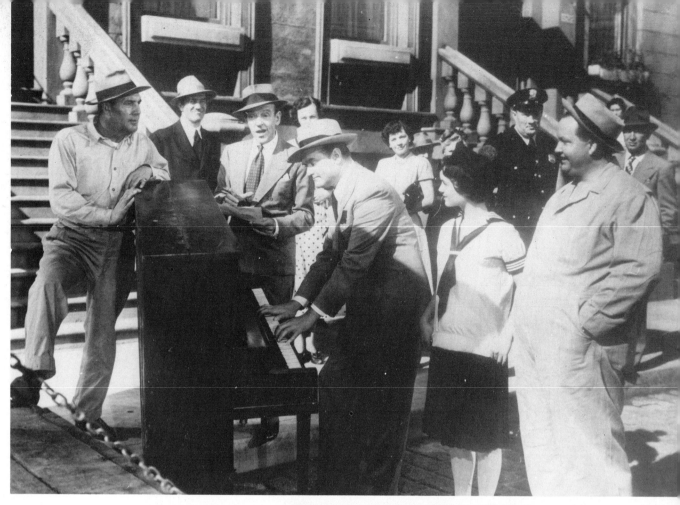

The accidental meeting with Helen Kane (Debbie Reynolds), as she provides the "boop-boop-a-doops" to "I Wanna Be Loved by You."

Yow! That's it! Harry rushes to the piano and starts fitting the words to his melody: "You are a dope. . . . Three little words. . . . It fits! Hey, Bert! Ya got it, Bert! The title of the song!"

Most of the other pieces were more formally introduced as part of vaudeville acts or Broadway shows. The number that opens the picture, "Where Did You Get that Girl?", is performed by Bert and Jessie at the Palace Theatre in 1919. It's a snappy routine, with both dancers attired in top hats, white ties, and tails. Another sequence at the Palace, "Mr. and Mrs. Hoofer at Home," is an extended ballet pantomine, which, according to *The New York Times*' Thomas M. Pryor, "for purity of motion would be hard to equal. With Vera-Ellen as his adept spouse, the incomparable Mr. Astaire nimbly demonstrates the domestic life

Red, as Harry Ruby, at the Washington Senators training camp.

Dancing with Vera-Ellen to "Thinking of You."

The real Harry Ruby makes a quickie appearance.

of a pair of married dancers. The hyphenated young lady beautifully complements her partner in this imaginative, exquisitely conceived and executed number."

In a Buffalo vaudeville house, Jessie Brown—who has gone out as a single because of Bert's knee injury—is "Sweet Marie from Gay Paree," singing and dancing "Come On, Papa," with a chorus of French sailors. Spotting Bert and Harry in the audience, Jessie invites them onstage to introduce their latest song, "Nevertheless"—thus unveiling the number some eleven years before it was actually written.

Two prominent stage personalities were depicted in *Three Little Words,* each with one song to sing. Debbie Reynolds (in her third screen role) played Helen Kane, the "boop-boop-a-doop" girl, whose voice was dubbed

Arlene Dahl singing "I Love You So Much."

Reunion at the film's fadeout.

for Miss Reynolds' singing of "I Wanna Be Loved by You." (Bert's sidewalk discovery of Miss Kane was amusingly done in the film, but the fact is that the baby-voiced singer had already been well established on Broadway before she introduced the song.) The other headliner shown in the movie was Mrs. Carter DeHaven, whose daughter, Gloria DeHaven, played the part and sang "Who's Sorry Now?" In a night club sequence, Gale Robbins, as one of Harry's briefly flickering flames, performs "All Alone Monday," and also gets to do it in the Broadway show, *The Ramblers*.

It was in the same night club scene that *Three Little Words* gave audiences the real lowdown on how songwriters get their big break. At least according to Hollywood. As Bert, Harry and Jessie are sitting at a table, along comes Charlie Kope (Keenan Wynn), the team's dynamic agent:

CHARLIE: Boys, that's Phil Goodman I'm sitting with. The big theatri-

cal producer. He loves your song and he wants it for his next show!

HARRY: Yeah?

CHARLIE: And that's not all. He wants you to write the whole score!

HARRY: A Broadway show?

CHARLIE: Sure!

BERT: Words and music by Kalmar and Ruby!

Reviewers found much to please them in *Three Little Words*. "With the stars at the top of their form," wrote Otis Guernsey, Jr., in the *New York Herald Tribune*, "the whole package is made into a cool and breezy diversion." In *The New York Times*, Thomas M. Pryor was of the opinion that "Mr. Astaire has drawn rich dividends from time and is dancing at peak form." *Variety* went so far as to call *Three Little Words* "unquestiontionably Fred Astaire's best picture in years." And from Astaire himself: "*Words* was an outstanding film and one of my top favorites. I'd like to be doing it all over again."

345

Between takes, Fred with composer-lyricist Frank Loesser.

LET'S DANCE

CAST

Kitty McNeil Everett	Betty Hutton
Don Elwood	Fred Astaire
Edmund Pohlwhistle	Roland Young
Carola Everett	Ruth Warrick
Serena Everett	Lucile Watson
Richard "Richie" Everett VII	Gregory Moffett
Larry Channock	Barton MacLane
Tim Bryant	Sheppard Strudwick
Charles Wagstaffe	Melville Cooper
Marcel (chef)	Harold Huber
Judge MacKenzie	George Zucco
Milton DeLugg	Milton DeLugg
Tommy (pianist)	Tommy Chambers
Bubbles Malone	Peggy Badey
Elsie	Virginia Toland
George (bartender)	James Burke
Dugan (detective)	Oliver Prickett
Mrs. Bryant	Nana Bryant

Producer: Robert Fellows for Paramount Pictures. Director: Norman Z. McLeod. Lyrics & Music: Frank Loesser. Screenplay: Allan Scott & Dane Lussier, from story, "Little Boy Blue," by Maurice Zolotow. Dance director: Hermes Pan. Art directors: Hans Dreier, Roland Anderson. Costumes: Edith Head. Music director: Robert Emmett Dolan. Orchestrations: Van Cleave. Vocal arrangements: Joseph J. Lilley. Cameraman: George Barnes. Editor: Ellsworth Hoagland. Color by Technicolor. Release date: August 11, 1950. Running time: 111 minutes.

MUSICAL NUMBERS: "Can't Stop Talking"—Hutton & Astaire; dance by Hutton & Astaire/ "Piano Dance" (including "Tiger Rag")—dance & piano playing by Astaire/ "Jack and the Beanstalk"—Astaire/ "Oh, Them Dudes"—Astaire & Hutton; dance by Astaire & Hutton/ "Why Fight the Feeling?"—Hutton; reprised as dance by Astaire & Hutton/ "The Hyacinth"—music box; dance by Astaire & Watson/ "Tunnel of Love"—Hutton & Astaire; dance by Hutton & Astaire, chorus. Unused: "The Ming Toy Noodle Company."

Let's Dance offered an invitation most people were reluctant to accept.

In the remarkably small company of minor Fred Astaire movies it may not have been the least worthy, but—despite an occasional high spot—it seems to have been the most ill-advised. Perhaps *Time* magazine put it best when it described the picture as "a talky musicomedy that takes its plot too seriously and its stars special talents too lightly."

Following her screen debut in 1945 in *The Fleet's In*, Betty Hutton had quickly blasted her way to become the zingiest singing and dancing attraction on the Paramount lot. Prior to making *Let's Dance*, her hoyden personality and buoyant good looks had sparked some fifteen films, including *Let's Face It, The Miracle of Morgan's Creek, Here Come the Waves*, and, in a loanout to M-G-M, *Annie Get Your Gun*. But in her one screen appearance opposite Astaire, she was given a role that did its best to dampen her customary flamboyance. Audiences simply could not adjust to a Betty Hutton whose chief concern was saving her fatherless child from the stifling clutches of Back Bay society. As for Fred Astaire's secondary—and second-billed—role, it offered him as a hoofer who, though earning a living dancing in a New York night club, is anxious to give up show business in favor of gambling and financial wheeler-dealering (one of his pet projects is to sell the Brooklyn Dodgers football team). Though this indicates kinship with *Swing Time*'s Lucky Garnett, *Let's Dance*'s Don Elwood turns out to be a more underhanded sort who is not above framing Miss Hutton as a gold digger in order to prevent her marrying his socially prominent friend.

But the most serious flaw in *Let's Dance* was simply that the personalities and styles of the two stars were not particularly well matched on the screen. ("Of the many partners Mr. Astaire has drawn in the movies, Miss Hutton is the least compatible," was the firm verdict of *The New York Times*' Thomas M. Pryor.) On the set, though, Fred found the association

Fred and Betty Hutton dancing to "Can't Stop Talking."

Fred proposes to Betty—only to find out she's already married.

highly stimulating. According to his autobiography, "Working with Betty Hutton keeps anybody on the move. She's so talented and conscientious that if you don't watch yourself you feel you're standing still and letting her do all the work."

On hand to create the songs for *Let's Dance* was Frank Loesser, an experienced Hollywood lyricist who had only recently—with the score for the Broadway musical *Where's Charley?*—established himself as a major composer as well (immediately following *Let's Dance* he wrote the songs for the classic *Guys and Dolls*). For this movie assignment, Loesser turned out a score that was far more attuned to the Hutton voice and delivery than to the Astaire. Every Betty Hutton movie had to have at least one slam-bang, pull-out-all-the-stops number, and *Let's Dance* was no exception (Loesser himself had previously contributed "Murder, He Says," "Papa, Don't Preach to me," and "Rumble, Rumble, Rumble"). The opening routine—performed in wartime London after an air-raid wail had turned into a Betty Hutton high note—was a rumbling item that began: "Can't stop talking about him, and talking about him, and talking about him, I can't stop talking about him, the man that I adore." (The song's sheet music is helpfully marked, "Tempo? You're on Your Own," and the instruction for the refrain is "Roll and Keep Rolling.") Also in the raucous vein were "Oh, Them Dudes," a sprightly lament of a couple of seedy cowpokes—Betty and Fred, both with droopy moustaches—

349

Fred's "Piano Dance,"
with Tommy Chambers at the piano.

who bemoan the affectations of Easterners who have taken to Western dances and clothes ("Look at those varmints wearin' our garmints"). For the finale, there was the equally Huttonized duet, "Tunnel of Love," all about a hot time in the old amusement park.

In a gentler style, "Why Fight the Feeling?" was intended to reveal Betty's more sensitive side, as well as provide a brief dream dance for Fred and Betty. There was also a dainty music-box piece, "The Hyacinth," which supplied the music for a dance between Astaire and Boston dowager Lucile Watson. (The complete lyric for that one would appear to be, "Ah, to be a hyacinth." At least that's all of it Fred sang.)

Fred Astaire did manage to be seen in two numbers of his own that stopped the show—unfortunately only temporarily. During a rehearsal at the night club where he works, Fred effortlessly taps, slides and glides all around, underneath, on top of, and inside a grand piano, which—to the accompaniment of "Tiger Rag"—even disgorges a half-dozen cats. Astaire also performs some jazzy playing at an upright, and ends by blithely sailing over the furniture (shades of *The Gay Divorcee*!). It's the kind of routine that evokes disbelief even while being seen.

The other Astaire specialty was his unorthodox bedtime story narrated to Betty Hutton's son. Because Fred devotes most of his nonhoofing hours to dreaming up outlandish business deals, he sings a nimble Wall Street version of "Jack and the Beanstalk" (during which he manages to roll and tear a newspaper into a beanstalk):

> Yes, Jack was a boy of financial immaturity
> Jack was a big mess in mortgages and liens
> Jack was a kid whose collateral security
> Amounted to a handful of beans.

Like any Fred Astaire movie, *Let's Dance* did have its highlights. It was just a matter of all those dreary stretches in between.

In the kitchen of the night club where she works, Betty puts on an act to convince dowager Lucile Watson that her child has disappeared.

Betty and Fred—"Oh Them Dudes."

The "Tunnel of Love" finale.

ROYAL WEDDING

CAST

Tom Bowen	Fred Astaire
Ellen Bowen	Jane Powell
Lord John Brindale	Peter Lawford
Anne Ashmond	Sarah Churchill
Irving Klinger/Edgar Klinger	Keenan Wynn
Jamie Ashmond	Albert Sharpe
Sarah Ashmond	Viola Roache
Purser	Henri Letondal
Cabby	James Finlayson
Pete Cumberly	Jack Reilly
Billy	John Hedloe
Dick	William Cabanne
Linda	Kerry O'Day
Barbara	Pat Williams
Chester (valet)	Alex Frazer
Charles Gordon (stage manager)	Francis Bethancourt
Telephone Operator	Mae Clarke

Producer: Arthur Freed for Metro-Goldwyn-Mayer. Director: Stanley Donen. Lyrics: Alan Jay Lerner. Music: Burton Lane. Screenplay: Alan Jay Lerner. Associate producer Roger Edens. Dance director: Nick Castle. Art directors: Cedric Gibbons, Jack Martin Smith. Costumes: uncredited. Music director: Johnny Green. Orchestrations: Conrad Salinger, Skip Martin. Cameraman: Robert Planck. Editor: Albert Akst. Color by Technicolor. Release date: February 14, 1951. Running time: 93 minutes.

MUSICAL NUMBERS: "Ev'ry Night at Seven"—Astaire; dance by Astaire & Powell, chorus/ "Sunday Jumps"—dance by Astaire/ "Open Your Eyes" —Powell; dance by Astaire & Powell/ "The Happiest Day of My Life"—Powell, with Astaire, piano/ "How Could You Believe Me When I Said I Love You When You Know I've Been a Liar All My Life?"—Astaire & Powell; dance by Astaire & Powell/ "Too Late Now"—Powell/ "You're All the World to Me"—Astaire; dance by Astaire/ "I Left My Hat in Haiti"—Astaire, chorus; dance by Astaire & Powell, chorus/ "What a Lovely Day for a Wedding"—Londoners.

Late in the summer of 1928, in the midst of a New York heat wave, Fred Astaire and his sister Adele closed their run in the musical *Funny Face* and took the show to London where it repeated its success. While there, Adele met Lord Charles Cavendish, whom she subsequently married, thereby ending her stage career.

Late in the summer of 1947, in the midst of a New York heat wave, Tom Bowen and his sister Ellen closed their run in the musical *Every Night at Seven,* and took the show to London where it repeated its success. On the ship going over, Ellen met Lord John Brindale, whom she married soon after the London opening, thereby ending her stage career.

So much for parallels between the real Fred and Adele Astaire and the roles played by Fred and Jane Powell in the movie called *Royal Wedding.* Alan Jay Lerner's original screenplay also added a romance for Fred—with a saloonkeeper's daughter—and had the film's four principals get married on the very same day as Princess Elizabeth and Philip Mountbatten, Duke of Edinburgh. It was, in fact, the real royal wedding that had first started producer Arthur Freed thinking about a musical with a London background; even before a word of the script had been written, he sent a camera crew to take color shots of the parades and processions. (Lest British audiences mistake the movie for a documentary, the title was changed in England to *Wedding Bells.*)

For a while, though, it looked as if the M-G-M *Royal Wedding* would never take place. Initially scheduled to co-star Fred Astaire and June Allyson, the movie was ten days into

"Ev'ry Night at Seven."

Jane Powell and Fred meet Peter Lawford during a transatlantic crossing.

357

shooting when Miss Allyson announced that she was pregnant and could not continue. Subsequent delays in finding a suitable replacement also resulted in the resignation of director Charles Walters to accept another assignment. Everything seemed set again when Judy Garland agreed to step in, but the actress, who had just completed *Summer Stock,* was in poor health and soon began missing rehearsals. As in the case of *The Barkleys of Broadway,* she was again fired. Over a month went by with neither co-star nor director, when Freed discovered that Jane Powell was available. "While Janie was not primarily a dancer," wrote Astaire in his autobiography, "I knew she could do what was required in this show. She surprised everyone by her handling of the dances." With the signing of director Stanley Donen, the picture, at long last, began to roll. Peter Lawford, Judy Garland's bland suitor in *Easter Parade* was cast as Jane's bland suitor in *Royal Wedding,* and Keenan Wynn repeated his aggressive theatrical agent of *Three Little Words,* only this time he was twice as aggressive, since he also played the agent's British-based (and influenced) twin brother. ("Tell me, old boy, how are things in the colonies these days?" was one of his nifties.) The surprise casting —after Moira Shearer proved unavailable for the part—was that of Sarah Churchill, the Prime Minister's daughter, as the saloonkeeper's daughter. Albert Sharpe, who was seen as the publican, had originated the role of Finian in the Broadway musical *Finian's Rainbow,* a part Fred Astaire would later play in the screen version.

Newspaper and magazine reviewers described the film in such terms as "engaging," "light-hearted," "lightweight," "pleasant," and "spirited," and *Time* maintained that "Fred Astaire has never danced with greater skill or ingenuity." *The New York Times'* critic, Bosley Crowther, however, dismissed the movie with: "It has one swell number built on the world's longest-titled song, three or four that are good, a laugh here, a laugh there, colored newsreels of the British royal wedding, and so long, pal."

358

The "Sunday Jumps" number
in the ship's gymnasium.

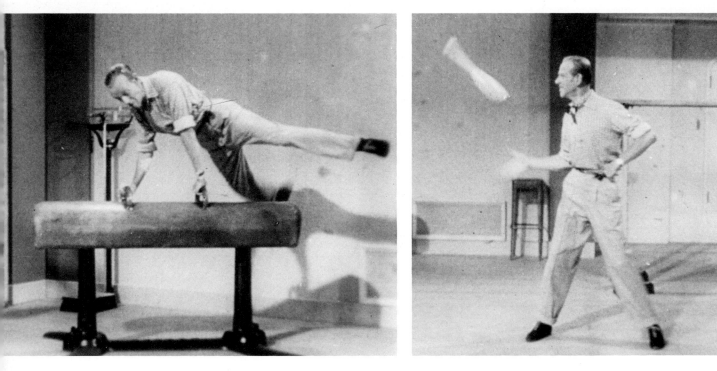

Collaborating on the score with lyricist Lerner was composer Burton Lane, whose *Finian's Rainbow* had opened on Broadway the same season as Lerner's *Brigadoon.* The team wrote nine songs for *Royal Wedding,* with only one, "Too Late Now," conceived with Jane Powell specifically in mind. That "one swell number" cited by Crowther was created almost by accident. Riding to the studio one day, Lerner turned to Lane and said, "You know, this picture is so damn charming it's going to delicate itself to death. What it needs is a real corny vaudeville number. How's this for a title? . . ." And on the spur of the moment he blurted out, "HowcouldyoubelievemewhenIsaidIloveyouwhenyouknowI'vebeenaliarallmylife?" Lane quickly hummed a melody, the two began improvising words and music, and by the time the writers reached the M-G-M lot they had completed almost the entire song. On the screen it turned out to be a suitably raffish Astaire-Powell follow-up to the Astaire-Garland "Couple of Swells" routine in *Easter Parade.*

Royal Wedding opens on a musical sequence in a Broadway revue. The scene is a throne room where "Ev'ry Night at Seven" a tap-dancing king puts aside affairs of state to enjoy a romp with a coquettish chambermaid. It is also the show's next-to-closing night; soon Broadway's royal pair, Tom and Ellen Bowen, are aboard ship en route to England for a West End repeat engagement. During the crossing, Tom takes advantage of the gymnasium to try a few terpsichorean exercises. At first accompanied solely by a metronome and later by the tune, "Sunday Jumps," he uses a clothestree, pulleys, dumbbells, and other gymnastic equipment to perform what *Time* called "a little masterpiece of grace, timing and inventiveness." Also during the crossing, as part of a benefit show for seamen, Ellen entertains by trilling "Open Your Eyes," followed by a brother-sister dance. Only the routine is ruined by the rocking motion of the ship which keeps the couple slipping and sliding

Dancing to "Open Your Eyes," before and after the ship begins to roll.

Sarah Churchill auditions for Fred's show.

The show-stopping "Liar" number.

The gravity-defying dance to
"You're All the World to Me."

362

363

A drink with saloonkeeper Albert Sharpe.
(Sharpe had originated the role of Finian that
Fred later played in the film, *Finian's Rainbow*.)

all over the dance floor. (The situation
was inspired by a similar incident in
1923 when Fred and Adele were on
the *Aquitania* sailing to appear in London in *Stop Flirting*.)

Once in London, there are hectic
days casting, rehearsing and sight-see-
ing (in order not to miss one of the
parades, Ellen is allowed to rehearse
"The Happiest Day of My Life" right
in her hotel room). On the show's
opening night, the curtains part to
reveal brother and sister (she's in a
black wig) as two gum-chewing tough
kids on a street corner trading insults:

ELLEN: Dintcha mudder never teach
ya no manners?

TOM: I never had no mudder. We
wuz too poor.

ELLEN: Say, whatsa matter witcha
lately? Ya used ta tell me ya loved
me. Ya used ta treat me like a high-
class dame. Well, usen'tcha?

TOM: So I used.

Thoroughly exasperated by the nagging filly, Tom demands to know:
"How could you believe me when I
said I love you when you know I've

been a liar all my life?" Ellen joins in
the song, there is a bit of a rowdy
dance—and we know that London
will love them.

At a party following the opening,
Ellen finds herself alone with her ardent suitor, Lord John Brindale (Peter
Lawford), who is fearful that he will
lose her. "Someday," he tells Ellen,
"you might look over your shoulder
and see someone else." And Ellen replies with melodic reassurance: "Too
late now to forget your smile,/ The
way we cling when we've danced a
while,/ Too late now to forget and go
on/ To someone new. . . ."

Tom, however, has been having a bit
tougher time wooing Anne Ashmond
(Sarah Churchill), a dancer in the
show. After removing her photograph
from a display case in front of the
theatre, he returns to his hotel room,
props it against a lamp, and sings the
sprightly Rand-McNally compilation,
"You're All the World to Me." In the
song he likens his beloved to Paris in
April or May, New York on a silvery
day, a Swiss Alp at sunset, Loch
Lomond in autumn, a moonlit night in

Happy newlyweds Peter and Jane and Fred and Sarah.

Capri, and Cape Cod looking out to sea—but no place in England! (The same tune with a different lyric had once been called "I Want to Be a Minstrel Man" when it was sung in the Eddie Cantor movie, *Kid Millions.*) Recalling that Anne had told him about a schoolgirl crush making her feel so good she pretended that she could dance on walls and ceilings, Tom decides to test the theory. And it really works! No pretense about it, either; he can actually dance all over the hotel-room walls and ceiling. (The illusion was created by having Fred dance in an upright position while the room itself revolved with the camera and furnishings anchored to the floor.)

The big production number in Tom and Ellen's musical revue is "I Left My Hat in Haiti," though its chug-chugging samba beat makes it sound rather more indigenously Brazilian than Haitian. Tom sings of his loss alone against a simple backdrop which, suddenly, dissolves into a gaudy set approximating the size of the entire island. There Tom leads the populace —including Ellen—in a brisk, buoyant

pursuit of his blue-grey fedora, and even finds it. A monkey had it.

Royal Wedding had several "firsts." It was the first screenplay written by Alan Jay Lerner (his next would be *An American in Paris*), and it was his first collaboration with composer Burton Lane (they would later write the score for *On a Clear Day You Can See Forever*). The movie also marked the first solo directorial effort of Stanley Donen, who had previously co-directed *On the Town* with Gene Kelly. As for Fred Astaire, this was his first— and only— screen appearance in which he had a sibling relation. Contrary to popular belief, the song title, "How Could You Believe Me When I Said I Love You When You Know I've Been a Liar All My Life?," did not have the distinction of being the world's longest. According to the *Guinness Book of World Records,* that mark was set by Hoagy Carmichael's "I'm a Cranky Old Yank in a Clanky Old Tank on the Streets of Yokohama with My Honolulu Mama Doin' Those Beat-o, Beat-o, Flat-on-My-Seat-o, Hirohito Blues."

THE BELLE OF NEW YORK

CAST

Charles Hill	Fred Astaire
Angela Bonfils	Vera-Ellen (sung by Anita Ellis)
Lettie Hill	Marjorie Main
Max Ferris	Keenan Wynn
Elsie Wilkins	Alice Pearce
Gilford Spivak	Clinton Sundberg
Dixie "Deadshot" McCoy	Gale Robbins
Frenchie	Lisa Ferraday
Frenchie's Girls	Carol Brewster, Meredith Leeds, Lyn Wilde
Officer Clancy	Henry Slate
Judkins	Roger Davis
Men in Welfare House	Tom Dugan, Percy Helton, Dick Wessel

Producer: Arthur Freed for Metro-Goldwyn-Mayer. Director: Charles Walters. Lyrics: Johnny Mercer. Music: Harry Warren. Screenplay: Robert O'Brien & Irving Elinson, adapted by Chester Erskine from stage musical by Hugh Morton (C. M. S. McLennan) & Gustave Kerker. Associate producer: Roger Edens. Dance director: Robert Alton. Art directors: Cedric Gibbons, Jack Martin Smith. Costumes: Helen Rose, Gile Steele. Music director: Adolph Deutsch. Orchestrations: Conrad Salinger, Maurice DePackh. Cameraman: Robert Planck. Editor: Albert Akst. Color by Technicolor. Release date: February 28, 1952. Running time: 82 minutes.

MUSICAL NUMBERS: "When I'm Out with the Belle of New York"—male New Yorkers; reprised as dance by Astaire & Ellen/ "Bachelor Dinner Song" —Astaire; dance by Astaire, Frenchie's girls/ "Let a Little Love Come In" (Roger Edens)—Daughters of Right/ "Seeing's Believing"—Astaire; dance by Astaire/ "Baby Doll"—Astaire; dance by Astaire & Ellen/ "Oops"—Astaire; dance by Astaire & Ellen/ "A Bride's Wedding Day Song" ("Thank You Mr. Currier and Thank You Mr. Ives")—Ellen (sung by Ellis); dance by Astaire & Ellen, chorus/ "Naughty but Nice"—Ellen (sung by Ellis); dance by Ellen; reprised by Pearce/ "I Wanna Be a Dancin' Man"—Astaire; dance by Astaire.

"I'll always remember this old gang of mine."

Making a contribution to Daughter of Right Vera-Ellen.

368

"Seeing's Believing."

Remember *The Belle of New York?*
The movie Fred Astaire was supposed
to make following *Yolanda and the
Thief* back in 1946? Because he had
felt so pessimistic about the project,
Astaire was happy to skip over to
Paramount to appear in *Blue Skies* in
order to avoid doing it. And then to
make certain he would never do it, he
retired from the screen.

All that had occurred six years before. Now that Fred was again an
M-G-M contract player, producer
Arthur Freed dusted off the script and
scheduled it to follow *Royal Wedding.*

The genesis of *The Belle of New
York,* however, went much further
back than 1946—all the way back, in
fact, to 1897, when the same basic
story, but with a different score, was
first presented on Broadway. Though
hardly a success, the tale of the playboy who loves a Salvation Army lass
was transported to London the following year to become not only the first
American musical to play the West
End but also a solid 700-perform-
ance smash. Repeating their original
roles were Harry Davenport (he would
later become one of Hollywood's dear
old codgers in such films as *Gone with
the Wind* and *Meet Me in St. Louis*)
and Edna May, who, though barely
remembered today, was so beloved as
the Belle of New York that she truly
became the Belle of London. The story
even got the silent-film treatment in
1919 when Marion Davies played the
title role and Raymond Bloomer
played the playboy.

As transferred to the musical screen,
The Belle of New York was outfitted
with a brand new Johnny Mercer–
Harry Warren score and a script that
kept the bare bones of the story but
changed all the names—and some of
the genders—of the characters. (There
was also an obvious similarity to Fred's
1930 Broadway show, *Smiles,* since
that one had been likened by many
to the original *Belle of New York.*)
One of the chief attractions of the new
film was the expansion of the fantasy
element of *Royal Wedding.* In the previous movie, to prove conclusively
that he was in love, Fred blithely
danced on the walls and ceiling of his
hotel room; in *The Belle of New York,*

love caused him to perform an even more amazing feat of gravitational defiance: he simply walked and danced on air.

Our tale takes place in the early days of the century—about the same period as *Easter Parade*. Angela Bonfils (Vera-Ellen), an officer in the Daughters of Right (apparently the Salvation Army refused permission to use its name), is so admired by the male population of New York that the men serenade her under her office window with "When I'm Out with the Belle of New York" (though, in truth, none has ever had the pleasure). In another part of the city, playboy Charles Hill (Fred Astaire) is enjoying a bachelor dinner, not with the customary gentlemen friends but with a bevy of call girls from the establishment of a lady known as Frenchie (Lisa Ferraday). To celebrate his forthcoming nuptuals to an Annie Oakley–type performer named Dixie "Deadshot" McCoy, Charles—in the "Bachelor Dinner Song"—invites all the girls to step up for a kiss and a dance all over the banquet table. Suddenly, his Aunt Millie (Marjorie Main), the leader of the Daughters of Right, bursts in on the wild party:

MILLIE: Charles, what is the meaning of this? (*She notices Frenchie's low-cut gown.*) Who is that unclad creature? And what are those obscene remarks she's making?

CHARLES: It's not obscene, it's French.

MILLIE: French *is* obscene.

FRENCHIE: What is the meaning of this "obscene"?

"Baby doll, you beautiful baby doll . . ."

Marjorie Main pays off Fred's jilted bride, Gale Robbins,
as lawyer Keenan Wynn looks on.

CHARLES: It means you'd better go.
FRENCHIE: Very well then. I obscene.

Once the girls have left, Aunt Millie
is appalled by a poster with the likeness of her nephew's intended bride.
"A marriage to a woman like that
ought to be prohibited by law," she
snorts.

Later that night, Charles sees—and
falls in love with—Angela Bonfils as
she is leading a street-corner meeting
near the Washington Square arch. He
brashly confesses his love, but Angela
tells him he doesn't know what love
is. "Love," she explains, "is an emotion that's live, exciting, vibrant. You
feel like a billowy cloud and you walk
on air." And, once Angela has left,
this is exactly what Charles does. Up
up up he goes, all the way to the top
of the arch, where he sings "Seeing's

Believing" to his departed beloved. He
even ventures a buoyant dance on and
around the ledge, and ends up sleeping
on the flagpole.

The next day Charles goes to Wel-
fare House, where Angela works, and
tells her he wants to join the cause
("Frankly, it's the uptrodden who
need saving these days"). To prove his
sincerity, he promises to do an honest
day's work because—as he explains in
the song "Baby Doll"—"To say I'm
fond of you would merely be an attitude,/ To say you're wonderful would
be a platitude. . . ." Then, continuing
his courtship through dance, Charles
gracefully breaks down Angela's resistance until they are in each other's
arms delicately gliding all over the
floor—and again we are treated to the
sight of Fred Astaire's wooing-and-
winning dance-floor technique.

"Oops! The moment that we met, my heart went oops . . ."

Charles gets a job as a streetcar conductor, which gives him the opportunity of following Angela down the street. He even tries charming her by offering a bag of peanuts, saying, "Here, peanuts, I only wish they were diamonds." (With this the writers pilfered a celebrated line first uttered by playwright Charles MacArthur upon meeting his future wife, Helen Hayes. Only MacArthur had wished for emeralds.) Angela calls Charles insane, and he answers: "I should say I am. From the moment I saw you." And he sings, "Oops!/ The moment that we met/ My heart went oops!/ I never will forget/ My heart turned hoops/ The moment that I met you . . ." This is also a logical spot for the couple to perform a bright, flirtatious dance all around the trolley car.

By now Angela as well as Charles is taking to defying the law of gravity. With mutual affection so graphically demonstrated, the next logical step is marriage. But first the two must have their pictures taken by Mr. Currier and Mr. Ives. As Angela sings of their coming nuptuals, the canvas autumnal backdrop becomes a real autumnal setting and the song develops into an extended dance sequence with appropriate Currier and Ives seasonal backgrounds. From badminton playing and swinging in swings, the principals and chorus shift to a winter scene on a Central Park ice-skating rink, and end on a Coney Island boardwalk, where Charles, in striped blazer, dances a clog dance with Angela to the tune of "When I'm Out with the Belle of New York." (Wrote Gilbert Seldes in the *Saturday Review:* "There is a series of scenes after Currier and Ives, all of entrancing beauty; one of them, a skating scene, has a breathless quality

"A Bride's Wedding Day Song."

"Darling, you need someone dependable, a man with both
feet on the ground." Fred tries to keep from rising
in the air by holding onto a table.

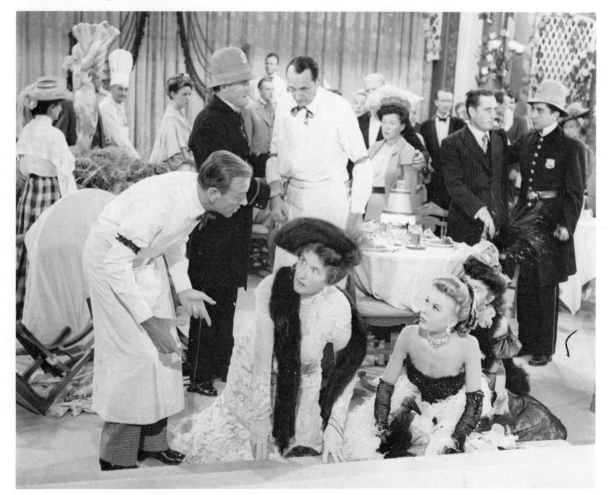

Fred, Marjorie and Vera get involved in a beer-garden brawl.

376

"I wanna be a dancin' man . . ."

Fred rushes after Vera as they both rise in the air . . .

not achieved by the best of the ballet scenes in *An American in Paris*.")

After Charles has a hangover and misses the wedding, he is filled with remorse and gets a job as a singing waiter at Weber's Casino. Somehow this inspires Angela to kick up her heels and go on the town. While dressing in sexy black underclothes and a sequined evening gown, she sings and dances "Naughty but Nice," and then makes a flashy entrance into Weber's. Charles, after being suitably shocked, entertains the patrons with an engaging song and dance, "I Wanna Be a Dancin' Man," which emerges as a particularly personal expression for Fred Astaire.

The last scene of *The Belle of New York* finds Charles and Angela quarreling in the street over Angela's apparent fall from grace. Despite their angry words, however, they rise higher and higher and higher. Once in mid-air, they change into wedding clothes and dance gaily off into the sky.

As she had in *Three Little Words*, Vera-Ellen again revealed herself to be a particularly adept dancing partner for Fred Astaire. And the reviewers were not unappreciative. *The New York Times'* Bosley Crowther found her to be "as graceful and pleasing a dancer as any that has gone before." According to *Newsweek*, "Possibly none of his opposites has ever matched Astaire's personal style so brilliantly." And from Seldes in the *Saturday Review:* "Vera-Ellen dances always as well as and sometimes better than any other partner of Astaire's."

But as with every other movie partner except for Ginger Rogers, two appearances with the master were to be the limit for the former Vera-Ellen Westmeyr Rohe.

378

. . . and dance off together.

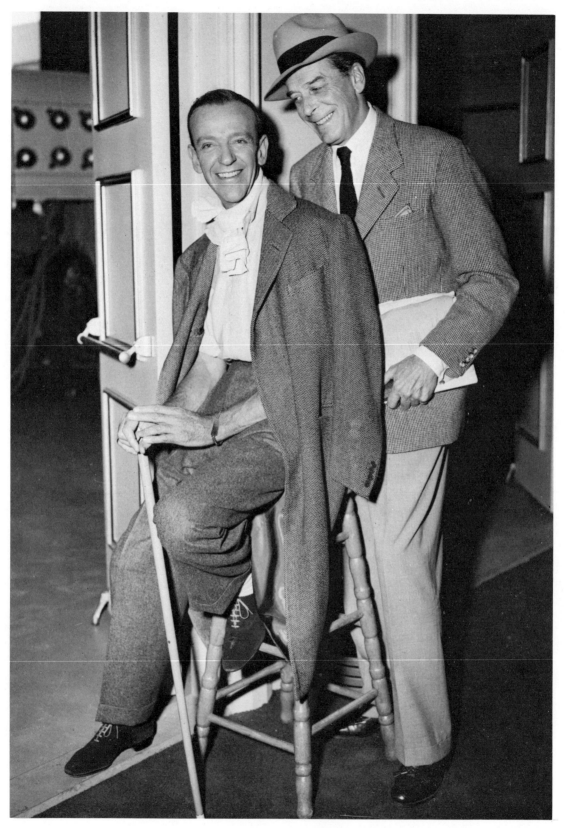

Fred and Jack Buchanan relaxing on the set.

THE BAND WAGON

CAST

Tony Hunter	Fred Astaire
Gabrielle Gerard	Cyd Charisse (sung by India Adams)
Lester Marton	Oscar Levant
Lily Marton	Nanette Fabray
Jeffrey Cordova	Jack Buchanan
Paul Byrd	James Mitchell
Hal Benton	Robert Gist
Col. Tide	Thurston Hall
Bootblack	LeRoy Daniels
Ava Gardner	Ava Gardner

Producer: Arthur Freed for Metro-Goldwyn-Mayer. Director: Vincente Minnelli. Lyrics: Howard Dietz. Music: Arthur Schwartz. Screenplay: Betty Comden & Adolph Green. Associate producer: Roger Edens. Dance director: Michael Kidd. Art directors: Cedric Gibbons, Preston Ames. Settings for musical numbers: Oliver Smith. Costumes: Mary Ann Nyberg. Music director: Adolph Deutsch. Orchestrations: Conrad Salinger, Skip Martin, Alexander Courage. Cameraman: Harry Jackson. Editor: Albert Akst. Color by Technicolor. Release date: July 7, 1953. Running time: 111 minutes.

MUSICAL NUMBERS: "By Myself"—Astaire/ "A Shine on Your Shoes"—Astaire; dance by Astaire & Daniels/ "That's Entertainment"—Buchanan, Fabray, Levant, Astaire; reprised as finale with Charisse (sung by Adams) added/ "Beggar Waltz" ("Giselle")—dance by Charisse, corps de ballet/ "Dancing in the Dark"—dance by Astaire & Charisse/ "You and the Night and the Music" —chorus; dance by Astaire & Charisse/ "Something to Remember You By"—party guests/ "High and Low"—party guests/ "I Love Louisa"— Astaire, with Levant, Fabray, party guests/ "New Sun in the Sky"—Charisse (sung by Adams)/ "I Guess I'll Have to Change My Plan"—Astaire & Buchanan; dance by Astaire & Buchanan/ "Louisiana Hayride"—Fabray, chorus/ "Triplets" —Astaire, Fabray, Buchanan/ "The Girl Hunt" Ballet (narration written by Alan Jay Lerner)— spoken by Astaire; dance by Astaire & Charisse, dancers. Unused: "Got a Bran' New Suit," "Sweet Music," "Two-Faced Woman."

Being greeted at Grand Central Station by
Oscar Levant and Nanette Fabray.

The movie opens in a Los Angeles auction gallery, where the personal effects of former screen star Tony Hunter are being displayed. "Remember these," the auctioneer says admiringly, holding up two items. "Perhaps the most famous top hat and stick of our generation." But the gallery audience is completely indifferent; despite his entreaties, the auctioneer cannot even get the bidding started at fifty cents.

Now everyone knows that the most famous top hat and stick of our generation belong to Fred Astaire. Thus the moviegoer right from the start is encouraged to identify the picture's supposedly forgotten movie star with the actor who is playing the part. And that's not the only link along the way. Tony Hunter is admittedly getting on in years and so is Fred Astaire. Tony's old pictures are being shown in museums and so are Fred's. Tony once had

a big stage hit at the New Amsterdam Theatre on Times Square and so had Fred. And what was the name of the show? *The Band Wagon,* which also happens to be the title of the film in which all this overlapping of identity is taking place.

But despite nagging signs that the movie is a *roman à clef,* it soon becomes clear that these are intended as no more than superficial resemblances. For the fact remains that, unlike Tony Hunter, Fred Astaire was certainly not washed up in Hollywood in 1953. Tony Hunter might not have made a picture in three years but Fred Astaire had been regularly appearing in at least one big budget musical a year since his return to the screen in 1948. And Tony Hunter to the contrary, Fred Astaire never had to return to Broadway to make a comeback.

The Band Wagon was the final film Fred made under his Metro contract.

382

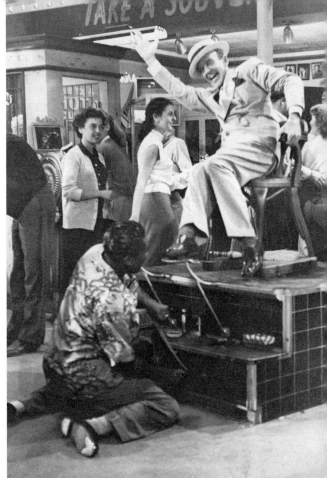

"A Shine on Your Shoes" with LeRoy Daniels.

Curiously, by detailing the preparations of a Broadway-bound musical, the story covered the familiar territory of hopes and setbacks and eventual triumph that had been the concern of Fred's very first movie, *Dancing Lady*. And while the film did have a bright overlay of show-business satire, it also had its moments of show-business bathos (such as the assembled cast serenading the star with "For He's a Jolly Good Fellow" following the musical's successful Main Stem opening).

Betty Comden and Adolph Green, the authors of *The Band Wagon*, had also written the screenplay for one other Fred Astaire film, *The Barkleys of Broadway*. That one had dealt with the problems confronting a married song-and-dance team when the wife decides to take a fling at serious drama. In *The Band Wagon*, Comden and Green took up the problem of what happens when a director of serious drama decides to take a fling at directing a song-and-dance show. Despite both films' insistence that there is no basic difference between musicals and dramas, they actually proved the reverse: the musical-comedy actress of *The Barkleys of Broadway* could only be happy in her accustomed field, and the director in *The Band Wagon* makes a total botch of staging his first musical—which is saved only when Tony and the gang give it that old Broadway know-how.

The inspiration of *The Band Wagon* was the successful Broadway revue of 1931 that had starred Helen Broderick and Frank Morgan along with Fred and Adele Astaire. Apart from Fred, however, all that remained of the show were five of the original seventeen Howard Dietz–Arthur Schwartz songs. To these were added eight other Dietz and Schwartz numbers from other shows (at least three more had to be cut because of time), plus a new song,

Jack Buchanan convinces James Mitchell to let his fiancée, ballerina Cyd Charisse, appear in a musical comedy.

Coached by director Buchanan, Fred goes dramatic during a rehearsal.

"That's Entertainment," and the extended "Girl Hunt" ballet. (A 1949 picture, *Dancing in the Dark,* had also utilized songs from *The Band Wagon* to augment a story about a washed-up actor, played by William Powell, who discovers a Broadway actress to star in a movie version of *The Band Wagon.*)

The picture also served to pair Fred Astaire with one of his loveliest-limbed co-stars, Cyd Charisse, who had briefly danced near him—but not with him—in *Ziegfeld Follies.* "Cyd is a terrific dancer, a wonderful partner," wrote Astaire in his autobiography. "She has precision plus—beautiful dynamite, I call it." Newspaper and magazine appraisers were equally admiring. Including the gentleman at *Time* who hailed her as "a new partner who can fill the shoes—and the nylons—of the best of Astaire's former dancing partners."

In addition to giving Fred Astaire a role that was inspired to a degree by Fred Astaire, writers Comden and Green wrote parts for Nanette Fabray and Oscar Levant that resembled writers Comden and Green. (For the scene at Grand Central Station, the idea of having Fabray and Levant greet Astaire carrying "fan-club" signs stemmed from an actual occasion in which Comden had once greeted Green at the same station carrying a "fan-club" sign.) Some of Levant's lines, however, sounded like pure—if repetitive—Levant. Such as his remark after being accidentally kicked: "I can stand anything but pain." Or his remark after the show's disastrous try-out opening: "I can stand anything but failure." In the role of the explosive director (originally earmarked for Clifton Webb), England's dapper Jack Buchanan played a character who, according to the film's director, Vincente Minnelli, was "a cross between Orson Welles, stage designer Norman Bel Geddes and José Ferrer, who had at that time done similar pretentious productions." Those who knew Minnelli, however, couldn't help but notice that Buchanan's clothes and the nervous way he smoked were copied from the director himself.

"I am not Nijinski. I am not Marlon Brando. I am Mrs. Hunter's little boy, Tony, song-and-dance man . . ." Fred tells off Buchanan before walking out on the show.

Despite carping about the tiredness of *The Band Wagon* plot, most reviewers turned in rave notices. Bosley Crowther in *The New York Times* maintained that it was "a show that respectfully bids for recognition as one of the best musical film ever made." Otis Guernsey, Jr., the *New York Herald Tribune* critic, called it "a big load of musical comedy pleasure." *Newsweek* put Astaire and Charisse on its cover and dubbed the film "a gala and witty enterprise with a brisk and funny original script. . . . Astaire is to show-dancing what Leonide Massine was in such elegant ballets as *Beau Danube*—all formal elegance, a steady demonstration of the exquisite restraint which permits the electrifying release." As for Fred Astaire himself, he was once quoted as saying, "I loved the picture. All except the first few minutes."

After those first few minutes during which the movie star's top hat and cane were being auctioned, *The Band Wagon* puts Tony Hunter on an eastbound train where he must endure some heavy-handed gaucheries about his being all washed up in pictures. Alone and ignored when he arrives at Grand Central Station, Tony ruefully acknowledges his solitude by singing "By Myself" as he jauntily walks down the station platform.

But his old pals Lily and Lester Marton (Nanette Fabray and Oscar Levant) haven't forgotten him. They greet him in the terminal with the exciting news that they have written the libretto for a musical that would be just perfect for him to do on Broadway. They have even persuaded the theatre's current wonderman, Jeffrey Cordova (Jack Buchanan) to produce and direct it. Lester assures Tony that even though Cordova has never done a musical before he would do a great job. Why, he's got three hits running and he's starring in one of them. Tony's only reaction is a mock-innocent, "Only one of them?"

Walking along Forty-second Street, Tony is appalled at the honkytonk atmosphere until he comes upon an

In a Central Park setting,
"Dancing in the Dark" with Cyd Charisse.

"We're gonna put this thing across, aren't we kids?"

exuberant bootblack (LeRoy Daniels) energetically shining and tapping away. Suitably inspired, Tony bucks up his spirits by bucking and winging "A Shine on Your Shoes" all around a garish amusement center.

Backstage at the theatre, where Jeffrey Cordova is starring in *Oedipus Rex,* Tony expresses bewilderment that he would be so anxious to direct a musical. Cordova has a stock anser: "In my mind there is no difference between the magic rhythms of Bill Shakespeare's immortal verse and the magic rhythms of Bill Robinson's immortal feet. I tell you, if it moves you, if it stimulates you, if it entertains you, it's theatre!"

But Cordova, apparently, still hasn't even read the script and Lily and Lester proceed to give him a brief outline of the fun-filled jamboree. Cordova, however, sees the show as a modern version of *Faust,* full of meaning and stature, and tries to sell the unimpresssed Tony on the idea:

JEFFREY: We're going to make you explode on the theatre scene like a skyrocket. Not just the old trademark with the top hat, white tie and tails, but a great artist at the peak of his powers. Tony Hunter 1953!

TONY: Well, whatever I am, whether it's a new me or an old me, remember I'm still just an entertainer.

JEFFREY: Well, what do you think I am? What do you think the theatre is? It's all entertainment. Believe me, there is no difference between the magic rhythms of Bill Robinson's immortal feet . . .

LESTER: You said that before.

JEFFREY: All right, all right. Well, what did Bill Robinson do? He danced on the stairs, didn't he? Now I happen to play Oedipus the King on the same stairs. What's the difference? We're all theatre. *(He begins to tap dance on the stairs.)* Show me the greatest tragic actor or the lowest red-dog comic in burlesque, and I'll show you an entertainer. We're all entertainers!

388

The old soft shoe to
"I Guess I'll Have to Change My Plan."

With the aid of Lily and Lester, Jeffrey convinced the reluctant Tony through the rapid-fire compilation, "That's Entertainment," in which just about everything in life is itemized as entertainment—for Oedipus Rex to a clerk losing his job, and from reading a will to waving a flag. Tony signifies his agreement by joining them both in song and in a series of wacky sight gags.

It's Jeffrey's idea to co-star Tony with the beautiful ballet dancer, Gabrielle Gerard (Cyd Charisse), and Lily, Lester, and Tony take in her performance as Giselle (set to the music of Arthur Schwartz's "Beggar Waltz"). Later that night, Tony meets Gabrielle at Jeffrey's home and compliments her on her dancing:

GABRIELLE: I'm a great admirer of yours, too.

TONY: Oh, I didn't think you'd ever heard of me.

GABRIELLE: Heard of you? I used to see all your pictures when I was a little girl. And I'm still a fan. I recently went to see a revival of them at the museum.

TONY *(his pride hurt)*: Museum? Step right this way, ladies and gentlemen, Egyptian mummies, extinct reptiles, and Tony Hunter, the grand old man of the dance.

The relationship between the two slides downhill from there until one day during rehearsal Tony tells everyone off and quits the show. After Gabrielle visits him at his hotel to apologize, they take a walk in Central Park where they hear a band playing "Dancing in the Dark." To find out if they really are able to dance together the two are soon in each other's arms gliding about tenderly to the strains of the melody. As they end up leaping into a horse-drawn carriage, there is no doubt that Tony will stay in the show if only to stay close to Gabrielle.

Fred, Nanette and Jack in the "Triplets" number.

390

"The Girl Hunt" ballet subway scene.

But their show, *The Band Wagon,* is a pretentious mess. A dress rehearsal of the dance to "You and the Night and the Music" is ruined when some weird explosive effects get out of hand, and the New Haven tryout opening the following night is a total disaster. Before the performance begins, a chattering, expectant throng is jamming its way into the theatre as Col. Tide (Thurston Hall), the show's blustering chief backer, dashes about inviting one and all to his after-theatre party ("Champagne's on me!"). The doors close and suddenly an eerie, doom-laden moaning is heard, accompanied first by the sight of a stark, repellent stage setting, then by a huge egg that fills the entire screen. The audience emerges with ashen, drawn faces, and Col. Tide, his wattles sagging, now has only the one desire to beat a hasty retreat back to New York. (As director Minnelli once told an interviewer: "All the out-of-town scenes, the moment when things go wrong at a first night, were terribly authentic, autobiographical.")

At the local hotel, the boys and girls of the chorus still go through with the traditional opening-night party, even though they know the show is a bomb. With Tony, Lily, and Lester leading, they clown through an old Tony Hunter number, "I Love Louisa" (which Astaire had first sung in *The Band Wagon* on Broadway). Once the singing is over, they are all again faced with grim reality, and Lester blurts out one of Hollywood's favorite show-business bromides: "Gosh, with all this raw talent around, why can't us kids get together and put on ourselves a show!" Bromide or not, it spurs Tony into action, and he tells Jeffrey they're not closing the show. "We're going on," Tony says. "We're

392

"The Girl Hunt" ballet barroom scene.

gonna keep it on the road and we're gonna redo it from top to bottom. It won't be a modern version of *Faust, Pilgrim's Progress,* or the *Book of Job* in swingtime. It'll be our show. The show we started out to do. The book the Martons wrote. It'll have laughs and entertainment."

And, by God, they do it! Even Jeffrey stays with them, but now, of course, he's just another member of the cast. Although Tony has insisted that they will go back to the original libretto, what emerges after six weeks on the road is obviously a revue: Gabrielle sings the exultant "New Sun in the Sky" at the first stop. . . . Hunter and Cordova, in top hat, white tie, and tails, strut through "I Guess I'll Have to Change My Plan" at the second. . . . Lily leads the chorus in proclaiming the joys of a "Louisiana Hayride" at another. . . . Lily, Jeff and Tony, wearing baby clothes and walking on their knees, sing of the woes of being "Triplets" at still another.

Opening night in New York does finally arrive. In the one number that we see—"The Girl Hunt" ballet—choreographer Michael Kidd evolved a takeoff on the Mickey Spillane school of literature. With Tony doing the offstage narration (written by an uncredited Alan Jay Lerner), the scene opens with Tony as white-suited private eye Rod Reilly prowling the early-morning streets ("The city was asleep. The joints were closed. The rats and hoods and killers were in their holes. I hate killers"). Suddenly he spots a frightened blonde, played by Gabrielle ("I can smell trouble a mile off. And this kid was in trouble. Big trouble. She was scared. Scared as a turkey in November"). After a hood has been blasted before his eyes, Rod is beaten up by a gang ("So that's the way they wanted to play it. All right. Somewhere in the city there was a killer. And that

"For he's a jolly good fellow . . ."

394

DADDY LONG LEGS

CAST

Jervis Pendleton	Fred Astaire
Julie André	Leslie Caron
Linda Pendleton	Terry Moore
Melissa Pritchard	Thelma Ritter
Griggs	Fred Clark
Sally McBride	Charlotte Austin
Ambassador Alexander Williamson	Larry Keating
Gertrude Pendleton	Kathryn Givney
Jimmy McBride	Kelly Brown
Mr. Bronson	Ralph Dumke
Miss Carrington	Kathryn Card
Guide	Joseph Kearns
Mme. Sevanne	Ann Codee
Larry Hamilton	Damian O'Flynn
Pat Withers	Sara Shane
Jeweler	David Hoffman
Athletic Girl Dancer	Janice Carroll
Band at Prom	Ray Anthony Orchestra

Producer: Samuel G. Engel for 20th Century-Fox. Director: Jean Negulesco. Lyrics & Music: Johnny Mercer. Screenplay: Phoebe & Henry Ephron, from novel & play by Jean Webster. Dance directors: David Robel, Roland Petit. Art directors: Lyle Wheeler, John DeCuir. Costumes: Charles Le-Maire, Kay Nelson, Tom Keogh. Ballet music: Alex North. Music director: Alfred Newman. Orchestrations: Edward Powell, Skip Martin, Earle Hagen, Bernard Mayers, Billy May. Vocal arrangements: Ken Darby. Cameraman: Leon Shamroy. Editor: William Reynolds. Filmed in CinemaScope. Color by Deluxe. Release date: May 4, 1955. Running time: 126 minutes.

MUSICAL NUMBERS: "History of the Beat"—Astaire; drumming & dance by Astaire/ "C-A-T Spells Cat"—Caron/ "Daddy Long Legs"—chorus/ "Welcome Egghead"—college students/ Daydream Sequence (Texas Millionaire-International Playboy-Guardian Angel)—dance by Astaire & Caron, chorus/ "Dream"—vocal quintet, Anthony Orchestra; dance by Astaire & Caron/ "Sluefoot"—vocal quintet, Anthony Orchestra; dance by Astaire & Caron, students/ "Something's Gotta Give"—Astaire; dance by Astaire & Caron/ "Dancing Through Life" ballet (Paris - Hong Kong - Rio de Janeiro (North)—Caron, dancers, with Astaire.

The success of *The Band Wagon* should have spurred Hollywood studios to start combing through their vaults in search of properties suitable for a middle-aged dancer to appear in playing a middle-aged dancer. But it didn't work out quite that way and, with his M-G-M contract expired, and no subsequent offers, Fred Astaire again contemplated permanent retirement. Surprisingly, it was 20th Century-Fox, where Astaire had never made a picture, that gave him reason to change his mind.

Daddy Long Legs had been around for a long time. Jean Webster's sentimental novel, which was published in 1912, dealt with a wealthy New Orleans businessman, who, to forestall possible gossip about the purity of his motives, becomes the anonymous sponsor of a young orphan-girl's education. Eventually, the two meet, fall in love, and head for marriage. The title refers to the fact that, initially, the only sight the girl has of her benefactor is his distorted, spidery shadow, thus prompting the lovable waif to dub him her Daddy Long Legs.

The author dramatized the story in 1914, with Ruth Chatterton as orphan Judy Abbott and Charles Waldron as benefactor Jervis Pendleton. Mary Pickford and Mahlon Hamilton appeared in the first film version in 1919, and Janet Gaynor and Warner Baxter were the May-December lovers in 1931. Since 20th Century-Fox owned the screen rights, studio head Darryl Zanuck had been toying with the idea of a musical version at least since 1951 when it was announced (but then abandoned) as a vehicle for Mitzi Gaynor. The following year, as *Love from Judy,* it did get a musical treatment, but on the London stage not the Hollywood screen. Jeannie Carson and Bill O'Connor appeared in it, with Hugh Martin and Timothy Gray responsible for the score.

Leslie Caron at the French orphanage.

398

In the "Daydream Sequence,"
Fred appears as a Texas Millionaire . . .

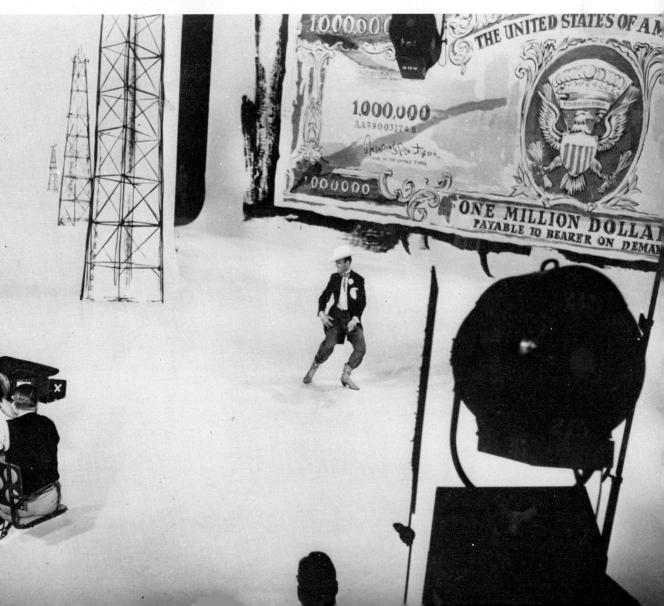

For the newly reincarnated—and updated—*Daddy Long Legs,* the story was kept basically the same except that instead of an American waif named Judy Abbott the girl became a French waif named Julie André. Why? Because Darryl Zanuck wanted the part played by Leslie Caron—who had recently scored impressively in *An American in Paris* and *Lili*—and Leslie Caron was unalterably French (she even referred to her Daddy Long Legs as "Papa Faucheux"). Actually, all that scriptwriters Phoebe and Henry Ephron had to do to accommodate the change in nationality was to put Jervis on some sort of State Department mission that takes him to France early in the film just so that he might discover the girl in an orphanage outside Paris. Later on, they worked in a bit about the suspicious American ambassador to France (Larry Keating), who questions Jervis's motives in sponsoring Julie's education in the United States. "You've changed her whole life, for which she must be very grateful," he tells the millionaire. Jervis protests. "She doesn't know I'm her Daddy. . . ." "Daddy what?" snaps the ambassador. "Daddy Sugar?"

According to Astaire, the script was "one of the best ever to come my way," and, in general, the critical consensus was favorable. "There could have been no happier choice for a dancing Daddy Long Legs than leaping, gliding, genial, warbling papa Fred Astaire," wrote Irene Thirer in the *New York Post.* "There's something about Fred Astaire that is always youthful, and he is ideally suited to this bright song and dance version," was the verdict of William K. Zinsser in the *New York Herald Tribune.* "At 55, Fred Astaire remains head man among American hoofers. His dancing is as graceful and as effortless as ever," claimed *Newsweek. "Daddy Long Legs* gives Fred Astaire one of his best opportunities in ages to display both his peculiar charm and his dancing skill," was Arthur Knight's view in the *Saturday Review.*

About Astaire's latest co-star (the only one, incidentally, whose back-

... and as Leslie Caron's Guardian Angel.

ground had been exclusively in ballet), there were conflicting opinions. Arthur Knight maintained: "With Leslie Caron, Fred Astaire has a dancing partner wholly worthy of his talent. Their numbers together rank with the best things he has ever done." But *Time* countered with: "Fred and Leslie dance prettily when separated, but when they get together the ballerina looks about as comfortable in a two-step as Fred would in a tutu." On the other hand, *Newsweek* held: "Leslie Caron becomes probably the most delightful partner Astaire has had on the screen." Then there was the verdict of *The New Yorker*'s John McCarten: "Although a capable enough practitioner of ballet, Leslie Caron is no Ginger Rogers when it comes to picking them up and putting them down in the breezy Astaire style." William Zinsser, however, was of the opposite opinion: "Fred Astaire has waited twenty years for the right partner to come along and now the search seems to be over. Let's hope he makes as many movies with Miss Caron as he did with Miss Rogers." But *Daddy Long Legs* turned out to be the first and last for the team of Fred Astaire and Leslie Caron.

It was Astaire who asked for Johnny Mercer to write the songs for the film primarily, he claimed, because he had long admired Mercer's languid, eleven-year-old ballad, "Dream," which provided the film with both a dance number for Astaire and Caron and a suitable theme for the girl's daydreams. Also prominently displayed was a new dance step, "Sluefoot," a collegiate successor to "The Carioca," "The Continental," "The Piccolino," "The Yam," and "The Shorty George." Then there was the chief new ballad, "Something's Gotta Give." Fred sang this amatory application of physical law ("When an irresistible force such as you/ Meets an old immovable object like me") in a hotel balcony scene to reveal how powerless he was to resist falling for Leslie. Then it's on the town for an all-night dancing spree.

401

The nature of the story provided French choreographer Roland Petit with the opportunity to create two extended dream sequences (either or both are all too often excised on television). Though Julie André has been writing to her unseen benefactor "John Smith" for two years, he has never answered any of her letters. Daydreaming in her room at college, she wonders if he is bald or if he is old. But then she decides it's more fun not to know; she can imagine him to be whatever she wants him to be. First she dreams that he is a Texas millionaire—and there is Jervis, in ten gallon hat and spurs, prancing about in a square dance. (That basso voice, of course, did not belong to Fred Astaire. It belonged to voice-dubber Thurl Ravenscroft.) Next—to a tango rhythm—Julie imagines Jervis to be an international playboy. Finally, he is her guardian angel (shades of *Yolanda and the Thief*), and Jervis materializes to perform an appropriately tender slow polka with Julie. (Despite the inventiveness and charm of these three dances, it would have been a bit difficult for Julie to dream of Jervis at that time, since she had no idea who he was, nor in fact had she even laid eyes on him.)

The second ballet sequence occurs two years later. Though Julie is still in the dark about the identity of her Daddy Long Legs, she has met Jervis and has fallen in love with him. Because of the stickiness of this romantic development, Jervis now spends most of his time traveling around the world, and Julie spends most of her time mooning over newspaper accounts of his travels. Once more—with the strains of "Dream" heard in the background—she dreams up a Roland

Doing the "Sluefoot."

402

"Something's Gotta Give."

"Dancing Through Life" in Paris,
Hong Kong and Rio de Janeiro.

Petit ballet. This time she pursues Jervis, first as a ballet dancer in the Paris Opera, then as a slinky demi-mondaine in a Hong Kong den, and finally as a Pierrette in a colorful Rio de Janeiro street carnival. But no matter where she dances, Jervis manages to elude her grasp. (In *A Star Is Born,* released some nine months before *Daddy Long Legs,* Judy Garland entertained husband James Mason by satirizing a spectacular movie production number in which a girl searches for a lover in Paris, China, Africa, and Brazil.)

Rehearsals for *Daddy Long Legs* began in July 1954, with the shooting scheduled for September. At about that time, Phyllis Astaire, Fred's wife, had to undergo an operation for cancer. Although at first she seemed to be recovering, her condition soon deteriorated and she died in mid-September. Fred desperately tried to get out of the new assignment but producer Samuel Engel and director Jean Negulesco per-suaded him to return early in October.

The 20th Century-Fox high command was well satisfied with the results of the film, and despite Fred's feeling that perhaps the time had really come for him to retire as an actor, the studio signed him for a second film. Tentatively titled *Dry Martini,* it was to be produced, directed and written by the same team responsible for *Daddy Long Legs,* but the plans fell through. Fred then signed a contract with Paramount calling for two pictures to be made over a period of three years. The first was to have been another co-starring venture with Bing Crosby, but Crosby took off to M-G-M to make *High Society,* and Paramount never heard from him again. Then they put *Papa's Delicate Condition* on Fred's schedule, but it also had to be abandoned (Jackie Gleason later did it, but without music) when Astaire became involved in still another project, this one co-starring him with Audrey Hepburn.

404

Adele and Fred in
the stage *Funny Face*.

Audrey and Fred in
the screen *Funny Face*.

406

FUNNY FACE

CAST

Jo Stockton	Audrey Hepburn
Dick Avery	Fred Astaire
Maggie Prescott	Kay Thompson
Prof. Emile Flostre	Michel Auclair
Paul Duval	Robert Flemyng
Marion	Dovima
Babs	Virginia Gibson
Dancers in "Pink" Number	Suzy Parker, Sunny Harnett
Lettie	Ruta Lee
Devitch	Alex Gerry
Hairdresser	Jean DeVal
Armande	Iphigenie Castiglioni
Sidewalk Café Patrons	Baroness Van Heemstra, Roger Edens
Laura	Sue England
Gigi	Karen Scott
Mimi	Diane DuBois
Mr. Baker	Nesdon Booth

Producer: Roger Edens for Paramount Pictures. Director: Stanley Donen. Lyrics: Ira Gershwin, Leonard Gershe. Music: George Gershwin, Roger Edens. Screenplay: Leonard Gershe, from his unproduced stage musical, *Wedding Day*. Dance director: Eugene Loring. Art directors: Hal Pereira, George W. Davis. Costumes: Edith Head, Hubert de Givenchy. Visual consultant: Richard Avedon. Music director: Adolph Deutsch. Orchestrations: Conrad Salinger, Van Cleave, Alexander Courage, Skip Martin. Cameraman: Ray June. Editor: Frank Bracht. Filmed in VistaVision. Color by Technicolor. Release date: March 28, 1957. Running time: 103 minutes.

MUSICAL NUMBERS: "Think Pink!" (Gershe-Edens) —Thompson, office workers/ "How Long Has This Been Going On?" (Gershwin-Gershwin)— Hepburn/ "Funny Face" (Gershwin-Gershwin)— Astaire; dance by Astaire & Hepburn/ "Bonjour, Paris!" (Gershe-Edens)—Astaire, Thompson, Hepburn, chorus/ "Basal Metabolism"—dance by Hepburn/ "Let's Kiss and Make Up" (Gershwin-Gershwin)—Astaire; dance by Astaire/ "He Loves and She Loves" (Gershwin-Gershwin)—Astaire; dance by Astaire & Hepburn/ "On How to Be Lovely" (Gershe-Edens)—Thompson & Hepburn/ "Marche Funebre" (Edens)—uncredited French singer/ "Clap Yo' Hands" (Gershwin-Gershwin) —Astaire & Thompson/ " 'S Wonderful"—Astaire & Hepburn; dance by Astaire & Hepburn.

"Think Pink!"

Funny Face was put together by combining the title and songs of one stage musical with the story intended for another—and was put on the screen by combining one Hollywood studio with the production personnel of another.

This hybrid genesis originated when screen writer Leonard Gershe wrote a story called *Wedding Day* which he planned to have produced as a Broadway musical. When the project fell through, he sold the rights to M-G-M producer Roger Edens, whose idea was to embellish the tale with songs the Gershwin brothers had written some thirty years before for the Broadway musical *Funny Face*. Edens promptly lined up director Stanley Donen and co-stars Audrey Hepburn and Fred Astaire and scheduled the movie for immediate production. And then he

was almost forced to abandon the whole thing.

Since Edens, Gershe, and Donen were all under contract to Metro, they assumed there would be little trouble borrowing the services of Hepburn and Astaire from Paramount and purchasing the Gershwin score from Warner Brothers, which controlled the music. But obstacles loomed so large that for a while they seemed insurmountable. Months dragged on as Edens tried to work out an agreement satisfactory to everyone. Eventually all the pieces fell into place when Warners agreed to sell the *Funny Face* songs to M-G-M, which then sold them—along with Messrs. Edens, Gershe, and Donen—to Paramount.

In a way it was fitting that Paramount get the nod, since the entire project really depended upon Miss

Fred and Kay Thompson take over
Audrey's Greenwich Village bookstore.

"How Long Has This Been Going On?"

Hepburn who, after four starring roles, had risen to become the brightest female star on the Paramount lot. It was she who had insisted that Fred Astaire appear opposite her in what was to be not only her first film musical but the only one in which she would be heard singing (her "voice" in *My Fair Lady* was Marni Nixon's). Though not primarily known as a dancer, Miss Hepburn had had extensive training in ballet schools in Holland and England, and also with Adele Astaire's coach, Buddy Bradley.

Funny Face was unquestionably the most stunningly photographed of any film in which Fred Astaire has appeared. For the first time color was used with a boldness and ingenuity that made the movie as much of a treat for its sheer aural sensations as it was for its songs, dances, and performances. There was good reason for this. Since the picture dealt with a fashion-magazine photographer on assignment in Paris and since the character of the photographer was based on a real fashion-magazine photographer, Richard Avedon, producer Edens hired Avedon as the film's "visual consultant." It was largely through his efforts that the movie achieved its extra dimension of pictorial excitement.

Many striking images are quickly recalled—the dazzling opening with its emphasis on pink as the new color rage in fashion . . . the dance between Audrey and Fred in a photographer's darkroom illuminated solely by the faint glow of a ruby lightbulb . . . the splitscreen views of Paris . . . the soft-focus, Corot-influenced scene on the lawn of a rustic French church . . . the way each scene photographed for a magazine layout was frozen as a still picture, first in negative, then as a black-and-white positive, and finally with spots of color added bit by bit to isolated areas. As *Newsweek* observed: "The charm, the elegance, the nutty pictorial poetry to be found in the classier fashion photographs have all been preserved on the screen. In fact, they have been enhanced by being stirred into lovely motion and bathed in a kind of springlike misty color, shot through with neon lights."

Back in 1928, while starring in *Funny Face,* on the stage, Fred and Adele Astaire had made a screen test for Walter Wanger, who was interested in filming the musical. Nothing, however, came of it. Nor was Fred's appearance in the screen *Funny Face* directly linked to his stage appearance, as had been the case of the equally altered movie version of *The Band Wagon.* Like *The Band Wagon,* however, the new *Funny Face* did possess the characteristics of a *roman à clef.* Apart from Fred Astaire's Dick Avery being modeled after Dick Avedon, Kay Thompson (in her screen debut) played a magazine editor, Maggie Prescott of *Quality,* who was inspired by Carmel Snow of *Harper's Bazaar.* Michel Auclair's Professor Flostre, the leader of the philosophical movement called Empathicalism, had a name intended to suggest both Jean-Paul Sartre, the leader of Existentialism, and the Café de Flore, Sartre's well-publicized hangout.

The movie *Funny Face* utilized four songs from the original *Funny Face*—"'S Wonderful," "Let's Kiss and Make Up," "He Loves and She Loves," and the title song—plus the Gershwins' "How Long Has This Been Going On?", which had been cut before the show's New York opening and was later added to *Rosalie.* Also included was "Clap Yo' Hands" from *Oh, Kay!* Augmenting these were three new ones by Messrs. Gershe and Edens: "Think Pink!" (melodically suggesting "High Hat," one of the numbers in the first *Funny Face* that was not being used), "Bonjours, Paris!", and "On How to Be Lovely."

As something of a prologue to the story, the film begins with Editor Maggie Prescott barging into her office at *Quality.* "Lettie, take an editorial," she commands her secretary. " 'To the Women of America . . .' No, make it, 'To the Women Everywhere: Banish the black, burn the blue, and bury the beige. From now on, girls, Think Pink!' " And they do, in the swirling

410

"Funny Face."

Audrey's "Basal Metabolism" dance.

number that evolves showing the pervasive influence of a fashion-magazine's royal decree. The whole country goes pink!

But a color fad is a color fad, and Maggie must now dream up something new to attract both readers and dress buyers. Her new campaign: "Clothes for the woman who isn't interested in clothes." To get dowdy intellectuals fashion conscious, Maggie sends her chief photographer, Dick Avery, to photograph a model in a "movingly dismal" Greenwich Village book store, run by bespectacled, black-wool-stockinged Jo Stockton (Audrey Hepburn). After the others leave, Dick stays behind to help clean up and Jo belittles him for wasting his time photographing "silly dresses on silly women." When Dick explains that he likes his job, particularly his annual trip to Paris, Jo tells him she would love to go there to hear the lectures of Professor Flostre, the high priest of Empatheticalism, a philosophy based on feeling what one thinks another person feels. Dick demonstrates his own brand of Empatheticalism by kissing Jo—and the girl is suddenly transformed! So much so, that once Dick has left, she puts on a wide-brimmed hat and dreamily dances all over the store singing "How Long Has This Been Going On?" (In the original song, the "This" of the title applied merely to kissing; the movie gave it a deeper romantic significance chiefly by adding new words to the verse.)

Now Maggie has a new scheme to tie in with the new campaign: she will choose a "Quality Woman," someone with real "bazazz," to be photographed in Paris wearing the new collection designed by France's leading couturier, Paul Duval. Dick proposes Jo for the job, and though initially appalled at the idea, Maggie looks the girl over and allows, "She might do." "Might do what?" asks Jo (recalling a similar exchange between Fred Astaire and Judy Garland at their first meeting in *Easter Parade*). When a horrified Jo becomes aware of what Maggie has in mind, she dashes out of her office

"Let's Kiss and Make Up."

415

and into a darkroom. And there is Dick developing a huge blowup of her face. Jo cannot understand what all the fuss is about, since she has always thought her face was funny.

"How could you possibly make a model out of that?" she asks looking at the photograph. "You can't be serious."

"When I get through with you," Dick reassures her, "you'll look like . . . Well, what do you call beautiful? A tree? You'll look like a tree."

And right on cue he sings the movie's title song in which Dick reveals his love for Jo's "sunny funny face."

So off they go to Paris, where Dick, Maggie, and Jo take in a split-screen tour of the city. Gaily singing "Bonjour, Paris!" Dick steps out on the Champs Élysées, Maggie window shops along the Rue St. Honoré and the Rue de la Paix, and Jo heads for the Left Bank in search of "the den of thinking men like Jean-Paul Sartre." (The only thinking man Jo is supposed to be thinking about is named Flostre, but Sartre certainly makes more sense in a song lyric. Besides, it rhymes with Montmartre.) After bounding about the city admitting, "I'm simply tourist and I couldn't care less," the three end up giggling on top of the Eiffel Tower.

Jo's failure to show up at Duval's salon the next day prompts Dick to track her down at an Empatheticalist bistro, where she is happily drinking in —and dancing in—the avant garde atmosphere. Dick and Jo have a row and he takes her back to her hotel. In the courtyard beneath her window, he serenades her with "Let's Kiss and Make Up," which he follows with a lightning matador-styled sword-and-cape dance using his umbrella and raincoat.

It isn't long, though, before Jo settles down and Dick photographs her all over Paris in a variety of outfits and moods. First she scampers through the Tuileries carrying a dozen balloons ("There's a sudden shower and you're very, very happy." "Why am I so happy?" "Because I say you are"). Next she is a tragic figure ("Today you're Anna Karenina") being en-

416

"He Loves and She Loves."

gulfed by the steam of an outgoing train. Dick continues to snap away at a carefree Jo visiting a flower market, a regal Jo leaving the Paris Opera, a girlish Jo fishing in the Seine, an ethereal Jo at the "Winged Victory" statue in the Louvre, and a dewy-eyed Jo as a bride outside a country church.

There, on a misty lawn, as birds twitter and swans majestically sail by on a nearby pond, Dick kisses Jo. "I *love* Paris," she exclaims, "and I *love* these clothes and this little church and I love you." With a confession like this in a setting like this, what else would a fellow do but sing? So Dick sings "He Loves and She Loves." Soon, the two are in each other's arms dancing ever so airily over the grass, around the pond, and onto a raft.

With the picture-taking sessions over, Maggie briefs Jo at Duval's salon on the fine points of receiving the press that evening. "They'll want to know who does your hair," she tells her, "what you eat, what you drink, what kind of sheets you sleep on. You will be an authority on how to be lovely." And Maggie sings her how, with Jo repeating the lessons after each line.

But that night Jo again slips off to hear Flostre lecture. She even gets a chance to talk to the great man, solemnly advising him, "You must see Greenwich Village. It's our Left Bank. People there think and do things, useful things." After Dick yanks her back to the press reception, Jo is so furious that she dunks him into a fountain and storms out. The following evening things look pretty bleak for the double

unveiling of the "Quality Woman" and Duval's collection. Knowing that Jo is at Flostre's home, Dick (in fake beard) and Maggie go in search of her by posing as Empatheticalists. They entertain the disciples with a rousing "Clap Yo' Hands," and are about to spirit Jo away when Flostre has them thrown out. Jo beats a hasty retreat herself once she discovers that the professior's interest in her is more carnal than cerebral.

Jo returns to Duval's and the fashion show is a huge success—but Dick, thoroughly disillusioned, is at Orly Airport to catch the next plane back to New York. Accidentally bumping into Flostre, he is relieved to learn that Jo still has her virtue and he dashes back to Duval's. No Jo. Maggie, however, has found the secret of Empatheticalism: "She put herself in your place. All you need to do is put yourself in her place and the two of you are bound to run into each other in somebody's place." That's clue enough for Dick, and off he rushes to the country church. She's there all right. Rapturously, Dick and Jo sing " 'S Wonderful"—and glide merrily off on a raft into the dewy mist.

Director Donen began shooting *Funny Face* on the Paramount lot in April 1956, and then moved the company to Paris in June. There they were confronted with one major unmanageable problem: the weather. For days it either rained or was extremely windy, which was hardly helpful since not one scene to be shot in Paris called for either rain or wind. Because it was raining when they shot the background at the Tuileries and it didn't rain when they shot the closeups, Fred and Audrey had to be sprayed with a hose in order to conform to the setting. For the churchyard scene in Chantilly, Donen used the setting around a hunting-lodge chapel which was made to look more churchlike simply by changing the windows and doors. But the lawn had no grass. After a hurry call to California had

418

"Clap Yo' Hands."

produced fast-growing grass seed, the rain came down so heavily that the entire area was turned into a quagmire. The problem was solved with the purchase of huge quantities of sod, which had to be kept in a greenhouse until the scene was ready to be filmed. Another unforseen problem was the crowds. Lacking police protection to control the curious Parisians who followed the shooting wherever it went, Donen simply put police uniforms on the French extras, who then managed to keep the gawkers from interfering with the takes. In all, the company remained in Paris about two months.

Apart from a devastating notice in *Time* ("one of those big Technicolor musicals that stagger toward the culminating nuptuals like a determined but overequipped bride"), most reviewers hailed *Funny Face* as the stylish treat that it was. *The New York Times'* critic, Bosley Crowther, wrote: "This is its major magnificence—appropriate decor and visual style that lend to this Cinderella story a modern Cinderella atmosphere." To William K. Zinsser in the *New York Herald Tribune*, "*Funny Face* is that rare thing on the screen—a polished musical. It is also great fun." In *The New Yorker*, John McCarten advised: "Put *Funny Face* down as an amiable bit of seasonal fluff, and rejoice that Mr. Astaire's middle-aged bones can still rattle with an infectious beat." And in the *Saturday Review*, Arthur Knight found *Funny Face* "literally brimming with wonderfully fresh and exhilarating moments. Altogether it is sparkling entertainment that sends one out of the theatre with the feeling that he can dance like Astaire—and is married to Audrey Hepburn. It's a glorious sensation, however fleeting."

419

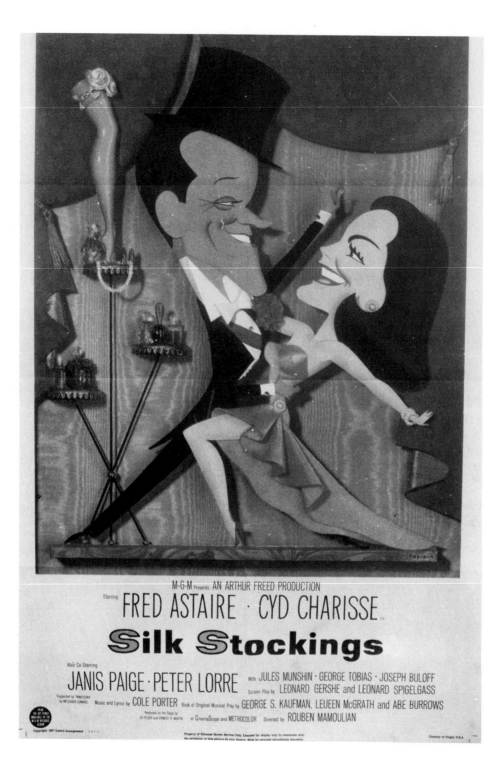

M-G-M Presents AN ARTHUR FREED PRODUCTION

Starring

FRED ASTAIRE · CYD CHARISSE

Silk Stockings

Also Co-Starring

JANIS PAIGE · PETER LORRE

With JULES MUNSHIN · GEORGE TOBIAS · JOSEPH BULOFF

Screen Play by LEONARD GERSHE and LEONARD SPIGELGASS

Suggested by "NINOTCHKA"
by MELCHIOR LENGYEL   Music and Lyrics by COLE PORTER   Book of Original Musical Play by GEORGE S. KAUFMAN, LEUEEN McGRATH and ABE BURROWS

Produced on the Stage by
CY FEUER and ERNEST H. MARTIN   in CinemaScope and METROCOLOR   Directed by ROUBEN MAMOULIAN

SILK STOCKINGS

CAST

Steven "Steve" Canfield	Fred Astaire
Nina "Ninotchka" Yoshenko	Cyd Charisse (sung by Carol Richards)
Peggy Dayton	Janis Paige
Brankov	Peter Lorre
"Bibi" Bibinski	Jules Munshin
Vassili Markovitch	George Tobias
Ivanov	Joseph Buloff
Peter Ilyitch Boroff	Wim Sonneveld
Suzette	Betty Uitti
Fifi	Barrie Chase
Gabrielle	Tybee Afra
Ballerina	Belita

Producer: Arthur Freed for Metro-Goldwyn-Mayer. Director: Rouben Mamoulian. Lyrics & Music: Cole Porter. Screenplay: Leonard Gershe & Leonard Spigelgass, from stage musical by George S. Kaufman, Leueen McGrath, Abe Burrows, based on story "Ninotchka" by Melchior Lengyal, & screen version by Charles Brackett, Billy Wilder, Walter Reisch, Ernst Lubitsch. Dance directors: Hermes Pan, Eugene Loring. Art directors: William A. Horning, Randall Duell. Costumes: Helen Rose: Music director: Andre Previn. Orchestrations: Conrad Salinger, Skip Martin, Al Woodbury. Vocal arrangements: Robert Tucker. Cameraman: Robert Bronner. Editor: Harold F. Kress. Filmed in CinemaScope. Color by Metrocolor. Release date: May 20, 1957. Running time: 117 minutes.

MUSICAL NUMBERS: "Too Bad"—Lorre, Munshin, Buloff, Astaire, Uitti, Chase, Afra/ "Paris Loves Lovers"—Astaire, Charisse (sung by Richards)/ "Stereophonic Sound"—Paige & Astaire; dance by Astaire & Paige/ "It's a Chemical Reaction, That's All"—Charisse (sung by Richards)/ "All of You"—Astaire; dance by Astaire & Charisse/ "Satin and Silk"—Paige/ "Silk Stockings"—dance by Charisse/ "Without Love"—Charisse (sung by Richards)/ "Fated to Be Mated"—Astaire; dance by Astaire & Charisse/ "Josephine" (incomplete) —Paige/ "Siberia"—Lorre, Munshin, Buloff/ "The Red Blues"—Sonneveld, Russians; dance by Charisse, Russians/ "The Ritz Roll and Rock"— Astaire; dance by Astaire, chorus. Background: "I've Got You Under My Skin," "Close," "You'd Be So Nice to Come Home To," "You Can Do No Wrong."

421

"Too bad we can't go back to Moscow" sing Barrie Chase, Peter Lorre, Joseph Buloff, Fred Astaire, Jules Munshin, Betty Uitti, and Tybee Afra.

Fred Astaire plays the role of an enterprising American whose work takes him to Paris. He is attracted to a plainly dressed, serious-minded girl who, at first, expresses no interest in romance and even belittles Fred's work and the world in which he lives. Eventually, under the influence of both Paris and Fred's singing and dancing, the girl develops a taste for worldly goods, particularly feminine finery. The two fall in love, surmount a breakup, and end in each other's arms.

Funny Face? Right. *Silk Stockings?* Right again. And the second was released within four months of the first.

The resemblances between these movies, however, were no more than coincidental (also no more than coincidental was the fact that Leonard Gershe, the author of *Funny Face,* was also the co-author of the *Silk Stock-*

ings screenplay). The progenitor of the new picture was actually the eighteen-year-old screen classic, *Ninotchka,* the film in which Greta Garbo, playing a dedicated Communist on a Parisian fling, was at last revealed as a skillful light comedienne. In 1955, Broadway librettists George S. Kaufman and his wife, Leueen McGrath, (later succeeded by Abe Burrows) coarsened the sophisticated lark into a profitable stage musical called *Silk Stockings,* which had songs by Cole Porter and a cast headed by Hildegarde Neff and Don Ameche. (To confuse things even more, a year later Katharine Hepburn and Bob Hope co-starred in *The Iron Petticoat,* a movie about a Soviet aviatrix who defects to the West after a spree in London.)

When producer Arthur Freed decided to make a screen-musical ver-

Lorre even tries a well-supported *prisiadka*.

Note that the only name on the record-album cover belongs to producer Arthur Freed.

sion of the stage-musical version of *Ninotchka,* he and director Rouben Mamoulian kept the story and songs pretty much the same except that—with Fred Astaire and Cyd Charisse in the leads—the emphasis became primarily choreographic. "I had two of the best dancers in the world," Mamoulian once said in an interview, "and what interested me was to give greater importance to the dancing than to the action proper. The psychological and dramatic development existed only in the dances." Because of this, two minor songs were discarded in favor of two new ones created specifically as dance routines. "Fated to Be Mated" was a joyous marriage proposal that was performed from one deserted movie studio sound stage to another, and "The Ritz Roll and Rock" was a bouncy, angular top-hatted Fred Astaire specialty, far more Ritz than rock. Mamoulian also added Cyd Charisse's sensuous dance, in which—to the unsung accompaniment of the film's title song—she symbolically removed her drab clothes and donned the newly purchased finery that she had hidden in various parts of her room.

The only actor to act in both Broadway and Hollywood *Silk Stockings* was George Tobias as the Soviet Commissar of Arts. Tobias even had a triple distinction, since he had also appeared in *Ninotchka* in the role of a Soviet passport official. The three Russian emissaries, whose behavior in Paris starts all the fuss, were played in *Silk Stockings* by the Hungarian-born Peter Lorre, the Russian-born Joseph Buloff, and the New York-born Jules Munshin. Lorre had the film's funniest line. Called to a meeting with the other agents at two in the morning, he arrives late, obviously because of a dalliance, and offers the lame excuse that he was having a manicure. At two o'clock in the morning? Lorre's ready explanation: "I cannot sleep with long fingernails."

One subtle touch in the screenplay was that the terms "Soviet" and "Communist" were each used only once.

423

The country was identified as Russia and the inhabitants thereof were known as Russians, a form of euphemism presumably intended to make the characters more sympathetic.

The major changes, of course, were what Kaufman, McGrath, Burrows, and Porter had wrought. As *Ninotchka,* the story had been a witty, civilized Ernst Lubitsch spoof at the expense of Communist venality. Three bungling Soviet representatives are in Paris to sell the court jewels once belonging to a former Grand Duchess (Ina Claire) now living in that city. Thanks to the lady's lover, Count Léon d'Algout (Melvyn Douglas), the three become not only legally thwarted but morally corrupted, and Moscow dispatches envoy extraordinary Nina Yakushova to bring them back into line. Léon accidentally meets Nina one night as she is trying to find her way to the Eiffel Tower, and before long he is calling her Ninotchka and they are falling in love. Aware of this, the Grand Duchess, having managed to recover her jewels, offers to hand them over to the Soviets once her romantic rival is safely back where she came from. Ninotchka agrees to return to Moscow, but Léon does not return to the Grand Duchess. Instead, he is able to get Ninotchka out of the U.S.S.R. by mailing an anonymous report that the three corruptible comrades—now on a mission to Constantinople—are up to their old tricks. Ninotchka is sent to investigate and finds not only the trio awaiting her but also faithful Léon.

Fred and movie star Janis Paige give a musical demonstration of "Stereophonic Sound."

424

When the musical-comedy librettists got hold of the story, they retained the basic theme of Communists succumbing to the lure of capitalism, and kept the characters of Ninotchka and the three emissaries just about the same—though all their last names were changed (Ninotchka went from Yakushova to Yoshenko). However, the suave Count Léon was turned into the brash Steve Canfield, a Hollywood agent (elevated to a Hollywood producer for the movie), whose client, an Esther Williams–type star named Peggy Dayton, is in Paris to make a film version of—that's right—*War and Peace*. The mission of the three Russians is now to bring home comrade-composer Peter Ilyitch Boroff, who has been signed to create the background score for the picture.

Why Boroff—no matter how esteemed he might be—is so indispensable to the filmmakers is never really made clear, but Steve goes about corrupting the three Russians as if the composer himself were the imperial court jewels. Steve, in fact, is a man of such easy malleability that when Peggy Dayton proposes that *War and Peace* be scrapped in favor of a vulgar musical about Napoleon and Josephine—to be called *Not Tonight*—he thinks it's a great idea. Nor has he any scruples about hiring a visiting American lyric writer to add words to Boroff's melodies without the composer's knowledge. When upbraided by the Russians for this devious practice, Steve shrugs off the complaint with the explanation: "In America we do this sort of thing all the time." (As an inside joke, the lyricist is called Archie Birch, a reference to Cary Grant, né Archie Leach, who played Cole Porter in his screen biography.)

Despite alterations in characters and story line, *Silk Stockings* was not above helping itself to some of *Ninotchka*'s dialogue—such as Ninotchka's remark upon seeing a hotel-lobby display case containing a pair of silk stockings: "How can such a civilization survive when women are permitted to wear things like that?" (in *Ninotchka* it had been a cornucopia-shaped lady's hat). Or her line to Steve: "As basic material you might not be bad but you are the unfortunate product of a doomed culture." Or Steve's reply: "You must admit that this doomed old civilization sparkles. . . . It glitters!" Or Ninotchka's balanced appraisal: "We have the high ideals but they have the climate."

The original movie also provided composer-lyricist Porter with lines and situations that helped cue in the musical numbers. In *Ninotchka,* the two had gone to the Eiffel Tower to take in the sights, but since *Silk Stockings* dispensed with on-location shooting (*Funny Face* had pretty well exhausted all the locales), it was essential that the hypnotic appeal of Paris be conveyed exclusively through dialogue and song, as in this early exchange in a hotel room:

NINOTCHKA: Why can't you understand that this is no laughing matter?
STEVE: Comrade. We're in Paris. In the spring. Why can't we make it a laughing matter?
NINOTCHKA: Really, Mr. Canfield, it is quite obvious what you have done to Bibinsky, Brankov, and Ivanov. But if you think you will do the same thing to me, you had better stop right now.
STEVE: I didn't do anything to the commissars. Paris did. It did it to them. It did it to me. It'll do it to you. Let me show you something. (*He opens a terrace door revealing the glittering sight of Paris at night.*) Comrade, face your enemy. (*He sings.*) "Gaze on the glistening lights below and above,/ Oh, what a night of nights for people in love. . . ."

"All of You," the dance that breaks down the
resistance of Soviet envoy Cyd Charisse.

Janis Paige's "Satin and Silk" number has the desired effect
on composer Wim Sonneveld.

428

"I want to make a speech."

A kiss before the "execution."
(below), "I have paid the penalty. I feel better."

With the conclusion of "Paris Loves Lovers," Ninotchka seems only concerned with the amount of wattage required for those glistening lights. But despite her air of indifference to the city's appeal, Ninotchka does recall the line, "the urge to merge with the splurge." And that's cue enough for Steve to reprise his song. This time, as counterpoint, Ninotchka interjects words and expressions that have been drummed into her head about the non-communist world—"Imperialistic . . . militaristic . . . bourgeois propaganda . . ."—and concludes by labeling love a "low totalitarian thing."

In the scene in the Garbo movie in which Léon tries to thaw the icy Russian, she tells him, "Love is a romantic designation for a most ordinary biological, or shall we say chemical, process." That was all the inspiration Cole Porter needed to write "It's a Chemical Reaction, That's All," whose lyric begins: "When the electric-magnetic of the he-male/ Meets the electro-magnetic of the female . . ."

The film, *Ninotchka,* continued the scene with Léon objecting to Ninotchka's "analyzing everything out of existence," and he went on to an oddly Cole Porterish description of the ways in which doves, snails, moths, and flowers all succumb to the "divine passion." But for *Silk Stockings,* instead of giving Steve a song about the amatory habits of the lower primates (which the composer had already covered in the song "Let's Do It," among others), Porter created a less biological, more cartographical expression of love in "All of You." Here his hero expresses admiration not only for the girl's arms, eyes, and mouth, but also for her East, West, North, and South. With his romantic tour concluded, Steve continues his efforts to win over the scientifically minded Russian through a display of dancing. Suddenly, he grabs the initially reluctant girl and whirls her about so ardently and gracefully that there is no doubt that she, too, has finally succumbed to the divine passion. At the conclusion of the dance, Steve kisses her. Completely his, Ninotchka murmurs, "That was restful. Again."

Probably the most famous scene in
Ninotchka occurred after Ninotchka's
first formal date with Léon. Both a
bit tipsy, they return to the hotel room
and Ninotchka is suddenly seized with
a feeling of guilt for enjoying herself
so much. She confesses that she has
betrayed the Russian ideal and should
be stood against the wall and shot.
Tying a napkin over her eyes, Léon
plays firing squad by popping the cork
out of a champagne bottle, and Ninotchka sinks into a chair. Having
thus atoned for her sins ("I have paid
the penalty"), she makes a speech,
a tender plea that the coming world
revolution wait a bit longer so that
lovers might have a little more time
in which to be happy.

In *Silk Stockings,* the scene was
completely reversed. It begins with
Ninotchka saying she wants to make
a speech but instead she changes her
mind and makes a confession—via the
song "Without Love"—of a woman's
deep need for love. It is then that
Steven blindfolds Ninotchka with his
handkerchief and stands her against
the wall. When he pops the cork, she
sinks to the floor saying "I have paid
the penalty"—and passes out.

In addition to writing two new songs
for the movie, Cole Porter also had to
rewrite some of the more censorable
lyrics sung by Janis Paige, playing
movie star Peggy Dayton. Most of the
raucous humor of "Satin and Silk"
and "Josephine" was retained, although the lady of the second piece
was now referred to as Napoleon's
little chum instead of his little bum.
The major tampering was made in
"Stereophonic Sound," a tribute to
Hollywood's latest affliction with technical elephantiasis.

Leading up to this song was a press

430

"We were fated to be mated, spotted to be knotted . . ."

Back home, Cyd leads her fellow Muscovites in "The Red Blues."

interview conducted by Peggy who has just arrived in Paris to start work on *War and Peace*:

PEGGY: It's gonna make a wonderful picture once it's boiled down. Of course, the title's gonna hafta go.

REPORTER: How do you feel about Tolstoy?

PEGGY: Who?

REPORTER: Tolstoy.

PEGGY: Who's that?

REPORTER: He wrote *War and Peace*.

PEGGY: Oh, *that* Tolstoy! There's absolutely no truth to the rumors. We're just good friends.

The reporters clamor for more information. Who will do the adaptation? Who is the director? Who will be in the cast? Peggy couldn't care less. "Those things don't mean a thing today," she tells them. "Today there are many other things that are much more important." And she sings:

Today to get the public to attend a
    picture show
It's not enough to advertise a
    famous star they know,
If you wanna get the crowds to
    come around
You gotta have glorious Tech-
    nicolor, breathtaking Cinema-
    Scope and Stereophonic Sound.

In adapting the song for movies, Porter removed the references to Zanuck (rival studio) and "Marilyn's behind," and a five-foot-wide bosom was replaced by a five-foot-wide mouth. A remark about Ava Gardner playing Godiva was kept in but a line about seeing her in the bare was changed to "they wouldn't even care."

Steve soon joins Peggy in singing the didactic ditty (including a one-line self-reference for Fred Astaire: "A fellow hugged his partner as they cuddled cheek to cheek"), and presently they are cavorting around the room as they simulate all the arduous activities that go into movie-making.

Reviews for *Silk Stockings* were a

432

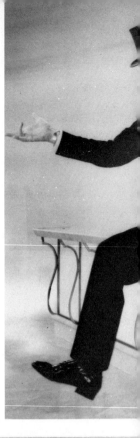

"The Ritz Roll and Rock."

pretty mixed bag. Alton Cook in the *New York World Telegram* led the yea-sayers with: "Like every other Fred Astaire movie, while the spell of seeing it is fresh, it seems to be the best one he has made." According to Archer Winsten in the *New York Post*, "Fred is almost as ageless as ever, those old bones flicking about like so many feathers, and Cyd Charisse, always a favorite of this connoisseur, resists the ravages with complete success." *The New York Times'* Bosley Crowther was equally delighted with the pair: "There should be legislation requiring that Fred Astaire and Cyd Charisse appear together at least once every two years. They are both in delightful fettle when they testily spar with the words, but are off in the blissful empyrean when they rise on their dancing shoes."

Crowther called the movie "an all-round refreshing show," but William K. Zinsser of the *New York Herald Tribune* felt, "somehow the plot seems less durable every time around. This is not the fault of the two stars. Astaire's feet are as nimble as ever, and as for Miss Charisse's legs, they are practically a national shrine." *Time* called it "a lisle version of a fairly spirited musical comedy in turn woven over an old velveteen original," while Arthur Knight in the *Saturday Review* felt that the plot, "although simplified to the point of imbecility, still remains too ponderous for a good musical."

Following *Silk Stockings*, after twenty-three and a half years before the cameras, Fred Astaire retired as a romantic song-and-dance man. Not counting his dance-on in *Dancing Lady* or the revue *Ziegfeld Follies*, he had wooed and won thirteen of the screen's fairest ladies in twenty-six movie musicals (Bing Crosby had handed him his only two romantic defeats). Permanent retirement, however, was out of the question. Very much in the question, though, was whether to concentrate on dramatic screen roles or to take the plunge into the burgeoning medium of television.

433

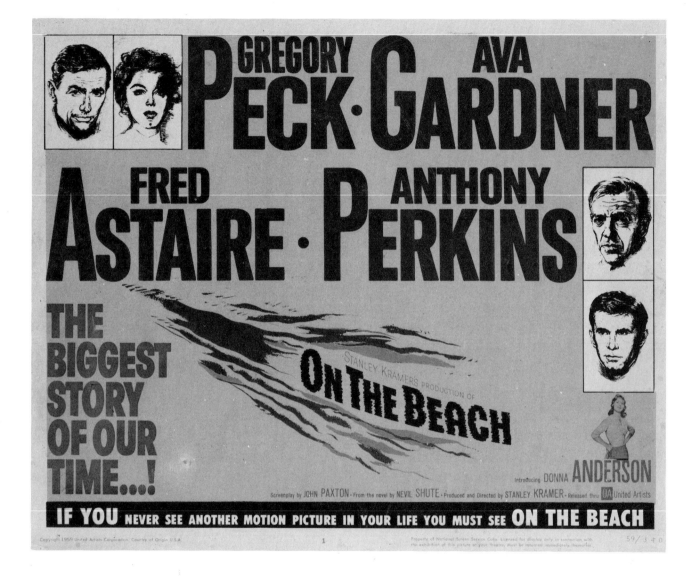

434

ON THE BEACH

CAST

Capt. Dwight Lionel Towers	Gregory Peck
Moira Davidson	Ava Gardner
Julian Osborn	Fred Astaire
Lt. Peter Holmes	Anthony Perkins
Mary Holmes	Donna Anderson
Adm. Bridie	John Tate
Lt. Hosgood	Lola Brooks
Farrel	Guy Dolman
Yeoman Swain	John Mellon
Sundstrom	Harp McGuire
Davidson	Lou Vernon
Benson	Ken Wayne
Davis	Richard Meikle
Morgan	Grant Taylor
Prof. Jorgenson	Peter Williams
Chrysler	Jim Barrett
Salvation Army Captain	John Casson

Producer: Stanley Kramer for United Artists. Director: Stanley Kramer. Screenplay: John Paxton, from novel by Nevil Shute. Art director: Fernando Carrere. Costumes: Fontana Sisters, Joe King. Background score (including "Waltzing Matilda" by Cowan-Paterson): Ernest Gold. Music director: Ernest Gold. Cameramen: Giuseppe Rotunno, Daniel Fapp. Editor: Frederick Knudtson. Release date: December 2, 1959. Running time: 133 minutes.

"I won't have it do you hear! There *is* hope!"
Donna Anderson is upset by Fred's prediction of doom
as husband Anthony Perkins tries to calm her.

Fred Astaire, at age fifty-eight, entered the world of television by appearing in a half-hour nonmusical comedy called *Imp on a Cobweb Leash*. Shown on the General Electric Theater series on December 1, 1957, this was a whimsical piece about a wealthy, staid business executive who revolts against convention by appearing at a board meeting sporting Bermuda shorts and a crew cut. It was on October 17, 1958, however, that Astaire first made an impact on the home screen by starring in his own musical special, *An Evening with Fred Astaire*. The show was just that, since apart from partner Barrie Chase (she had appeared briefly in *Silk Stockings*) and the Jonah Jones Quartet, the hour-long Chrysler-sponsored program was all Astaire. It was also the most acclaimed television entertainment of the year, garnering nine "Emmy" awards from the Television Academy of Arts and Sciences (Fred offered to give back the "best actor" trophy but the Academy wouldn't let him). Three months later, Astaire was back on the box for the GE Theatre in *Man on a Bicycle*.

The actor was pleased with his varied television appearances. But nothing could have prepared him—or the public—for his next screen assignment.

In September 1957, producer-director Stanley Kramer read a novel by Nevil Shute called *On the Beach* while it was still in galley form. Convinced that its theme—the annihilation of mankind in 1964 through a nuclear war—was the most vital one the screen could tackle, he quickly secured the film rights. Just a little over a year later, he took his crew to Melbourne, Australia, where the bulk of the movie was shot. In the cast were Gregory Peck as a stalwart American submarine captain, Ava Gardner as a morose lady who sleeps around, Anthony Perkins as an embittered naval officer, and in the role of an alcoholic English scientist, the former "Mr. Top Hat, White Tie, and Tails."

The choice of Fred Astaire for the part of Julian Osborne, while offbeat, was nonetheless understandable. Fred didn't sing or dance or crack jokes, but he did provide a welcome change

436

Gregory Peck and Ava Gardner in a playful moment on the beach.

"I've never been pushed around in such a nice way."
Ava realizes that Gregory is the man for her.

from the sight of grim-faced Peck, Gardner, and Perkins stoically accepting their fate. Sardonic, philosophical Julian, deeply troubled by the responsibility of science for the holocaust, finds some measure of relief in drink and in racing his Ferrari—and in railing melodramatically against the stupidity of mankind. At a party early in the film there was this exchange with an officer named Morgan (Grant Taylor):

MORGAN: You built the bomb. You experimented with it. Tested it. And exploded it.

JULIAN: Now just a moment, Morgan . . .

MORGAN: Thanks to you chaps, a moment is about all we have.

JULIAN: Every man who ever worked on this thing told you what would happen. The scientists signed petition after petition. But nobody listened. There *was* a choice. It was to build the bombs and use them. Or hope the United States and the Soviet Union and the rest of us would find some way to go on living.

MORGAN: Look, they pushed us too far. They didn't think we'd fight no matter what they did.

JULIAN: And they were wrong. We fought. We expunged them. We didn't do such a bad job on ourselves, either. With the interesting result that the background level of radiation in this very room is nine times what it was a year ago. Don't you know that? Nine times! We're all doomed, you know. The whole silly, pathetic lot of us! Doomed by the air we are about to breathe. We haven't got a chance!

Most of the footage in *On the Beach* was devoted to the mission of a nuclear submarine following a war that has wiped out all life in the Northern Hemisphere. Under the command of Capt. Dwight Lionel Towers (Gregory Peck), and with Julian on board as "a sort of scientific cruise director," the *Sawfish* is sent northward from Melbourne to determine how much atomic dust is in the atmosphere and to see if there might possibly be any

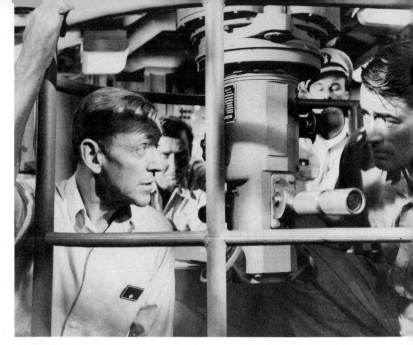

Aboard the submarine to check radioactivity in the northern Pacific.

Fred as racing car enthusiast Julian Osborn wins his last race.

438

Watching the submarine begin its final journey.

signs of life. After exploring Point Barrow, San Francisco and San Diego, and realizing that there is no hope left, the ship returns to Melbourne. There the crew votes to go back to the United States to die, Julian speeds to his death following a suicidal auto race, and Peter Holmes (Anthony Perkins) and his wife take suicide pills. As the film ends, the only sign of movement is the flapping of a banner across a Melbourne street with the ironic message: "THERE IS STILL TIME . . . BROTHER."

Kramer hoped, of course, that the message would be accepted as a reminder that there still was time for nations to outlaw the use of atomic weapons. After the film's international world premieres—showings were held in twenty cities, including New York, London, Paris, Tokyo, and even Moscow—the movie was greeted by a generally appreciative press, at least in the United States. Reviews, however, ran the gamut from the *Saturday Review*'s "a picture that aims at something big and emerges as something tremendous" (Arthur Knight) to *The New Yorker*'s "If you were the only

girl in the world and I were the only boy, God forbid we should wind up on the littoral of Australia in the gluey attitudes of the doomed characters" (John McCarten).

Fred Astaire's work in his first non-musical film was well received. Bosley Crowther in *The New York Times* termed his performance "amazing," and added that he "conveyed in his self-effacing manner a piercing sense of the irony of his trade." Arthur Knight felt "Astaire's work is not only reminiscent of but compares favorably to an Alec Guinness performance," and *Newsweek* stated unequivocally: "Astaire has never performed better."

Though some predicted a new career for Fred Astaire in dramatic roles, *On the Beach* remains his only sortie in the field of message-delivering filmmaking. And it certainly didn't make him hang up his dancing shoes. In fact, following *On the Beach*, he devoted almost all of his professional time during 1960 to two more highly acclaimed television specials: *Another Evening with Fred Astaire* (shown in May) and *Astaire Time* (October), both with Barrie Chase again as Fred's partner.

A dance with Debbie Reynolds.

THE PLEASURE OF HIS COMPANY

CAST

Biddeford "Pogo" Poole	Fred Astaire
Jessica Poole	Debbie Reynolds
Kate Dougherty	Lilli Palmer
Roger Henderson	Tab Hunter
Jim Dougherty	Gary Merrill
Mackenzie Savage	Charlie Ruggles
Toy	Harold Fong
Mrs. Mooney	Elvira Allman
Dress Designer	Edith Head

Producer: William Perlberg for Paramount Pictures. Director: George Seaton. Screenplay: Samuel Taylor, from play by Cornelia Otis Skinner & Samuel Taylor. Art directors: Hal Pereira, Tambi Larsen. Costumes: Edith Head. Background score: Alfred Newman. Song: "Lover" by Richard Rodgers & Lorenz Hart. (Sung by Fred Astaire.) Music director: Alfred Newman. Orchestrations: Herbert Spender, Edward Powell. Cameraman: Robert Burks. Editor: Alma Macrorie. Color by Technicolor. Release date: May 8, 1961. Running time: 114 minutes.

Debbie Reynolds beams as daddy
Fred meets fiancé Tab Hunter.

Fred's wedding gift to daughter Debbie:
a necklace of emeralds and pearls.
Looking on are Gary Merrill, Lilli Palmer and Charlie Ruggles.

Marjorie Main had once played his aunt, Jane Powell had been his sister, and he had been married three times to Ginger Rogers and once to Vera-Ellen. But for the most part, the on-screen Fred Astaire has been singularly unencumbered by familial ties. Even in *The Pleasure of His Company,* Fred's second nonmusical picture, he had to settle for an ex-wife (Lilli Plamer), a former father-in-law (Charlie Ruggles), and a daughter (Debbie Reynolds), whom he hadn't seen in fifteen years.

The film did, however, involve Fred in a particularly domestic situation, the preparations for his daughter's wedding. Adapted by Samuel Taylor from his play written with Cornelia Otis Skinner, *The Pleasure of His Company* starred Fred Astaire in a role that was well suited to his style —even though his dancing was limited to ballroom turns with Misses

Reynolds and Palmer, and his singing to snatches of "Lover" as he vainly tried to romance his ex-wife. (For the record, this was the only Rodgers-and-Hart song Fred ever sang on stage or screen.) Astaire's Biddeford "Pogo" Poole was a gadabout, a cultivated international playboy, who while shunning the responsibilities of fatherhood, was not above trying to dissuade daughter Jessica from marrying Roger the rancher so that he might sweep her off with him to Europe.

The original stage production had opened on Broadway in 1958, and ran for almost five hundred performances. Cyril Ritchard created the role of Pogo, Cornelia Otis Skinner was ex-wife Kate Dougherty, Dolores Hart played Jessica, and George Peppard was the fiancé. Charlie Ruggles, who had appeared in stage as Pogo's former father-in-law, Mackenzie Savage, was the only actor to recreate his role in

Fred flies off
with a painting
of Debbie as a child

442

the movie (which somehow never bothered to clear up the mystery of how his daughter, Lilli Palmer, got that German accent).

In general, the lighthearted film script closely followed the original, except for the ending. Onstage, after Pogo had used all of his considerable charm to convince Jessica to spend a carefree, hedonistic year with him, she chucks the wedding and the two dash off on their madcap spree. But this irresponsible denouement would never do in a 1961 movie. So, although Jessica is won over ("He needs me to fill up the emptiness in his life"), Pogo gallantly tells her not to sacrifice herself for him. And so he flies off—with two acquisitions: a painting of Jessica as a child and Kate's multitalented Oriental cook.

Early in 1960, producer William Perlberg and director George Seaton took their crew and cast for location-shooting in San Francisco. When the strike of the Screen Actors Guild halted production in March, Perlberg and Seaton were faced with a dilemma. Since they were committed to filming *The Counterfeit Traitor* in Europe immediately following *The Pleasure of His Company,* they could either scrap the movie they were working on or postpone its completion until after the second picture was finished. They chose to postpone it. So it was that eight months later—and a loss of $500,000 caused by the delay—*The Pleasure of His Company* resumed production with the same cast at the same spot it had left off.

Some of the dialogue was considered pretty sophisticated stuff at the time. In describing her fiancé to her recently arrived father, Jessica says, "He's very progressive. He has all sorts of ideas about artificial insemination and all that sort of thing. He breeds all over the world." To which Pogo replies, "You must be very proud."

One night Pogo tries to flirt with his former wife:

POGO: What are we going to do tonight while the young are out dancing?
KATE: We're going to bed.
POGO: Is that the best you can offer?
KATE: It wasn't an offer.

After a tour of San Francisco, during which Pogo has done everything to make Roger look like a clod in Jessica's eyes, the young couple quarrel over the dinner that Pogo had ordered for them at a French restaurant:

ROGER (*mocking Jessica*): "*Épatant! Merveilleux La salade était magnifique!*" It was salad. Plain, ordinary salad!
JESSICA: It wasn't plain, ordinary salad! It had upland cress in it and wild dandelion leaves!
ROGER: That's what my cattle eat!

Although the film was hardly a box-office smash, Astaire received favorable notices. In *The New York Times,* Bosley Crowther called the movie "a lot of fun" and admitted "it was hard to imagine anyone else better qualified to play the prodigal parent than Fred Astaire." Edith Oliver in *The New Yorker* allowed that "Fred Astaire is as wonderful as ever which makes it doubly sad that the picture, for all its surface glitter, is a very shoddy piece of work." *Time,* however, gave the movie its most scathing notice, referring to its "undertones of incest and overtones of Andy Hardy," and saving its deadliest on-target blast for the former Mrs. Eddie Fisher: "Debbie Reynolds, after ten years in pictures and a highly publicized scandal-divorce, is still playing the head pom-pom girl at Beverly Hills High."

Jack Lemmon, Kim Novak and Fred.

THE NOTORIOUS LANDLADY

CAST	
Carlye Hardwick	Kim Novak
Bill Gridley	Jack Lemmon
Franklin Armbruster	Fred Astaire
Inspector Oliphant	Lionel Jeffries
Mrs. Dunhill	Estelle Winwood
Miles Hardwick	Maxwell Reed
Mrs. Brown	Philippa Bevans
Minister	Henry Daniell
Coroner	Ronald Long
Lady Fallott	Doris Lloyd
Dillings	Richard Peel
Colonel	Frederick Worlock
Old Man	Carter DeHaven, Sr.

Producer: Fred Kohlmar for Columbia Pictures. Director: Richard Quine. Screenplay: Larry Gelbart & Blake Edwards, from novel by Margery Sharp. Art director: Cary Odell. Costumes: Kim Novak. Background score (including "A Foggy Day" by Gershwin-Gershwin & medley from *The Pirates of Penzance* by Gilbert & Sullivan): George Duning. Music director: George Duning. Orchestrations: Arthur Morton. Cameraman: Arthur Arling. Editor: Charles Nelson. Release date: June 26, 1962. Running time: 123 minutes.

Part of 1961 and most of 1962 found Fred Astaire primarily occupied in hosting—and occasionally acting in —*Fred Astaire's Première Theatre*, an ALCOA-sponsored television series over the ABC network. He did, however, return to the more standard form of movie-making once during that period to co-star with Kim Novak and Jack Lemmon in *The Notorious Landlady*. In the role of Franklin Armbruster, a worldly American diplomat stationed in London, Astaire endowed the character with a causticity and even breeziness that perfectly suited a murder mystery far more kooky than spooky. And he had some of the best lines in the witty script that Blake Edwards and Larry Gelbart had adapted from the novel by Margery Sharp.

Early in the film, Armbruster summons to his office a young official, Bill Gridley (Jack Lemmon), upon receiving word that he has been seen escorting the notorious Carlye Hardwick (Kim Novak):

ARMBRUSTER: Tell me, what sort of a woman do you find her? You can speak off the record if you like.

BILL: Well, this is for the record, sir. I find her absolutely heavenly.

ARMBRUSTER: Were you able to find out anything about *Mister* Hardwick?

BILL: Yes, sir, they're separated.

ARMBRUSTER: She told you that?

BILL: Yes . . . sir.

ARMBRUSTER: Don't you think that would be adding insult to injury?

BILL: How's that?

ARMBRUSTER: Gridley, Mrs. Hardwick murdered her husband.

BILL: Well, that's certainly grounds for div . . . She *what*?

ARMBRUSTER: I said that absolutely heavenly woman killed her husband. A sort of permanent trial separation.

Since Gridley has rented a flat in Carlye Hardwick's house in Mayfair, Armbruster wants him—undetected, of course—to keep an eye on the lady. That night, in Carlye's backyard, Bill accidentally sets fire to an awning while barbecuing a steak, and the fire department is summoned to put it out. The following morning, Armbruster

again sends for Gridley. "When I instructed you to keep your presence in Mrs. Hardwick's house absolutely secret," he says through clenched teeth, "did you feel you could best carry out that order by trying to set fire to London?" Then, pulling rank on the hapless subordinate, Armbruster tries to be helpful: "I think the answer to our frustrations is that we be in different countries. I pick England. Let's see what we can find for you." And he threatens to have Bill sent to Tierra del Fuego, on the southernmost tip of South America. Armbruster also offers some senior-officer advice. "You will learn, Gridley," he says sweetly, "that the higher your position, the more mistakes you are allowed. In fact, if you make enough of them it's considered your style. Now you happen to be in what I would call a one-mistake position. And you've made it."

Before long, the diplomat does meet Mrs. Hardwick and finds himself in complete agreement with Gridley: she is indeed a heavenly woman. Together the two men set out to clear Carlye's name. And they do—but not before Mr. Hardwick is killed (he really hadn't been before), Carlye gets into a slugging match with a two-ton lady bruiser, and there is a wild Keystone Kops chase in Penzance (accompanied by suitable Gilbert and Sullivan music).

The nation's press appraisers took a generally bright view of the film's comedy—but a dim one of its confused plotting. *Newsweek* held that "these shenanigans get more involved than Casey Stengel at a press conference, and the mystery's solution is preposterous and underhanded." But *Time* called it "a beguiling if hokey mystery," and *The New Yorker*'s John McCarten enjoyed himself so much that he declared: "I don't see how anyone could help but have a good time. . . . Casting Fred Astaire as a seasoned trouble-shooting State De-

Fred quizzes Jack Lemmon about his notorious landlady.

On the coast of Penzance, Kim Novak knocks out a lady bruiser (Philippa Bevan) . . .

446

partment man was absolutely inspired."

Equally inspired was the casting of Jack Lemmon as the cocky but befuddled hero, who opens the movie by answering a newspaper ad for a flat in Mrs. Hardwick's house. In order to conceal her identity, the notorious landlady greets him in dustcap and featherduster, and announces—in Kim Novak's approximation of Cockney—"Oy'm the parlor myde." At first she tells Bill that her mistress wishes to rent only to a married couple:

BILL: Believe me, I'd do nothing to harm her reputation as long as you're around.

CARLYE: Coo, you are a one, sir You Yanks, you come raht aout wiv it, don'tcha?

BILL: Most of it, anyway. . . . Tell me, Hilda, do you sleep in?

CARLYE: In an' aout. Off an' on.

BILL: Catch as catch can?

CARLYE: You moyt call it that sir.

Notwithstanding the movie's English locale, all the city exteriors were shot on the backlot of Columbia Pictures, and all the Penzance exteriors were shot in the Big Sur woods near Monterey. Though intended to help establish the London atmosphere, the background sound of "A Foggy Day (in London Town)" served even more to recall the occasion—almost a quarter of a century before—when Fred Astaire, in white tie and tails, had first sung it in *A Damsel in Distress*.

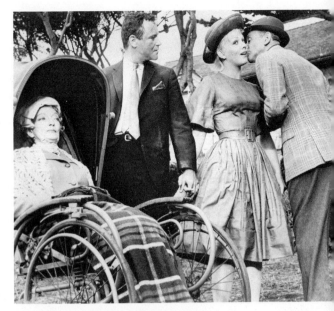

. . . and saves the life of invalid Estelle Winwood with the help of Jack and Fred.

At film's end, however, Miss Winwood's invalid chair accidentally starts rolling toward the sea again—with Lionel Jeffries, Fred, Kim, and Jack in pursuit.

447

FINIAN'S RAINBOW

CAST

Finian McLonergan	Fred Astaire
Sharon McLonergan	Petula Clark
Og	Tommy Steele
Woody Mahoney	Don Francks
Judge Rawkins	Keenan Wynn
Howard	Al Freeman, Jr.
Susan	Barbara Hancock
Buzz Collins	Ronald Colby
Sheriff	Dolph Sweet
District Attorney	Wright King
Henry	Louis Silas
Sharecropper	Brenda Arnau
Pilgrim Gospeleers	Avon Long, Roy Glenn, Jester Hairston

Producer: Joseph Landon for Warner Brothers-7 Arts. Director: Francis Ford Coppola. Lyrics: E. Y. Harburg. Music: Burton Lane. Screenplay: E. Y. Harburg & Fred Saidy, from their stage musical. Dance director: Hermes Pan. Art director: Hilyard M. Brown. Costumes: Dorothy Jeakins. Music director: Ray Heindorf. Associate: Ken Darby. Cameraman: Philip Lathrop. Editor: Melvin Shapiro. Filmed in PanaVision. Color by Technicolor. Release date: August 27, 1968. Running time: 145 minutes.

MUSICAL NUMBERS: "This Time of the Year"—chorus/ "How Are Things in Glocca Morra?"—Clark/ "Look to the Rainbow"—Clark & Astaire; dance by Astaire/ "If This Isn't Love"—Francks, Clark, Astaire, chorus; dance by Astaire/ "Something Sort of Grandish"—Steel & Clark/ "That Great Come-and-Get-It Day"—Francks, Clark, chorus/ "Old Devil Moon"—Francks & Clark/ "When the Idle Poor Become the Idle Rich"—Astaire, chorus; dance by Astaire, chorus/ "When I'm Not Near the Girl I Love"—Steele/ "Rain Dance"—dance by Hancock, chorus/ "The Begat"—Wynn, Long, Glenn, Hairston. Unused: "Necessity."

After an absence from the Hollywood screen of over six years, the sixty-eight-year-old Fred Astaire returned to the familiar territory of the movie musical.

Only it wasn't so familiar. *Finian's Rainbow,* Astaire's thirty-first musical, was so far removed from any other song-and-dance entertainment the actor had ever appeared in that his role was almost the complete reverse of his accustomed musical-comedy character.

As a scraggly Irish immigrant named Finian McLonergan, Fred was called upon to speak with a brogue, wear nondescript clothes, go unshaven, and possess a unique form of simpleminded logic: having stolen a crock of gold from a leprechaun, he believed that planting it in the earth near the buried gold at Fort Knox would make it grow and make him rich. But Astaire's worldly air, his jaunty, almost levitational walk, and his blithe singing and dancing style could never be submerged. "Fred Astaire's Finian is almost pure Astaire," commented *Newsweek*'s Joseph Morgenstern, "and that is a good thing for any Finian to be." Morgenstern's admiration was also shared by the *Saturday Review*'s Arthur Knight, who observed: "Astaire remains forever graceful and relaxed, never pushing for more than is required, never giving less than is due."

Casting Astaire as Finian did, however, necessitate some obvious changes from the way the role had been performed in the original 1947 Broadway production. On stage, *Finian's Rainbow* called for only a minimal amount of singing and dancing; on screen they made sure to give Fred ample opportunity to buck, wing, jig, jog, strut, hop, leap, skip, and tap as he pranced merrily about to the delight of the good folks of Rainbow Valley, Missitucky.

All the well-remembered songs from the original score were retained for the movie, except for "Necessity," which though filmed and recorded,

Fred as Finian McLonergan and Petula Clark as his daughter, Sharon, end their wandering in Rainbow Valley.

450

was cut from the final print. The only instances of lyrical updating occurred in "If This Isn't Love" (references to "Carmen Miranda" and "red propaganda" gave way to "Glocca Morra" and "Zsa Zsa Gaborra"), and in "The Begat" ("the misbegotten G.O.P." became rather pointlessly, "the misbegotten V.I.P."). As Finian's daughter, Sharon, English recording star Petula Clark was given most of the songs, although she had only one solo, the wistful "How Are Things in Glocca Morra?" With Astaire, she sang "Look to the Rainbow"; with hero Don Francks, "If This Isn't Love," "That Great Come-and-Get-It Day," and the main love duet, "Old Devil Moon"; and with Tommy Steele, as Og the leprechaun, she was heard in the perky minuet, "Something Sort of Grandish." Steele's solo was his swooping confession of amatory fickleness, "When I'm Not Near the Girl I Love" ("I love the girl I'm near"). The satirical depiction of a world of social equality, "When the Idle Poor Become the Idle Rich," was sung almost entirely by Astaire as he enumerated the effect of money as a great social leveler ("No one will see/ The Irish or the Slav in you,/ For when you're on Park Avenue/ Cornelius and Mike/ Look alike").

The story of *Finian's Rainbow* evolved from the desire of co-librettist and lyricist E. Y. Harburg to satirize an economic system dependent upon keeping gold reserves buried in the ground at Fort Knox. "Gold made us think of a pot of gold," Harburg once explained. "And the pot of gold reminded us of leprechauns and their crock of gold that was good for three wishes. Then it occurred to us that it would be funny to have a simpleminded Irishman believe that since America got rich by burying gold so could he. The three wishes gave us our conflict and a chance to kid the social system since the first wish makes a bigoted Southern senator turn black."

The "Look to the Rainbow" dance—first Fred with Petula, then with all the good citizens of Rainbow Valley.

The tale, of course, had the overriding theme of brotherhood with black-and-white sharecroppers sharing songs and dances, plus a bounty of material things that they are somehow able to buy on credit because of the buried crock.

In its original stage form, *Finian's Rainbow* opened on Broadway January 10, 1947, and had a successful run of 725 performances. Singing the Yip Harburg–Burton Lane score were Ella Logan as Sharon, Donald Richards as Woody, and David Wayne as the leprechaun. Finian was played by Albert Sharpe, who made his American movie debut playing Fred Astaire's prospective father-in-law in *Royal Wedding*.

There were seven previous attempts to make a movie out of *Finian's Rainbow*. A cartoon version had actually been started—Frank Sinatra, Judy Garland, Ella Fitzgerald, and Louis Armstrong were to supply the voices—but the project was eventually scrapped. Another attempt that never got off the ground occurred in 1965 when producer Harold Hecht secured the rights for a movie to star Dick Van Dyke. It was not until two years later—and twenty years after the initial stage presentation—that *Finian's Rainbow*, thanks to the determination of neophyte producer Joseph Landon, finally went into production at Warner Brothers. Under the direction of Francis Ford Coppola (he had directed only one previous film, *You're a Big Boy Now*), the company went through an intensive five-week rehearsal period, followed by seven weeks of actual shooting. The picture also marked the sixteenth film for which Hermes Pan shared choreographic chores with Fred Astaire.

Coppola was responsible for many imaginative touches. He used a quick-cutting technique for musical sequences such as "Woody's Here" (shots of Don Francks in various positions all over a train) and "The Begat" (a black

Fred digs his own private Fort Knox.

Botanist Al Freeman, Jr., demonstrates to Petula Clark and Don Francks his latest discover, mintolated tobacco.

454

Celebrating the day "When the Idle Poor Become the Idle Rich."

quartet riding in a car, getting it repaired, pushing it up a hill, etc.). For the romantic duet, "Old Devil Moon," he tried the soft-focus bit, which, since the sequence used many close-ups of Clark and Francks, proved particularly helpful as a wrinkle remover.

The only major character added for the film was the Negro botanist (played by Al Freeman, Jr.) who tries crossing tobacco with mint to make mintolated tobacco. First, it won't burn; then it burns but won't produce smoke. Possibly the movie's funniest scene—borrowed from the stage—occurs when Freeman gets a job as a servant for the Southern senator (played by Keenan Wynn). After being carefully coached in the approved shuffling manner for serving mint julep, Freeman also takes his Stepin Fetchit time in serving a Bromo Seltzer while the senator, choking from high blood pressure, desperately pleads with him to move faster.

Released in the fall of 1968, *Finian's Rainbow* was initially shown on a reserved-seat basis. Most reviewers were disapproving of what they felt was the film's outdated message. "The simplistic notion of the '40s that Negroes are just like whites beneath the skin is more than an embarrassment now," was the observation of *Time* magazine. Although Morgenstern in *Newsweek* called it "a shuffling relic that tries hard to be modern," Arthur Knight in *Saturday Review* was delighted that "they have not updated it." "My, how progressive it all seemed twenty years ago!" he wrote. "My, how quaint it all appears today! How well-meaning! How simple-minded!" But that's the way Knight liked it, and he concluded his notice with: "They have left it just the lovely show it was—tuneful, well-intended, occasionally funny, always appealing. By staying completely in its period, and doing everything supremely well, this *Finian's Rainbow* transcends time. Like Astaire himself, it seems ageless."

Og, the leprechaun (Tommy Steele), now loves Susan the Silent because, as he sings, "When I'm not near the girl I love, I love the girl I'm near."

455

MIDAS RUN

CAST

John Pedley	Fred Astaire
Sylvia Giroux	Anne Heywood
Mike Warden	Richard Crenna
Wister	Roddy McDowall
Henshaw	Sir Ralph Richardson
Dodero	Cesar Romero
Aldo Ferranti	Adolfo Celi
Crittenden	Maurice Denham
Wells	John LeMesurier
Co-Pilot	Fred Astaire, Jr.
Giroux	Jacques Sernas
Dietrich	Karl Otto Alberty
Pfeiffer	George Hartman
Mrs. Pfeiffer	Caroline de Fonseca
Pilot	Stanley Baugh
Gordon	Bruce Beeby
The Dean	Robert Henderson

Producer: Raymond Stross for Selmur Pictures Director: Alf Kjellin. Screenplay: James Buchanan & Ronald Austin, from story by Berne Giler. Art directors: Arthur Lawson, Ezio Cescotti. Costumes: Franco Antonelli. Background score: Elmer Bernstein. Lyric of title song: Don Black. (Sung by Anne Heywood.) Cameraman: Ken Higgins. Editor: Frederick Steinkamp. Release date: May 7, 1969. Running time: 106 minutes.

Midas Run was Fred Astaire's thirty-fifth movie and the fourth in which he played a nonsinging or dancing role. It was hardly among the imperishable ones, but it did offer Fred Astaire a part that was understandably appealing: a debonair British Secret Service officer who masterminds the hijacking of a government shipment of fifteen-million-dollars' worth of gold ingots being transported from Zurich to Tanzania via Italy. Apart from allowing him to be devilishly clever, the assignment also allowed Astaire to spend some free time in Europe in the company of his son, Fred, Jr., who had a small role in the film. Most of the action was shot on location in Italy, primarily in Venice, Terrentia, Rome, Milan, Florence, and Siena.

Reviewers were not exactly in a fedora-flinging mood following the picture's release, early in May 1969. "Despite its amiable 14-karat good intentions, *Midas Run* contains more dross than gold," revealed A. H. Weiler in *The New York Times,* and there were few to quarrel with his appraisal. Astaire, however, was well received under the circumstances. According to Alan Kriegsman in the *Washington Post,* "What keeps this mishmash from being a total loss is mainly Fred Astaire," and like-minded Ronald Gold in *Variety* commented, "the film is a spotty effort that is salvaged occasionally by Fred Astaire's ability to overcome a strictly pedestrian script."

Like *Finian's Rainbow, Midas Run* involved Fred Astaire in a scheme to turn gold into money, and again the effort paid off in an entirely unexpected manner. Seems that John Pedley (Fred Astaire), a veteran officer in Her Majesty's Secret Service, is mighty peeved at being constantly passed over for a knighthood. So he decides to do something that will really make everyone take notice. Plotting

Anne Heywood and Richard Crenna.

458

Fred with accomplices Crenna and Heywood.

with an American friend, Mike Warden (Richard Crenna), and a French girl, Sylvia Giroux (Anne Heywood), Pedley devises a daringly dramatic caper: the theft of 350 gold ingots while they are being flown over Italy in a plane chartered by a group of English tourists. Collaborating with the heisting gang are an ex-Nazi Luftwaffe pilot (Karl Otto Alberty), who is to head off the chartered plane and force it to land, and an ex-Fascist general (Adolfo Celi), who is to arrange for the sale of the gold.

Plans become further complicated when Henshaw (Sir Ralph Richardson), Pedley's superior, assigns Pedley the responsibility of protecting the in-gots, which means he must become a passenger on the flight. But the hijacking works smoothly enough: the German buzzes the chartered plane, the plane lands where it's supposed to, and Mike and Sylvia unload the gold onto waiting trucks. Pedley now finds himself in the ironic position of being in charge of tracking down the loot. He does such a perfectly splendid job of it that he even gets the authorities to drop charges against Mike and Sylvia by convincing them that the two are government agents. Because of his role in recovering the ingots that he had been responsible for stealing, John Pedley, at long last, is dubbed Sir John Pedley.

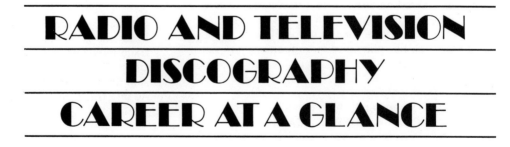

RADIO AND TELEVISION

DISCOGRAPHY

CAREER AT A GLANCE

NETWORK RADIO AND TELEVISION APPEARANCES

RADIO

August 12, 1935 *(series)*
YOUR HIT PARADE
Musical variety program with Fred Astaire,
Lennie Hayton Orchestra.
Sponsor: Lucky Strike Cigarettes.
NBC

September 15, 1936 *(39-week series)*
THE PACKARD HOUR
Variety program with Fred Astaire (host),
Charles Butterworth, Johnny Green
Orchestra, guest stars.
Sponsor: Packard Motor Car Company.
NBC

May 4, 1947
THE ANIMAL KINGDOM
Play by Philip Barry, adapted by
Arthur Arent.
Theatre Guild of the Air
Director: Homer Fickett.
Sponsor: U.S. Steel.
CAST: Fred Astaire, Wendy Barrie, Roger
Pryor, Carol Goodner, Carl Frank, Bill
Adams, Maria Manton, Cathleen Cordell,
Chester Stratton.
ABC

TELEVISION

April 3, 1955
THE TOAST OF THE TOWN
Variety program with Ed Sullivan (host),
Fred Astaire (TV debut), Will Mastin Trio
starring Sammy Davis, Jr., Dorothy
Dandridge, Julius La Rosa, Jackie Miles,
British champion strongwoman Joan
Rhodes.
CBS

December 1, 1957
IMP ON A COBWEB LEASH
Play by Jameson Brewer, John Keasler.
General Electric Theatre
Producer: William Frye, MCA-Revue
Productions. Director: Robert B. Sinclair.
Sponsor: General Electric.
CAST: Fred Astaire, Joan Tetzel, Rhys
Williams, Joyce Meadows, Howard Smith,
Margaret Irving, Walter Woolf King.
CBS

October 17, 1958
(repeated January 28, 1959)
AN EVENING WITH FRED ASTAIRE
Executive producer: Fred Astaire, Ava
Productions, Inc. Producer-director: Bud
Yorkin. Dance director: Hermes Pan.
Assistants: Gino Malerba, David Robel,
Pat Denise. Special material: Herbert
Baker. Music director: David Rose. Art
director: Edward Stephenson. Costumes:
Ray Aghayan. Sponsor: Chrysler Corp.
CAST: Fred Astaire, Barrie Chase, Jonah
Jones Quartet.
MUSICAL NUMBERS: "Svengali"—
Astaire, dancers/ "Change Partners"—
Astaire, Chase/ "Prop Dance"—Astaire/
"Baubles, Bangles and Beads," "Mack the
Knife"—Jones Quartet/ "Man with the
Blues"—Astaire, Chase, dancers/ "Old
MacDonald"—dancers/ "St. James
Infirmary"—Astaire, Chase, dancers/
Medley: "Oh, Lady, Be Good," "Cheek
to Cheek," "A Fine Romance," "They
Can't Take That Away from Me," "Nice
Work if You Can Get It," "A Foggy Day,"
"I Won't Dance," "Something's Gotta
Give," "Night and Day," "Top Hat, White
Tie and Tails"—Astaire/ "Isn't This a
Lovely Day?"—Astaire
NBC
*Note: Above program won nine Emmy
awards, plus Peabody award.*

September 3, 1959
MAN ON A BICYCLE
Play by Jameson Brewer, Victor Canning.
General Electric Theatre.
Producer: William Frye, MCA-Revue
Productions. Director: Herschel
Daugherty. Sponsor: General Electric.
CAST: Fred Astaire, Roxanne Berard,
Ann Codee, Linda Watkins, Stanley
Adams, David Hoffman, Jan Arvan.
CBS

Broadcasting *The Packard Hour* with Charles Butterworth

In *Imp on a Cobweb Leash,* Fred's first appearance in a television play (1957).

A special microphone was needed for Fred's tap dancing on the *Hit Parade* radio series (1935).

463

Dancing with Barrie Chase in *An Evening with Fred Astaire* (1958).

November 4, 1959
ANOTHER EVENING WITH FRED ASTAIRE
Executive producer: Fred Astaire, Ava Productions, Inc. Producer-director: Bud Yorkin. Dance director: Hermes Pan. Assistants: Gino Malerba, David Robel, Pat Denise. Music director: David Rose. Choral director: Bill Thompson. Art director: Edward Stephenson. Costumes: Ray Aghayan, Jean Louis. Sponsor: Chrysler Corp.
CAST: Fred Astaire, Barrie Chase, Jonah Jones Quartet, Bill Thompson Singers.
MUSICAL NUMBERS: "The Afterbeat"—Astaire/ "That Face"—Astaire, Chase/ "Drum Solo Dance"—Astaire/ "Girl in Calico," "When the Saints Go Marching In," "Night Train"—Jones Quartet/ "My Baby"—Astaire, Chase, narrated by Ken Nordine/ "Waltzing Matilda"—dancers/ "Sophisticated Lady"—Astaire, Chase/ Medley: "Fascinating Rhythm," "Dancing in the Dark," "The Way You Look Tonight," "Dearly Beloved," "Steppin' Out with My Baby," "Let's Face the Music and Dance," "The Carioca," "The Continental," "One for My Baby," "By Myself"—Astaire
NBC
Note: Above program won the TV Guide award.

September 28, 1960
ASTAIRE TIME
Producer: Fred Astaire, Ava Productions, Inc. Director: Greg Garrison. Dance director-Associate producer: Hermes Pan. Production coordinator: Gil Rodin. Music director: David Rose. Art director: Edward Stephenson. Costumes: Grady Hunt, Jean Louis. Sponsor: Chrysler Corp.
CAST: Fred Astaire, Barrie Chase, Count Basie Orchestra, Joe Williams, Ruth and Jane Earl.
MUSICAL NUMBERS: "Romeo and Juliet Overture"—Astaire, Chase/ "Miss Otis Regrets"—Astaire/ "Not Now"—Basie Orch./ "Sweet Georgia Brown"—Astaire, Basie Orch./ "Valse triste"—Chase/ "We Have to Dance"—dancers/ "The Sheik of Araby"—Astaire, Earl Twins/ "It's a Wonderful World"—Williams, Basie Orch./ "Blues"—Astaire, Chase, Williams, Basie Orch./ Medley: "Thank You So Much, Mrs. Lowsborough—Goodby," "Funny Face," "I Love Louisa," "Flying Down to Rio," "I'm Putting All My Eggs in One

Basket," "They All Laughed," "Lovely to Look At," "Let's Call the Whole Thing Off," "Easter Parade," "A Shine on Your Shoes"—Astaire
NBC
Note: Above program won two Emmy awards.

October 10, 1961—September 18, 1962
October 4, 1962—September 12, 1963
Mr. Astaire was host of Fred Astaire's Premier Theatre for two years and appeared in five plays.
Producer: ABC-Revue Productions.
Sponsor: Aluminum Corp. of America.

February 13, 1962
MR. EASY
Play by Jameson Brewer, Matt Taylor, Claude Binyon.
Director: John Newland.
CAST: Fred Astaire, Joanna Barnes, David White, George Petrie, Harold Fong, Fredd Wayne, Howard Wendell.

July 10, 1962
MOMENT OF DECISION
Play by Larry Marcus, Peter Tewksbury, James Leighton.
Director: John Newland.
CAST: Fred Astaire, Maureen O'Sullivan, Harry Townes, Oliver McGowan, Cathleen Cordell, Connie Gilchrist, Katherine Henryck.

October 11, 1962
GUEST IN THE HOUSE
Play by James Dunn, Philip MacDonald.
Director: Ted Post.
CAST: Fred Astaire, Lloyd Bochner, Philip Abbott, Susan Gordon, Phyllis Avery.

November 1, 1962
MISTER LUCIFER
Play by Alfred Bester.
Director: Alan Crosland, Jr.
CAST: Fred Astaire, Elizabeth Montgomery, Frank Aletter, George Petrie, Joyce Bulifant.

December 27, 1962
BLUES FOR A HANGING
Play by John and Ward Hawkins.
Director: Benard Girard.
CAST: Fred Astaire, Janis Paige, Richard Shannon, Lurene Tuttle, Lory Patrick, TylerMcDuff, Shelly Manne, Robert H. Harris.
ABC

October 2, 1964
THINK PRETTY
Play by Gary Marshall, Jerry Belson, Bill Persky, Sam Denoff.
Bob Hope's Chrysler Theatre
Producer: Richard Lewis. Director: Jack Arnold. Music: Tommy Wolf. Dance director: Hermes Pan. Sponsor: Chrysler Corp.
CAST: Fred Astaire, Barrie Chase, Roger Perry, Louis Nye, Reta Shaw, Linda Foster, Marilyn Wayne, Jack Bernardi.
NBC

November 22/ 23/ 29/ 30, 1965
DR. KILDARE
Play by William Fay.
Producer: Douglas Benton. Director: Herschel Daugherty.
Mr. Astaire appeared in a four-part episode of the series under the following titles: *Fathers and Daughters, A Gift of Love, The Tent Dwellers, Going Home.*
CAST: Fred Astaire, Richard Chamberlain, Raymond Massey, Laura Devon, Audrey Totter, Spring Byington, Norman Fell, Harry Morgan.
NBC

January 22, 1966
HOLLYWOOD PALACE
Variety program with Fred Astaire (host), Barrie Chase, Mickey Rooney and Bobby Van, Petula Clark, The Nitwits, The Lenz Chimps, comic Ray Hastings. Music director: Mitchell Ayres.
ABC

March 12, 1966
(repeated September 10, 1966)
HOLLYWOOD PALACE
Variety program with Fred Astaire (host), Ethel Merman, Jack Jones, Marcel Marceau, comic Pat Morita, acrobats Hardy Family. Music director: Mitchell Ayres.
ABC

April 30, 1966
HOLLYWOOD PALACE
Variety program with Fred Astaire (host), Barrie Chase, Herb Alpert and the Tijuana Brass, Louis Nye, Helen O'Connell, The Muppets, juggler Bela Kremo, lion tamer John Zerbini. Music director: Mitchell Ayres.
ABC

February 7, 1968
THE FRED ASTAIRE SHOW
Producers: Fred Astaire, Gil Rodin. Director: Robert Scheerer. Dance director: Herbert Ross. Music director: Neal Hefti. Music coordinators: Betty Walberg, Joseph Lipman. Art director: James Trittipo. Costumes: Bob Mackie. Sponsor: Foundation for Commercial Banks.
CAST: Fred Astaire, Barrie Chase, Sergio Mendes and Brasil '66, The Young-Holt Unlimited, The Gordian Knot, Simon and Garfunkel.
MUSICAL NUMBERS: "I've a Shooting Box in Scotland"—Astaire/ "I Love to Quarrel with You"—Astaire/ "Look to the Rainbow"—Astaire/ "When the Idle Poor Become the Idle Rich"—Astaire/ "Top Hat, White Tie and Tails"—Astaire/ "Oh, You Beautiful Doll," "The Look of Love," "Limehouse Blues," "Chinatown, My Chinatown"—Astaire, Chase/ "Pinky's Dilemma"—Simon and Garfunkel, Astaire
NBC

IT TAKES A THIEF
Plays by Glen A. Larsen.
Producer: Glen A. Larsen. Executive producer-director: Jack Arnold.
Mr. Astaire appeared as Alistair Mundy, father of the series' hero, in four episodes.
October 16, 1969
(repeated February 16, 1970)
THE GREAT CASINO CAPER
CAST: Fred Astaire, Robert Wagner, Adolfo Celi, Edward Binns, Francesco Mule, Gerard Herter, Francoise Prevost.
November 6, 1969
(repeated April 20, 1970)
THREE VIRGINS OF ROME
CAST: Fred Astaire, Robert Wagner, Victor Buono, Edmund Purdom, Karin Dor, Massimo Serato.
December 4, 1969
(repeated April 27, 1970)
THE SECOND TIME AROUND
CAST: Fred Astaire, Robert Wagner, Malachi Throne, Adolfo Celi, Edward Binns, Alice Ghostley, Martin Kosleck.
March 9, 1970
AN EVENING WITH ALISTAIR MUNDY
CAST: Fred Astaire, Robert Wagner, Edward Binns, Francesco Mule, Lynn Kellogg, Logan Ramsey.
ABC

Rehearsing with Barrie Chase.

November 10, 1970
THE DICK CAVETT SHOW
Mr. Astaire was the sole guest on the
90-minute program.
ABC

November 17, 1970
THE OVER-THE-HILL GANG RIDES AGAIN
Play by Richard Carr.
Movie of the Week
Executive producers: Aaron Spelling,
Danny Thomas. Director: George
McCowan. Music: David Raksin.
CAST: Walter Brennan, Fred Astaire,
Edgar Buchanan, Andy Devine, Chill Wills,
Paul Richards, Lana Wood.
ABC

December 13, 1970
*(repeated December 3, 1971;
December 1, 1972)*
SANTA CLAUS IS COMING TO TOWN
Play by Romeo Muller. Songs by Maury
Laws and Jules Bass.
Animated cartoon with voices of Fred
Astaire, Mickey Rooney, Keenan Wynn,
Paul Frees.
ABC

October 13, 1971
THE DICK CAVETT SHOW
Mr. Astaire again was the sole guest on
the 90-minute program.
ABC

January 17, 1972
**'S WONDERFUL 'S MARVELOUS
'S GERSHWIN**
Bell System Family Theatre
Executive producer: Joseph Cates.
Producer–writer–co-director: Martin
Charnin. Co-director: Walter C. Miller.
Dance director: Alan Johnson. Music
director: Elliot Lawrence. Dance arrange-
ments: John Morris. Sponsor: American
Telephone and Telegraph Co.
CAST: Jack Lemmon, Fred Astaire, Ethel
Merman, Leslie Uggams, Peter Nero,
Linda Bennett, Larry Kert, Robert
Guillaume, Alan Johnson.
NBC

September 9, 1972
MAKE MINE RED, WHITE AND BLUE
Executive producers: David L. Wolper,
Warren V. Bush. Producers: Bill Hobin,
George Sunga. Director: Bill Hobin.
Writers: Ed Haas, Jack Lloyd. Music
director: David Rose. Sponsor: Timex.
CAST: Fred Astaire, The 5th Dimension,
Michele Lee, Bob Crane. Jan Arvan, Irwin
Charone, Jason Johnson, Iron Eyes Cody,
Jimmy Joyce Singers, Tom Hansen
Dancers.
NBC

GUEST APPEARANCE IN FILM

January 11, 1973
IMAGINE
Film by John Lennon and Yoko Ono
Mr. Astaire appeared in Riverdale party
sequence along with Jack Palance, Dick
Cavett, and George Harrison. Sequence
directed by Jonas Mekas.

Son Fred Junior and daughter Ava visit Fred
on the set of *Man on a Bicycle* (1959).

Fred as Robert Wagner's father in *The Great Casino Caper*, from the television series, *It Takes a Thief* (1969).

Appearing on *The Dick Cavett Show* (1970).

DISCOGRAPHY

Compiled by Howard Levine

Following abbreviations used: E.Col. for English Columbia, WRC for World Record Club, M-E for Monmouth-Evergreen, Br. for Brunswick. 78 & 45 rpm record numbers appear in Roman type, followed by 33¹/₃ rpm record numbers in italics. An asterisk indicates dance solo.

RECORDED FOR 78 (OR 45) RPM RELEASES

1923 THE WHICHNESS OF THE
    WHATNESS
    OH, GEE! OH, GOSH!
        Vocals with Adele Astaire
        HMV B1719/ *WRC 125; M-E 7037*
1926 FASCINATING RHYTHM
        Vocal with Adele Astaire
    THE HALF OF IT, DEARIE,
        BLUES*
        George Gershwin, piano
        E.Col. 3969/ *WRC 124; M-E 7036*
    HANG ON TO ME
    I'D RATHER CHARLESTON
        Vocals with Adele Astaire
        George Gershwin, piano
        E.Col. 3970/ *WRC 124; M-E 7036*
    SWISS MISS
        Vocal with Adele Astaire
        E.Col. 3979/ *WRC 124; M-E 7036*
1928 HIGH HAT
    MY ONE AND ONLY*
        E.Col. 5173/ *WRC 125; M-E 7037*
    FUNNY FACE
    THE BABBITT AND THE
        BROMIDE
        Vocals with Adele Astaire
        E.Col. 5174/ *WRC 125; M-E 7037*
1929 NOT MY GIRL
    LOUISIANA
        Al Starita Orchestra
        E.Col. 5355/ *WRC 124; M-E 7036*
1930 PUTTIN' ON THE RITZ*
    CRAZY FEET*
        E.Col. DB96/ *WRC 124; M-E 7036*
1931 I LOVE LOUISA
    NEW SUN IN THE SKY
        Leo Reisman Orchestra
        Victor 22755/ *Vik 1001*
    WHITE HEAT
    HOOPS
        Vocals with Adele Astaire
        Leo Reisman Orchestra
        Victor 22836/ *Vik 1001;* Side 2
        also *RCA LPV 565*

1932 NIGHT AND DAY
    I'VE GOT YOU ON MY MIND
        Leo Reisman Orchestra
        Victor 24193/ *Vik 1001;* Eng.
        RCA RD 7756; RCA Intl. 1037;
        Side 1 also *RCA LPV 565*
1933 MAYBE I LOVE YOU TOO MUCH
        Leo Reisman Orchestra
        Victor 24262/ *Vik 1001;* Eng.
        RCA RD 7756; RCA Intl. 1037
    GOLD DIGGER'S SONG
    MY TEMPTATION
        Leo Reisman Orchestra
        Victor 24312/ *Vik 1001;* Eng.
        RCA RD 7756; RCA Intl. 1037;
        Side 1 also *RCA LPV 565*
    NIGHT AND DAY
    AFTER YOU
        E.Col. DB1215/ *WRC 124; M-E
        7036*
    FLYING DOWN TO RIO
    MUSIC MAKES ME*
        Col. 2912D; E.Col. DB1329/ *WRC
        124; M-E 7036;* Side 2 also
        Epic L2N 6072
    A HEART OF STONE
        Leo Reisman Orchestra
        Victor 24358/ *Vik 1001;* Eng.
        RCA RD 7756; RCA Intl. 1037
1935 CHEEK TO CHEEK
    NO STRINGS*
        Leo Reisman Orchestra
        Br. 7486/ Side 1 also *Epic FLM
        13103; Harmony 30549*
    ISN'T THIS A LOVELY DAY?
    TOP HAT, WHITE TIE AND TAILS*
        Johnny Green Orchestra
        Br. 7487
    THE PICCOLINO
        Leo Reisman Orchestra
        Br. 7488

1936 LET'S FACE THE MUSIC AND
DANCE
LET YOURSELF GO*
Johnny Green Orchestra
Br. 7608
I'M PUTTING ALL MY EGGS IN
ONE BASKET
WE SAW THE SEA
Johnny Green Orchestra
Br. 7609
I'D RATHER LEAD A BAND*
I'M BUILDING UP TO AN
AWFUL LET-DOWN
Johnny Green Orchestra
Br. 7610; Col. 3118D
A FINE ROMANCE
Johnny Green Orchestra
Br. 7716/ Epic FLM 13103
THE WAY YOU LOOK TONIGHT
PICK YOURSELF UP*
Johnny Green Orchestra
Br. 7717
NEVER GONNA DANCE
BOJANGLES OF HARLEM*
Johnny Green Orchestra
Br. 7718/ Side 2 also Epic L2N
6064
1937 THEY CAN'T TAKE THAT AWAY
FROM ME
(I'VE GOT) BEGINNER'S LUCK
Johnny Green Orchestra
Br. 7855/ Side 1 also Epic FLM
13103
THEY ALL LAUGHED
SLAP THAT BASS*
Johnny Green Orchestra
Br. 7856/ Epic FLM 13103; Side
2 also Epic FLM 15105
LET'S CALL THE WHOLE THING
OFF
SHALL WE DANCE?*
Johnny Green Orchestra
Br. 7857/ Side 1 also Epic FLM
13103
A FOGGY DAY
I CAN'T BE BOTHERED NOW*
Ray Noble Orchestra
Br. 7982/ Epic FLM 13103
THINGS ARE LOOKING UP
NICE WORK IF YOU CAN
GET IT*
Ray Noble Orchestra
Br. 7983/Epic FLM 13103
1938 CHANGE PARTNERS
I USED TO BE COLOR BLIND
Ray Noble Orchestra
Br. 8189/ Side 1 also Epic FLM
13103
THE YAM*
THE YAM STEP*
Ray Noble Orchestra
Br. 8190

1940 WHO CARES?
JUST LIKE TAKING CANDY
FROM A BABY*
Benny Goodman Orchestra
Col. 35517/ Col. CSM 891
LOVE OF MY LIFE
ME AND THE GHOST
UPSTAIRS*
Orchestra, Perry Botkin cond.
Col. 35815
POOR MISTER CHISHOLM
(I AIN'T HEP TO THAT STEP
BUT I'LL) DIG IT*
Orchestra, Perry Botkin cond.
Col. 35852/ Side 2 also Epic FLM
13103
1941 SO NEAR AND YET SO FAR
SINCE I KISSED MY BABY
GOODBYE
Vocal with Delta Rhythm Boys
Orchestra, Harry Sosnik cond.
Decca 18187/ Side 1 also Voc.
3716
DREAM DANCING
THE WEDDING CAKE-WALK
Vocal with Delta Rhythm Boys
Orchestra, Harry Sosnik cond.
Decca 18188/ Voc. 3716
1942 I'LL CAPTURE YOUR HEART
SINGING*
Vocal with Bing Crosby, Margaret
Lenhart
Bob Crosby Orchestra
Decca 18427/ Decca 4256
YOU'RE EASY TO DANCE WITH
I CAN'T TELL A LIE
Decca 18428/ Decca 4256; Side 1
also Voc. 3716
LET'S SAY IT WITH
FIRECRACKERS*
Bob Crosby Orchestra
Decca (unissued)
YOU WERE NEVER LOVELIER
ON THE BEAM
Orchestra, John Scott Trotter
cond.
Decca 18489/ Voc. 3716
I'M OLD FASHIONED
WEDDING IN THE SPRING
Orchestra, John Scott Trotter
cond.
Decca 18490/ Side 1 also Voc.
3716
DEARLY BELOVED
THE SHORTY GEORGE
Orchestra, John Scott Trotter
cond.
Decca 18491/ Voc. 3716
1944 THIS HEART OF MINE
IF SWING GOES, I GO TOO
Orchestra, Albert Sack cond.
Decca 23388/ Voc. 3716

Leo Reisman

471

1945 ONE FOR MY BABY
OH, MY ACHIN' BACK
Orchestra, Albert Sack cond.
Decca (unissued)
1946 PUTTIN' ON THE RITZ
A COUPLE OF SONG AND
DANCE MEN*
Vocal with Bing Crosby
Orchestra, John Scott Trotter
cond.
Decca 23650/ Side 1 also *Voc.*
3716; Side 2 also *Decca 4259*
1948 EASTER PARADE
Vocal with Judy Garland
MGM Orch., Johnny Green cond.
MGM 30185/ *MGM E3227; Eng.*
MGM 2353 076
A COUPLE OF SWELLS
I LOVE A PIANO/ SNOOKY
OOKUMS/ WHEN THE
MIDNIGHT CHOO-CHOO
LEAVES FOR ALABAM'
Vocals with July Garland
MGM Orch., Johnny Green cond.
MGM 30186/ *MGM E3227; Eng.*
MGM 2353 076
IT ONLY HAPPENS WHEN I
DANCE WITH YOU
MGM Orch., Johnny Green cond.
MGM 30187/ *MGM E3413*
STEPPIN' OUT WITH MY BABY
MGM Orch., Johnny Green cond.
MGM 30188/ *MGM E3227; MGM*
E3413; Eng. *MGM 2353 076*
1949 YOU'D BE HARD TO REPLACE
MY ONE AND ONLY HIGHLAND
FLING
Vocal with Ginger Rogers
MGM Orch., Lennie Hayton cond.
MGM 50016/ Side 1 also *MGM*
E3413
THEY CAN'T TAKE THAT AWAY
FROM ME
SHOES WITH WINGS ON*
MGM Orch., Lennie Hayton cond.
MGM 50017/ *MGM E3413*
1950 WHERE DID YOU GET THAT
GIRL?
Vocal with Anita Ellis
MGM Orch., André Previn cond.
MGM 30239/ *MGM E3768; Eng.*
MGM 2353 033
NEVERTHELESS
Vocal with Anita Ellis, Red
Skelton
MGM Orch., André Previn cond.
MGM 30240/ *MGM E3768; Eng.*
MGM 2353 033

MY SUNNY TENNESSEE/ SO
LONG, OO-LONG/ THREE
LITTLE WORDS
Vocals with Red Skelton
MGM Orch., André Previn cond.
MGM 30241/ *MGM E3768; Eng.*
MGM 2353 033
1951 HOW COULD YOU BELIEVE ME
WHEN I SAID I LOVE YOU
WHEN YOU KNOW I'VE
BEEN A LIAR ALL MY
LIFE?
Vocal with Jane Powell
MGM Orch., Johnny Green cond.
MGM 30316/ *MGM E3235*
I LEFT MY HAT IN HAITI
YOU'RE ALL THE WORLD TO ME
MGM Orch., Johnny Green cond.
MGM 30317/ *MGM E3235;* Side 1
also *MGM E3413*
EV'RY NIGHT AT SEVEN
MGM Orch., Johnny Green cond.
MGM 30319/ *MGM E3235; MGM*
E3413
1952 BABY DOLL
MGM Orch., Adolph Deutsch
cond.
MGM 30517/ *MGM E3413*
OOPS!
SEEING'S BELIEVING
MGM Orch., Adolph Deutsch
cond.
MGM 30518/ Side 2 also *MGM*
E3413
BACHELOR DINNER SONG
I WANNA BE A DANCIN' MAN*
MGM Orch., Adolph Deutsch
cond.
MGM 30520
1953 A SHINE ON YOUR SHOES*
I LOVE LOUISA
MGM Orch., Adolph Deutsch
cond.
MGM 30792/ *MGM E3051; MGM*
E3413
BY MYSELF
THAT'S ENTERTAINMENT
Vocal with Nanette Fabray, Jack
Buchanan, Oscar Levant, India
Adams
MGM Orch., Adolph Deutsch
cond.
MGM 30793/ *MGM E3051;* Side 1
also *MGM E3413*
TRIPLETS
Vocal with Nanette Fabray, Jack
Buchanan
MGM Orch., Adolph Deutsch
cond.
MGM 30794/ *MGM E3051*

I GUESS I'LL HAVE TO CHANGE
  MY PLAN
    Vocal with Jack Buchanan
    MGM Orch., Adolph Deutsch
    cond.
    MGM 30795/ *MGM E3051*
1955 SOMETHING'S GOTTA GIVE
SLUEFOOT
    Orchestra, Russ Garcia cond.
    RCA Victor 20-6140/ Side 1 also
    Reader's Digest 49-5
1956 HELLO, BABY
THERE'S NO TIME LIKE THE
  PRESENT
    Buddy Bregman Orchestra
    Verve 2009/ *Verve MGV 2114*
SWEET SORROW
JUST LIKE TAKING CANDY
  FROM A BABY
    Buddy Bregman Orchestra
    Verve 2019/ *Verve MGV 2114*
CLAP YO' HANDS*
    Vocal with Kay Thompson
    Orch., Adolph Deutsch cond.
    Verve 10041X45/
    Verve MGV 15001
HE LOVES AND SHE LOVES
FUNNY FACE*
    Orch., Adolph Deutsch cond.
    Verve 10042X45/
    Verve MGV 15001
1957 THAT FACE
CALYPSO HOORAY
    Buddy Bregman Orchestra
    Verve 10051X45/ Side 1 also
    Verve MGV 2114
1959 I'LL WALK ALONE
THE AFTERBEAT
    Orchestra, Pete King cond.
    Kapp 311X(45)
THAT FACE
THANK YOU SO MUCH, MISSUS
  LOWSBOROUGH-GOODBY
    Orchestra, David Rose cond.
    Choreo 100(45)/ *Choreo A-1*
1962 THE NOTORIOUS LANDLADY
THE MARTINI
    Orchestra, Dick Hazard cond.
    Choreo 104(45)
IT HAPPENS EVERY SPRING
YOU WORRY ME
    Orchestra, Dick Hazard cond.
    Ava 125(45)

Ray Noble.

RECORDED FOR 33⅓ RPM RELEASES
1931 *Victor L 24003* (10″)
  THE BAND WAGON
    Leo Reisman Orchestra
  SWEET MUSIC
    Vocal with Adele Astaire
  HOOPS
    Vocal with Adele Astaire
  I LOVE LOUISA
  WHITE HEAT
    Arthur Schwartz, piano
1952 *Clef MGC 1001/2/3/4*
  THE ASTAIRE STORY
    Produced by Norman Granz
    Oscar Peterson Group
  ISN'T THIS A LOVELY DAY?#
  PUTTIN' ON THE RITZ
  I USED TO BE COLOR BLIND##
  THE CONTINENTAL
  LET'S CALL THE WHOLE
    THING OFF#
  CHANGE PARTNERS#
  'S WONDERFUL#
  LOVELY TO LOOK AT
  THEY ALL LAUGHED
  CHEEK TO CHEEK
  STEPPIN' OUT WITH BY BABY#
  THE WAY YOU LOOK
    TONIGHT##
  I'VE GOT MY EYES ON YOU
  DANCING IN THE DARK
  THE CARIOCA
  NICE WORK IF YOU CAN
    GET IT
  NEW SUN IN THE SKY##
  I WON'T DANCE#
  FAST DANCE*#
  TOP HAT, WHITE TIE AND
    TAILS#
  NO STRINGS
  I CONCENTRATE ON YOU##
  I'M PUTTING ALL MY EGGS IN
    ONE BASKET
  A FINE ROMANCE#
  NIGHT AND DAY#
  FASCINATING RHYTHM
  I LOVE LOUISA
  SLOW DANCE*#
  MEDIUM DANCE*
  THEY CAN'T TAKE THAT AWAY
    FROM ME#
  YOU'RE EASY TO DANCE
    WITH##
  A NEEDLE IN A HAYSTACK
  SO NEAR AND YET SO FAR##
  A FOGGY DAY#
  OH, LADY BE GOOD!
  I'M BUILDING UP TO AN
    AWFUL LET-DOWN##
  NOT MY GIRL
    #also *Verve MGV 2010; ##also
    Verve MGV 2114*

1953 *MGM E3051* (film soundtrack)
THE BAND WAGON
  MGM Orch., Adolph Deutsch
    cond.
THE GIRL HUNT BALLET
  Narrated by Fred Astaire
  (For vocals, see 78 rpm list.)

1956 *Verve MGV 15001* (film soundtrack)
FUNNY FACE
  Orchestra, Adolph Deutsch cond.
FUNNY FACE*
BONJOURS, PARIS!
  Vocal with Audrey Hepburn, Kay
    Thompson
CLAP YO' HANDS*
  Vocal with Kay Thompson
HE LOVES AND SHE LOVES
LET'S KISS AND MAKE UP
'S WONDERFUL
  Vocal with Audrey Hepburn

1957 *MGM E3542ST* (film soundtrack)
    English MGM 2353 034
SILK STOCKINGS
  MGM Orch., André Previn cond.
TOO BAD
  Vocal with Peter Lorre, Joseph
    Buloff, Jules Munshin
PARIS LOVES LOVERS
  Vocal with Carol Richards
STEREOPHONIC SOUND
  Vocal with Janis Paige
ALL OF YOU
FATED TO BE MATED
THE RITZ ROLL AND ROCK

1959 *Kapp KL 1165/ KS 3049*
NOW
  Orchestra, Pete King cond.
CHANGE PARTNERS
ISN'T THIS A LOVELY DAY?
A FOGGY DAY
THE GIRL ON THE MAGAZINE
    COVER
I LOVE TO QUARREL WITH YOU
ALONG CAME RUTH
THE AFTERBEAT
THEY CAN'T TAKE THAT AWAY
    FROM ME
THEY ALL LAUGHED
I'LL WALK ALONE
ONE FOR MY BABY
OH, LADY BE GOOD!
PUTTIN' ON THE RITZ
TOP HAT, WHITE TIE AND TAILS
LADY OF THE EVENING
SOMETHING'S GOTTA GIVE

1960 *Choreo A-1* (TV soundtrack)
**THREE EVENINGS WITH FRED
ASTAIRE**
  Orchestra, David Rose cond.
OH, LADY BE GOOD!/ CHEEK
TO CHEEK/ A FINE ROMANCE/
THEY CAN'T TAKE THAT AWAY
FROM ME/ NICE WORK IF YOU
CAN GET IT/ A FOGGY DAY/ I
WON'T DANCE/ SOMETHING'S
GOTTA GIVE/ NIGHT AND DAY/
TOP HAT, WHITE TIE AND TAILS/
FASCINATING RHYTHM/
DANCING IN THE DARK/ THE
WAY YOU LOOK TONIGHT/
DEARLY BELOVED/ STEPPIN'
OUT WITH MY BABY/ LET'S
FACE THE MUSIC AND DANCE/
THE CARIOCA/ THE
CONTINENTAL/ ONE FOR MY
BABY/ BY MYSELF/ THAT FACE/
MISS OTIS REGRETS/ THANK
YOU SO MUCH, MISSUS
LOWSBOROUGH-GOODBY/
FUNNY FACE/ I LOVE LOUISA/
FLYING DOWN TO RIO/ I'M
PUTTING ALL MY EGGS IN
ONE BASKET/ THEY ALL
LAUGHED/ LOVELY TO LOOK
AT/ LET'S CALL THE WHOLE
THING OFF/ EASTER PARADE/
A SHINE ON YOUR SHOES

1968 *Warner BS2550* (film soundtrack)
FINIAN'S RAINBOW
  Orchestra, Ray Heindorf cond.
LOOK TO THE RAINBOW
  Vocal with Petula Clark
IF THIS ISN'T LOVE
  Vocal with Don Francks, Petula
    Clark
WHEN THE IDLE POOR
    BECOME THE IDLE RICH
  Vocal with Petula Clark

1971 *Daybreak 2009* (TV soundtrack)
**'S WONDERFUL, 'S MARVELOUS,
'S GERSHWIN**
  Orchestra, Elliot Lawrence cond.
'S WONDERFUL
OH, LADY BE GOOD!
THEY ALL LAUGHED
FASCINATING RHYTHM
A FOGGY DAY
LET'S CALL THE WHOLE
    THING OFF
THEY CAN'T TAKE THAT AWAY
    FROM ME

LP COLLECTIONS FROM PREVIOUS RELEASES

World Record Club 124
Monmouth-Evergreen 7036
LADY, BE GOOD!
World Record Club 125
Monmouth-Evergreen 7037
FUNNY FACE
Vik 1001
English RCA Victor RD 7756
RCA International 1037
THE BAND WAGON
MGM E3227
English MGM 2353 076
EASTER PARADE
MGM E3768ST
English MGM 2353 033
THREE LITTLE WORDS
Epic FLM 13103
**NOTHING THRILLED US HALF
AS MUCH**
Vocalion VL 3716
FRED ASTAIRE
MGM E3413
SHOES WITH WINGS ON
Verve MGV 2010
MR. TOP HAT
Verve MGV 2114
EASY TO DANCE WITH

SPECIAL 2-RECORD LP COLLECTION OF ALL BRUNSWICK RELEASES, 1935-38

Columbia SG32472
STARRING FRED ASTAIRE
CHEEK TO CHEEK/ NO STRINGS/ ISN'T THIS A LOVELY DAY?/ TOP HAT, WHITE TIE AND TAILS/ THE PICCOLINO/ LET'S FACE THE MUSIC AND DANCE/ LET YOURSELF GO/ I'M PUTTING ALL MY EGGS IN ONE BASKET/ WE SAW THE SEA/ I'D RATHER LEAD A BAND/ I'M BUILDING UP TO AN AWFUL LET-DOWN/ A FINE ROMANCE/ THE WAY YOU LOOK TONIGHT/ PICK YOURSELF UP/ NEVER GONNA DANCE/ BOJANGLES OF HARLEM/ WALTZ IN SWING TIME (ORCH. ONLY)/ THEY CAN'T TAKE THAT AWAY FROM ME/ (I'VE GOT) BEGINNER'S LUCK/ THEY ALL LAUGHED/ SLAP THAT BASS/ LET'S CALL THE WHOLE THING OFF/ SHALL WE DANCE?/ A FOGGY DAY/ I CAN'T BE BOTHERED NOW/ THINGS ARE LOOKING UP/ NICE WORK IF YOU CAN GET IT/ CHANGE PARTNERS/ I USED TO BE COLOR BLIND/ THE YAM/ THE YAM STEP

Fred and Johnny Green (1936).

CAREER AT A GLANCE

Note: Mr. Astaire choreographed all his own routines.

I. ON STAGE, NEW YORK & LONDON (L)

YEAR	PRODUCTION	NAME	DANCING PARTNER	WORDS & MUSIC	BOOK OR SKETCHES
1917	Over the Top	———	Adele Astaire	W: Charles Manning Matthew Woodward M: Sigmund Romberg Herman Timberg	Philip Bartholomae, Harold Atteridge
1918	Passing Show of 1918	———	Adele Astaire	W: Harold Atteridge M: Sigmund Romberg Jean Schwartz	Harold Atteridge
1919	Apple Blossoms	Johnnie	Adele Astaire	W: William LeBaron M: Fritz Kreisler Victor Jacobi	William LeBaron
1921	The Love Letter	Richard Kolner	Adele Astaire	W: William LeBaron M: Victor Jacobi	William LeBaron
1922	For Goodness Sake	Teddy Lawrence	Adele Astaire	W: Arthur Jackson M: William Daly Paul Lannin	Fred Jackson
1922	The Bunch and Judy	Gerald Lane	Adele Astaire	W: Anne Caldwell M: Jerome Kern	Anne Caldwell, Hugh Ford
1923	Stop Flirting (L) (For Goodness Sake)	Teddy Lawrence	Adele Astaire		
1924	Lady, Be Good!	Dick Trevor	Adele Astaire	W: Ira Gershwin M: George Gershwin	Guy Bolton, Fred Thompson
1926	Lady, Be Good! (L)	Dick Trevor	Adele Astaire		
1927	Funny Face	Jimmie Reeves	Adele Astaire	W: Ira Gershwin M: George Gershwin	Fred Thompson, Paul Gerard Smith
1928	Funny Face (L)	Jimmie Reeves	Adele Astaire		
1930	Smiles	Bob Hastings	Adele Astaire Marilyn Miller	W: Clifford Grey Harold Adamson Ring Lardner M: Vincent Youmans	William Anthony McGuire
1931	The Band Wagon	———	Adele Astaire Tilly Losch	W: Howard Dietz M: Arthur Schwartz	George S. Kaufman, Howard Dietz
1932	Gay Divorce	Guy Holden	Claire Luce	W & M: Cole Porter	Dwight Taylor
1933	Gay Divorce (L)	Guy Holden	Claire Luce		

DIRECTOR	DANCE DIRECTOR	PRODUCER	THEATRE	PERFORMANCES
Joseph Herbert	Allan K. Foster	Messrs. Shubert	44th St. Roof	78
J. C. Huffman	Jack Mason	Messrs. Shubert	Winter Garden	124
Fred Latham	Edward Royce	Charles Dillingham	Globe	256
Edward Royce	Edward Royce	Charles Dillingham	Globe	31
Priestley Morrison	Allan K. Foster	Alex A. Aarons	Lyric	103
Fred Latham	uncredited	Charles Dillingham	Globe	65
Felix Edwardes	Gus Sohlke	Alfred Butt	Shaftesbury, Queens, Strand	418
Felix Edwardes	Sammy Lee	Alex A. Aarons & Vinton Freedley	Liberty	330
Felix Edwardes	Max Scheck	Alfred Butt, Aarons & Freedley	Empire	326
Edgar MacGregor	Bobby Connolly	Alex A. Aarons & Vinton Freedley	Alvin	250
Felix Edwardes	Bobby Connolly	Alfred Butt, Lee Ephraim, Aarons & Freedley	Prince's	263
William Anthony McGuire	Ned Wayburn	Florenz Ziegfeld	Ziegfeld	63
Hassard Short	Albertina Rasch	Max Gordon	New Amsterdam	260
Howard Lindsay	Carl Randall & Barbara Newberry	Dwight Deere Wiman & Tom Weatherly	Ethel Barrymore Shubert	248
Felix Edwardes	Carl Randall & Barbara Newberry	Lee Ephraim	Palace	180

II. ON SCREEN

YEAR	FILM	NAME	OCCUPATION	DANCING PARTNER	WORDS & MUSIC
1933	Dancing Lady	Fred Astaire	dancer	Joan Crawford	multiple
1933	Flying Down to Rio	Fred Ayres	band musician	Ginger Rogers Dolores Del Rio	W: Edward Eliscu, Gus Kahn M: Vincent Youmans
1934	The Gay Divorcee	Guy Holden	dancer	Ginger Rogers	multiple
1935	Roberta	Huck Haines	band leader	Ginger Rogers	W: Otto Harbach Dorothy Fields M: Jerome Kern
1935	Top Hat	Jerry Travers	dancer	Ginger Rogers	W & M: Irving Berlin
1936	Follow the Fleet	Bake Baker	dancer, sailor, band leader	Ginger Rogers	W & M: Irving Berlin
1936	Swing Time	Lucky Garnett	dancer	Ginger Rogers	W: Dorothy Fields M: Jerome Kern
1937	Shall We Dance	Pete Peters	dancer	Ginger Rogers Harriet Hoctor	W: Ira Gershwin M: Jerome Kern
1937	A Damsel in Distress	Jerry Halliday	dancer	Burns & Allen	W: Ira Gershwin M: George Gershwin
1938	Carefree	Tony Flagg	psychiatrist	Ginger Rogers	W & M: Irving Berlin
1939	The Story of Vernon & Irene Castle	Vernon Castle	dancer	Ginger Rogers	multiple
1940	Broadway Melody of 1940	Johnny Brett	dancer	Eleanor Powell George Murphy	W & M: Cole Porter
1940	Second Chorus	Danny O'Neill	band leader, trumpeter	Paulette Goddard	W: Johnny Mercer M: multiple
1941	You'll Never Get Rich	Robert Curtis	director, draftee	Rita Hayworth	W & M: Cole Porter
1942	Holiday Inn	Ted Hanover	dancer	Virginia Dale Marjorie Reynolds	W & M: Irving Berlin
1942	You Were Never Lovelier	Robert Davis	dancer	Rita Hayworth	W: Johnny Mercer M: Jerome Kern

478

SCREENPLAY	DIRECTOR	DANCE DIRECTOR	PRODUCER	STUDIO
Allen Rivkin, P. J. Wolfson	Robert Z. Leonard	Sammy Lee Eddie Prinz	David O. Selznick	M-G-M
Cyril Hume, H. W. Hanemann, Erwin Gelsey	Thornton Freeland	Dave Gould	Louis Brock	RKO
George Marion, Jr., Dorothy Yost, Edward Kaufman	Mark Sandrich	Dave Gould	Pandro S. Berman	RKO
Jane Murfin, Sam Mintz, Glenn Tryon, Allan Scott	William A. Seiter	Hermes Pan	Pandro S. Berman	RKO
Dwight Taylor, Allan Scott	Mark Sandrich	Hermes Pan	Pandro S. Berman	RKO
Dwight Taylor, Allan Scott	Mark Sandrich	Hermes Pan	Pandro S. Berman	RKO
Howard Lindsay, Allan Scott	George Stevens	Hermes Pan	Pandro S. Berman	RKO
Allan Scott, Ernest Pagano	Mark Sandrich	Hermes Pan Harry Losee	Pandro S. Berman	RKO
P. G. Wodehouse, Ernest Pagano, S. K. Lauren	George Stevens	Hermes Pan	Pandro S. Berman	RKO
Allan Scott, Ernest Pagano	Mark Sandrich	Hermes Pan	Pandro S. Berman	RKO
Richard Sherman	H. C. Potter	Hermes Pan	George Haight	RKO
Leon Gordon, George Oppenheimer	Norman Taurog	Bobby Connolly	Jack Cummings	M-G-M
Elaine Ryan, Ian McL. Hunter	H. C. Potter	Hermes Pan	Boris Morros	Paramount
Michael Fessier, Ernest Pagano	Sidney Lanfield	Robert Alton	Samuel Bischoff	Columbia
Claude Binyon	Mark Sandrich	Danny Dare	Mark Sandrich	Paramount
Michael Fessier, Ernest Pagano, Delmar Daves	William A. Seiter	Val Roset	Louis F. Edelman	Columbia

YEAR	FILM	NAME	OCCUPATION	DANCING PARTNER	WORDS & MUSIC
1943	The Sky's the Limit	Fred Atwell	fighter pilot	Joan Leslie	W: Johnny Mercer M: Harold Arlen
1945	Yolanda and the Thief	Johnny Riggs	con man	Lucille Bremer	W: Arthur Freed M: Harry Warren
1946	Ziegfeld Follies ✓	———	———	Lucille Bremer Gene Kelly	multiple
1946	Blue Skies ✓	Jed Potter	dancer	Olga San Juan	W & M: Irving Berlin
1948	Easter Parade	Don Hewes	dancer	Judy Garland Ann Miller	W & M: Irving Berlin
1949	The Barkleys of Broadway	Josh Barkley	dancer-actor, director	Ginger Rogers	W: Ira Gershwin M: Harry Warren
1950	Three Little Words	Bert Kalmar	dancer, lyricist	Vera-Ellen	W: Bert Kalmar M: Harry Ruby
1950	Let's Dance	Don Elwood	dancer	Betty Hutton	W & M: Frank Loesser
1951	Royal Wedding	Tom Bowen	dancer	Jane Powell	W: Alan Jay Lerner M: Burton Lane
1952	The Belle of New York	Charles Hall	playboy	Vera-Ellen	W: Johnny Mercer M: Harry Warren
1953	The Band Wagon	Tony Hunter	dancer-actor, director	Cyd Charisse Jack Buchanan	W: Howard Dietz M: Arthur Schwartz
1955	Daddy Long Legs	Jervis Pendleton	businessman	Leslie Caron	W & M: Johnny Mercer
1957	Funny Face	Dick Avery	photographer	Audrey Hepburn	W: Ira Gershwin Leonard Gershe M: George Gershwin Roger Edens
1957	Silk Stockings	Steve Canfield	film producer	Cyd Charisse	W & M: Cole Porter
1959	On the Beach	Julian Osborn	scientist		
1961	The Pleasure of His Company	Pogo Poole	playboy		
1962	The Notorious Landlady	Franklin Armbruster	U.S. diplomat		
1968	Finian's Rainbow	Finian McLonergan	Irish immigrant		W: E. Y. Harburg M: Burton Lane
1969	Midas Run	John Pedley	British agent		

SCREENPLAY	DIRECTOR	DANCE DIRECTOR	PRODUCER	STUDIO
Frank Fenton, Lynn Root	Edward H. Griffith	Fred Astaire	David Hempstead	RKO
Irving Brecher	Vincente Minnelli	Eugene Loring	Arthur Freed	M-G-M
multiple	Vincente Minnelli	Robert Alton	Arthur Freed	M-G-M
Arthur Sheekman	Stuart Heisler	Hermes Pan	Sol C. Siegel	Paramount
Sidney Sheldon, Frances Goodrich, Albert Hackett	Charles Walters	Robert Alton	Arthur Freed	M-G-M
Betty Comden & Adolph Green	Charles Walters	Robert Alton Hermes Pan	Arthur Freed	M-G-M
George Wells	Richard Thorpe	Hermes Pan	Jack Cummings	M-G-M
Dane Lussier, Allan Scott	Norman Z. McLeod	Hermes Pan	Robert Fellows	Paramount
Alan Jay Lerner	Stanley Donen	Nick Castle	Arthur Freed	M-G-M
Robert O'Brien, Irving Elinson	Charles Walters	Robert Alton	Arthur Freed	M-G-M
Betty Comden & Adolph Green	Vincente Minnelli	Michael Kidd	Arthur Freed	M-G-M
Phoebe & Henry Ephron	Jean Negulesco	David Robel Roland Petit	Samuel G. Engel	20th Century-Fox
Leonard Gershe	Stanley Donen	Eugene Loring	Roger Edens	Paramount
Leonard Gershe, Leonard Spigelgass	Rouben Mamoulian	Hermes Pan Eugene Loring	Arthur Freed	M-G-M
John Paxton	Stanley Kramer		Stanley Kramer	United Artists
Samuel Taylor	George Seaton		William Perlberg	Paramount
Larry Gelbart, Blake Edwards	Richard Quine		Fred Kohlmar	Columbia
E. Y. Harburg & Fred Saidy	Francis Ford Coppola	Hermes Pan	Joseph Landon	Warner Bros.
James Buchanan, Ronald Austin	Alf Kjellin		Raymond Stross	Selmur

SONGS WITH MUSIC COMPOSED BY FRED ASTAIRE

TITLE	LYRICIST	YEAR	PRODUCTION
AFTERBEAT, THE	Johnny Mercer	1959	
BLUE WITHOUT YOU	Mitchell Parish, Jim Altemus	1930	
CALYPSO HOORAY	Fred Astaire	1957	
GIRLS LIKE YOU Co-composer: Tommy Wolf	Fred Astaire, Tommy Wolf	1962	
HELLO, BABY	Moe Jaffe, Walter Ruick	1956	
I LOVE EVERYBODY BUT YOU	Ava Astaire, Fred Astaire	1962	
IF SWING GOES, I GO TOO	Fred Astaire	1944	ZIEGFELD FOLLIES (film, 1946) Sung by Fred Astaire (unused)
I'LL NEVER LET YOU GO	Dave Dreyer, Jack Ellis	1936	
I'M BUILDING UP TO AN AWFUL LET-DOWN	Johnny Mercer	1936	RISE AND SHINE (London) Sung by Binnie Hale & Jack Whiting
JUST LIKE TAKING CANDY FROM A BABY	Gladys Shelley	1940	
JUST ONE MORE DANCE, MADAME	Dave Dreyer, Paul Francis Webster	1936	
LOVELY MELODY	Gladys Shelley	1956	
MORE AND MORE Co-composer: Richard Myers	Johnny Mercer	1930	TATTLE TALES (Boston) Sung by Odette Myrtil
NOT MY GIRL Co-composer: Van Phillips	Desmond Carter	1935	
OH, MY ACHIN' BACK	Willy Shore, Morey Amsterdam	1945	
SWEET SORROW	Gladys Shelley	1940	
TAPPIN' THE TIME	Jock Whitney, Jim Altemus	1927	SHAKE YOUR FEET (London) Sung by Joyce Barbour, company
THERE'S NO TIME LIKE THE PRESENT	Walter Ruick	1952	
YOU WORRY ME	Fred Astaire	1962	
YOU'VE SUCH A LOT	Austin Melford	1924	THE CO-OPTIMISTS (London) Sung by Phyllis Monkman & Austin Melford

INDEX

Aarons, Alex, 21-22, 25, 28, 39, 40, 42, 59, 477
Abbott, Philip, 465
ABC-Revue Productions, 465
Abel, David, 69, 97, 100, 119, 133, 151, 231
Abel, Walter, 231
Aber Twins, 40
"Abraham," 231, 239
Ackerman, P. Dodd, 38, 39
Adams, Bill, 462
Adams, India, 381, 472
Adams, Stanley, 462
Adamson, Harold, 40, 47, 476
Adler, Larry, 40
Adrian, 47, 201
Afra, Tybee, 421
"After You, Who?," 41, 42
"Afterbeat, The," 465, 473, 474, 482
"Again," 41
Aghayan, Ray, 462, 465
"Ah, che a voi perdoni iddio," 163
Ainslee, Marian, 173
Akst, Albert, 265, 303, 319, 355, 367, 381
Alberni, Luis, 57, 83
Alberty, Karl Otto, 457, 459
Albright, Lola, 303
Albro, Arthur, 38
Aletter, Frank, 465
Alexander, Ben, 151, 158
Alexander, Rod, 265
"Algerian Girl," 38
"All Alone Monday," 333, 345
"All by Myself," 289, 300
"All to Myself," 39, 42
"All of You," 421, 429, 474
Allen, Fred, 269
Allen, Gracie, 21, 163, 165, 167, 168-170, 478
Allister, Claud, 42
Allman, Elvira, 441
Allwyn, Astrid, 119
Allyson, June, 356, 358
"Along Came Ruth," 303, 474
Altemus, Jim, 482
Alton, Robert, 221, 265, 274, 303, 319, 320, 367, 479, 481
"Always," 289
Amatore, Pearl, 163
Ameche, Don, 422
American in Paris, An, 304, 365, 400
Ames, Leon, 279
Ames, Preston, 381
Amsterdam, Morey, 482
Anchors Aweigh, 304
Anderson, Donna, 435
Anderson, Roland, 231, 347

André Charlot's Revue of 1924, 274
"Angel," 279, 319
Angelo, Waldo, 289
Animal Crackers, 335
Animal Kingdom, The, 304, 462
Annie Get Your Gun, 348
Another Evening with Fred Astaire, 439, 465
Antonelli, Franco, 457
"Any Bonds Today," 289, 300
"Any Girl," 39
Anything Goes, 228
"Anyway We Had Fun," 40
Apple Blossoms, 18, 39, 476
Arden, Eve, 47, 52
Arden, Vic, 40
Arent, Arthur, 462
Arlen, Harold, 1, 257, 258, 480
Arling, Arthur, 445
Armstrong, Louis, 454
Arnau, Brenda, 449
Arnaud, Leo, 201, 303, 333
Arnold, Edward, 265, 270
Arnold, Jack, 466
Arnold, Joan, 231
Arren, Charlotte, 201
Arvan, Jan, 462, 468
As Thousands Cheer, 232
Ash, Paul, 59
Ash, Walter, 198
"A-stairable Rag," 221
Astaire, Adele, 11-35, 38, 39, 40, 41, 42, 192, 222, 356, 410, 470, 473, 476
Astaire, Ava, 482
Astaire, Fred, Jr., 457
Astaire, Phyllis, 37, 404
Astaire Story, The, 473
Astaire Time, 439, 465
"At the Devil's Ball," 303
Atkinson, Brooks, 34, 35
Atteridge, Harold, 38, 476
Atwell, Roy, 39
Auclair, Michel, 407, 410
"Audition Dance," 245
August, Joseph H., 163
Austerlitz, Ann Geilus, 11
Austin, Charlotte, 397
Austin, Ronald, 457, 481
Austin, William, 69
Ava Productions, Inc., 462, 465
Avedon, Richard, 407, 409, 410
Avery, Phyllis, 465
Ayers, Lemuel, 265
Ayres, Mitchell, 466

"Babbitt and the Bromide, The," 31, 40, 42, 265, 276, 277, 470

"Baby Doll," 367, 372, 472
"Bachelor Dinner Song," 367, 370, 472
Bacon, Irving, 201, 231
Bacon, Shelby, 231
Badey, Peggy, 347
Baker, Herbert, 462
Ball, Lucille, 83, 97, 104, 119, 126, 130, 265, 268, 277
Ballard, Shirley, 303
Band Wagon, The, 21, 34-35, 41, 49, 275, 304, 381-395, 410, 480
Banks, Lionel, 221, 245
Baravalle, Victor, 39, 163, 173, 187
Barbour, Joyce, 482
Bari, Lynn, 47
Barker, John, 41
Barkleys of Broadway, The, 199, 304, 319-331, 358, 384, 480
Barlow, Reginald, 57
Barnes, George, 347
Barnes, Howard, 149, 155, 192-193, 317
Barnes, Joanna, 465
Barnes, T. Roy, 38
Barratt, Watson, 38
Barrett, Jim, 435
Barrie, Wendy, 462
Barris, Harry, 231, 333
Barry, Pete, 265
Barry, Philip, 304, 462
Barthelmess, Richard, 120
Bartholomae, Philip, 476
"Basal Metabolism," 407
Bass, Jules, 468
Bassman, George, 163
Bates, Jimmy, 303
"Baubles, Bangles and Beads," 462
Baugh, Stanley, 457
Baxter, Warner, 398
"Be Careful, It's My Heart," 231, 239
"Be Good to Me," 40
Beatty, Roberta, 39
Beavers, Louise, 231
Beavers, Richard, 303
Beaumont, Glori, 42
"Beautiful Faces Need Beautiful Clothes," 303
"Because I Love You," 289
Beebe, Lucius, 35
Beeby, Bruce, 457
Beecher, Janet, 187
"Begat, The," 449, 452, 454-455
"Beggar Waltz, The," 35, 41, 275, 381, 390
"Begin the Beguine," 201, 204, 210
"Beginner's Luck," 151, 471, 475
Bel Geddes, Norman, 40

498